CHARLES XII's KAROLINERS

Volume 2: The Swedish Cavalry of the Great Northern War, 1700–1721

Sergey Shamenkov

'This is the Century of the Soldier', Fulvio Testi, Poet, 1641

Helion & Company

Helion & Company Limited
Unit 8 Amherst Business Centre
Budbrooke Road
Warwick
CV34 5WE
England
Tel. 01926 499 619
Email: info@helion.co.uk
Website: www.helion.co.uk
Twitter: @helionbooks
Visit our blog http://blog.helion.co.uk/

Published by Helion & Company 2023
Designed and typeset by Serena Jones
Cover designed by Paul Hewitt, Battlefield Design (www.battlefield-design.co.uk)

Text © Sergey Shamenkov 2023
Illustrations © as individually credited
Colour artwork by Sergey Shamenkov © Helion & Company 2023

Every reasonable effort has been made to trace copyright holders and to obtain their permission for the use of copyright material. The author and publisher apologise for any errors or omissions in this work, and would be grateful if notified of any corrections that should be incorporated in future reprints or editions of this book.

ISBN 978-1-804513-51-4

British Library Cataloguing-in-Publication Data.
A catalogue record for this book is available from the British Library.

All rights reserved. No part of this publication may be reproduced, stored in a retrieval system, or transmitted, in any form, or by any means, electronic, mechanical, photocopying, recording or otherwise, without the express written consent of Helion & Company Limited.

For details of other military history titles published by Helion & Company
Limited, contact the above address, or visit our website: http://www.helion.co.uk

We always welcome receiving book proposals from prospective authors.

Contents

Preface and Acknowledgements ... iv
1. Organisation, Recruitment, and Tactical Handling of the Swedish Cavalry ... 6
2. Arms and Equipment of Troopers and NCOs of Cavalry and Dragoons ... 21
3. The Headwear of Troopers, Hat and *Karpus* ... 44
4. The Uniform of the Cavalry and Dragoons ... 47
5. The Uniform of Cavalry and Dragoon NCOs ... 79
6. Officers' Uniform of the Cavalry and Dragoons ... 83
7. Officers' Gorgets of Rank ... 110
8. The Uniform and Equipment of the Drabant Corps (*Drabantkåren*) ... 112
9. The Uniform of the Musicians of the Cavalry and Dragoons ... 127
10. Musical Instruments: Their Decoration and Banners ... 142
11. Horse Furniture for Troopers and Distinctions for Officers ... 150

Colour Plate Commentaries ... 158
Bibliography ... 162

Preface and Acknowledgements

This is the second volume dedicated to the Swedish Army of the Great Northern War, and this volume covers the uniforms and equipment of the cavalry. This book is based on the articles, books and reference books on the subject of Swedish uniforms and equipment of the Swedish Army of the Great Northern War, listed in the corresponding section and in the Bibliography. To the authors already mentioned in the first volume, published in 2022, is added a remarkable work by Anders Larson, which contains important for the reconstruction of the appearance of Swedish officers and soldiers and clarifying much information. Unfortunately Swedish researchers in their works have paid little attention to documents, artefacts, and iconographic sources in the archives and museums of Russia and Ukraine, on the subject of the Swedish Army of period. As a result, readers and researchers interested in the topic do not have a complete picture in front of them; in this book I will try to fill this gap as much as possible.

On the basis of iconographic and written sources, I have endeavoured to show the development of, and differences in, the uniforms and equipment of officers, non-commissioned officers, troopers, and musicians of the cavalry and dragoon regiments, as well as cavalry equipment. At the beginning of the book I have given a brief overview of Swedish cavalry organisation, tactics, and exercises. There is also a separate chapter on the uniforms and equipment of the dragoon regiments. Each chapter is accompanied by graphic and pictorial reconstructions of Swedish cavalry uniforms and equipment. The illustrative material is supplemented by details from paintings and engravings created during the Great Northern War showing images of Swedish cavalry. Many details of these canvases the reader will, I think, be seeing for the first time. Some of the photos were taken by me, and others were taken at exhibitions and provided to me by friends and colleagues and museum staff, for which I am immensely grateful to them.

As with the first volume of the study, that devoted to infantry, I have included photos of archaeological finds from the battlefields. Photos of original surviving items of uniforms and equipment from museums in Russia, Sweden, and from the collection of the Poltava Battle Museum in Poltava, Ukraine, complete the illustrative material. The photographs of portions of the painting by D. Martin and items from the museum in Poltava are here published for the first time with the kind permission of the Museum Director, N. Bilan. The items are remarkable because many are unique artefacts from the period of the Northern War, and have no parallels in other

PREFACE AND ACKNOWLEDGEMENTS

museum collections. Additionally, some rare items from the collection of the Hermitage Museum in Russia, necessary for understanding the development, details of cut and decoration of uniforms of the Great Northern War period, are given in the form of the author's colour studies.

I would like to express my gratitude to the friends and colleagues mentioned above for providing photos and material: B. Megorsky, Kirill Nagorny, S. Minchenkov, N. Bilan, S. Makarenko, H. Henriksson, A. Yushkevich.

1

Organisation, Recruitment, and Tactical Handling of the Swedish Cavalry

The cavalry of Charles XII was perhaps the most effective cavalry of its time, combining the fastest possible speed during an attack with a more cohesive squadron formation than any other army could achieve.

Organisation

The Swedish cavalry of the Great Northern War was divided into horse and dragoons. By the beginning of the war, dragoons had actually lost their original purpose of being mounted infantry, and more often acted in battle in the same way as horse. At the same time, dragoons sometimes still fought dismounted supported by hand-held mortars, which will be discussed in detail below.

Horse were recruited under the *indelta* system of land conscription. When regiments mobilised under the *indelta* system moved to the theatre of war at the start of mobilisation, they were replaced by regiments of the next 'class'.[1] Thus, if necessary, regiments of the second, third, fourth, and even fifth 'class' could be formed. Part of the horse went to recruit the regiment of the first 'class'. The establishment of cavalry regiments was not uniform and the strength of a regiment could vary from 600 to 1,000 men.

The *Indelta* (Provincial) cavalry regiments included:

Livregementet till Häst
Västgöta Kavalleriregemente
Adelsfanan i Sverige och Finland
Åbo och Björneborgs Läns Kavalleriregemente

---

1   In the way that conscription in France during the Revolution and First Empire was by 'Class.'

ORGANISATION, RECRUITMENT, AND TACTICAL HANDLING OF THE SWEDISH CAVALRY

Nylands och Tavastahus Läns Kavalleriregemente
Smålands Kavalleriregemente
Östgöta Kavalleriregemente
Norra Skånska [North Scania] Kavalleriregementet
Karelska (Viborgs och Nyslotts län) Kavalleriregementet
Södra Skånska [Scouth Scania] Kavalleriregementet
Riksänkedrottningens [Queen Dowager's] Livregemente till Käst
Bohus Dragonskvadron
Jämtlands Kavallerikompani

Territorial cavalry regiments:

Upplands (Livregementet och Östgöta) Tremänningsregemente till Häst
Skånska och Småländska Tremänningsregementet till Häst
Västgöta (och Bohus läns) Tremänningsregemente till Häst
Åbo, Nylands och Viborgs Läns Tremänningsregemente till Häst
Upplands Ståndsdragonregemente
Skånska Ståndsdragonregementet
Västgöta Ståndsdragonregemente
Upplands (Livregementet och Östgöta) Femmänningsregemente till Häst
Karelska (Viborgs län) Fördubblingsregementet till Häst

Equestrian portrait of Charles XII at Narva, Johan Klopper.

Drawing of Charles XI's *Exercisreglementet*, Krigsarkivet, 1691–1707.

Key to illustration (note, there is no figure '1'):

2: Advance troopers; 3: Troop Captain; 4: Quartermaster; 5: First Lieutenant;

6: Second Lieutenant; 7: First Cornet; 8: Second Cornett; 9: Provost; 10: Junior Quartermaster;

11: Senior Corporal of the 1st corporalship; 12: Junior Corporal of the 1st corporalship;

13: Senior Corporal of the 2nd corporalship; 14: Junior Corporal of the 2nd corporalship;

15: Senior Corporal of the 3rd corporalship; 16: Junior Corporal of the 3rd corporalship.

ORGANISATION, RECRUITMENT, AND TACTICAL HANDLING OF THE SWEDISH CAVALRY

125 Mann mit completten ober
effen oder Schwengen soll.

Equestrian portrait of Charles XII at the Battle of Narva. Johan Klopper (1670–1734).

The nobility and the owners of estates, manors, and farms, raised mounted companies of the militia at their own expense – Adelsfanan. Horse could be noblemen, but by the beginning of the war, they had changed to paid cavalry with full equipment, uniforms and horses. Armament and equipment did not differ from the regiments of horse. In case of capture or death of a cavalry trooper, a replacement was to be sent. Swedish and Finnish Adelsfanan (Adelsfanan i Sverige och Finland) formed two companies. In the Baltic provinces two regiments were formed from such cavalry. The Adelsfan of Pomerania (Adelsfanan i Pommern) and Bremen (Adelsfanan i Bremen-Verden) each had a single company of 100–150 men.

The *indelta* horse regiment consisted of eight companies. Each company was divided into three platoons of 125: 124 troopers and one trumpeter.

Dragoons differed from the horse in the way they were formed. The clergy, tenant farmers of the King's lands, according to rules similar to those for raising horse, provided dragoons to form dragoon regiments. As in the case of the Adelsphan formation, farmers and clergy could pay for the

ORGANISATION, RECRUITMENT, AND TACTICAL HANDLING OF THE SWEDISH CAVALRY

maintenance, equipment and armouring of the dragoon, but the difference lay in this being a one-time formation, with further recruitment costs borne by the Crown. Thus three regiments and one independent company were formed from such dragoons. Under the same conditions eight companies were formed in Finland, divided into two squadrons. In the Baltic provinces three squadrons were formed.

The next method of forming cavalry regiments was straightforward recruitment. The recruited regiment of the Swedish *läns* was the Kunglig Majestäts Livregemente Dragoner; Livdragonregementet. By the start of the war there were a total of five 'recruited' cavalry regiments in the Swedish Army, later the number of recruited regiments and individual companies increased.

By the beginning of the war, the Swedish cavalry had 16 horse regiments, 10 of which were indelta regiments, three Adelsfan regiments, three recruited regiments, two dragoon regiments, and three dragoon 'battalions'. After the outbreak of the war, the formation of the next succession of indelta regiments, the formation of class dragoon regiments, and recruited regiments began in all provinces. Recruiting regiments:

Drabantkåren
Adelsfanan i Estland och Ingermanland
Adelsfanan i Livland och pä Ösel
Adelsfanan i Pommern
Adelsfanan i Bremen-Verden
Kunglig Majestäts Livregemente Dragoner; Livdragonregementet
Pommerska Kavalleriregementet
Drottningens [The Queen's] Livregemente till Häst; or Estniska Kavalleriregementet
Bremiska Kavalleriregementet
Bremiska Dragonregementet
Karelska Lantdragonskvadronen
Livländskt Dragonregemente
Ingermanländska Dragonregementet
Livländskt Dragonregemente
Öselska Lantdragonskvadronen
Pommerska Dragonregementet
Meierfelts Dragonregemente
Stenbocks Dragonregemente
Meierfelts Dragonregemente
Taubes or Schlesiska Dragonregementet
Dückers or Preussiska Dragonregementet
Bassewitz Dragonregemente or Dragonregemente i Wismar
Schwerins Dragonregemente
Vietinghoff's or Barthska Dragonregementet
Görtz Dragonregemente
Tyska Dragonregementet
Polska Regementet till Häst

Swedish Cavalry Tactics

The tactics of the Swedish cavalry under Charles XII developed within an already existing tradition. Earlier, during the reign of Charles XI, officers were authorised to train their men no more than three times a year, but not in larger units than companies. Even general musters were usually held in rotation, company by company. Before troops went to war, they had to assemble in their home town.[2]

Charles XII raised his cavalry to a high level of proficiency through intensive training of both riders and horses, using and perfecting the

---

2 *Kungl. Lifregementets Till Häst Historia: Utarbetad Efter Samlingar Generalmajoren M. M. O. M. F. Bjornstjerna Och Rlksheraldikern M. M. C. A. Klingspor. Uppsala & Stockholm Lifregementet Till Häst Aren 1667–1723*, p.126.

ORGANISATION, RECRUITMENT, AND TACTICAL HANDLING OF THE SWEDISH CAVALRY

Detail of a dragoon regiment drawn up, from the plan of the Battle of Gadebusch, 9 December 1712.

tactical formation introduced by his father. By constant exercises to achieve coherence, and a compact squadron formation with its characteristic form in the form of a wedge. Success on the battlefield was achieved by aggressive actions and the rapid transition to attack with 'cold steel'.

The tactic of conducting a caracole attack was still in use, at least in peacetime exercises, in the cavalry instructions of both Charles XI and Charles XII. According to the regulation drill, the first rank would fire first their carbine, then their right-hand pistol, and then their left-hand pistol, after which the rank would turn and retire to the rear of the company, at which point the second rank would advance to fire its carbines and pistols, etc.. According to the regulations, between each shot, however, the sword was drawn and the men prepared to advance to attack with cold steel.[3]

Depending on the situation on the battlefield, the regiments also practised another variant of attack method. According to the regulations of 1695, the Swedish cavalry company, lined up in three ranks, starting the attack at between 200 and 300 paces, at a trot. Troopers fired their pistols at a distance of 75 to 50 paces and then drew swords, and followed up with the attack. In some cases pistols might not be used at all, and the cavalry immediately attacked only with cold steel. Companies and squadrons in the early years of the Great

---

3 *Kungl. Lifregementets Till Häst Historia*, p.120.

Battle of Narva, 1700, painting by unknown artist. City Museum, Tallinn.

Northern War did not charge at full gallop, but at a trot. It is believed that only around 1705 did the gallop become normal for the last phase of the attack.[4]

In order to understand the tactical evolutions, it is appropriate to cite a picture of the Carolingian cavalry. For example, a picture from the *ekserzia* of the time of Charles XI is written: '*Ett kompani på 125 man kompletta med kompaniofficerare och underofficerare när det skall "träffa" (strida) eller svänga. Kompaniet är uppställd på tre led i plogformation. Varje cirkel motsvarar en ryttare med Häst*' (A company of 125 men, complete with company officers and non-commissioned officers, in the phase before the attack when it is necessary to fight. The company is shown in the formation phase of the formation in the form of a so-called wedge. Each circle corresponds to a cavalryman.)

Later, in another sketch, the circle schematic was replaced by horsemen. This is how Charles XI imagined the company formation in battle, and this is how it was used by Charles XII and his generals. The famous plan of the battle of Gadebusch, 9 December 1712, shows dragoon companies (judging by the distinctive dragoon guidons) also arranged in three ranks, and the companies can be clearly seen drawn up one behind the other.

---

4   G. Arteus, Krigsteori och historisk forklaring II, 'Karolinsk och europeisk. stridstaktik 1700–1712', *MHI*, 5. 1972, p.170.

ORGANISATION, RECRUITMENT, AND TACTICAL HANDLING OF THE SWEDISH CAVALRY

Cavalryman from the portrait of Charles XII. Narva Art Gallery.

So, at the beginning of the attack, the company was formed in platoon formations in three ranks, in the centre of the formation of the first line was *Andre Kornett*, the second cornet with the standard, the squadron commander, the *Förste Ryttmästaren*, was on the left of the standard, next to the captain, *Estandar-Junkaren*. To the right of the standard was the *Förste Korpralen*. A trumpeter was positioned on the flank. When moving, the troopers holding the formation, knee-to-knee pressed from the flanks, as a result, the centre was pushed forward and thus formed a wedge, the so-called 'plough'. At the same time they reached the limit density of the formation which allowed for a successful attack and dispersal of the enemy formation. The follow-up ranks pushed into the gap in the enemy formation. In the tactics of the time this was already a precursor to the defeat of the enemy, the enemy formation scattered, it lost cohesion and began the capture of standards, panic and pursuit of the enemy. To attack, a cavalry regiment could be deployed in a column with a sequential arrangement of companies, or deployed in squadron lines.

A detailed study of the cavalry regulations is beyond the scope of this book, but it is worthwhile to quote some fragments. The exercises contained a number of commands and instructions and knowledge of them and obedience to them was demonstrative of the training of the Swedish cavalry. To give an example, this quote is only a small part of the exercise of the attack:

> When they want to strengthen the front, it is necessary to do so, namely: That the lieutenant or quartermaster behind the company divide the rear line into four parts, and as soon as it is ordered: 'To the right and to the left strengthen your

Formation at Klishov, detail of a contemporary engraving.

fronts! and it is ordered 'march!' then one part of a quarter, that on the right hand, advances in the first line to the right, and the other part of a quarter, that on the left, rides up to the left in the first line; and the two middle quarters, one on the left and the other on the right in the second line. And then, when it is commanded, 'To the right' and 'To the left' you stand again in the former line, and it is said to march, the two middle quarters turn off first, and then the other two that went forward in the front rank. But when the squadrons meet the enemy, then the first only line draws its pistols, the sword in the left hand, and the other two lines draw the sword, tightly closing the line, moving with the last two lines united together. And when they advance on the squadron, the officers must keep the horse in the squadron line, and not immediately fire, and when they do fire, immediately return their pistols to their holsters and take their sword into the right hand. At the same time, if they meet when they have their carbine in hand, lower the carbine at once and immediately draw the sword ready to attack.[5]

Although Charles XII favoured attacking with the sword, with a minimal use of pistols and carbines, a number of paintings from the Great Northern War period show Swedish cavalrymen firing firearms during the battle. This is how Swedish cavalrymen are shown, for example, in these details on the following paintings:

The regulations on exercises, taking into account the realities of the ongoing war, are summarised in manuscript rules, in Ravic, as well as in the rules drawn up at Altransstadt in 1706–1707. These regulations divided the army into two arms, mounted and foot. A squadron usually consisted of one company, but could consist of two. The statute of 2 June 1707 mentions squadrons of no more than 160 horsemen.[6] Images of Charles XI's cavalry from the 1691–1707 Regulations show a company of 125 horsemen.

---

5   *Kungl. Lifregementets Till Häst Historia*, p.122.
6   *Kungl. Lifregementets Till Häst Historia*, p.122.

In addition to combat formations, there was also a parade formation, where the rank was straight, i.e. the riders were lined up knee-to-knee, and the distance between the ranks had to be large enough that two riders could pass between them. This was required for easy passage of the inspecting officer and the unit commander.[7]

In addition to the mounted exercises, training was planned and carried out dismounted. Service on foot was intended mainly as a preliminary necessary preparation for service in a mounted formation. However, especially for training in firing a carbine or musket, it should be noted that it was envisaged that the cavalrymen would fight on foot in the field as well. The frequent shortage of horses sometimes made service on foot a last resort, albeit a necessary one. In this case 'horseless' troopers were to be lined up on foot in front of the mounted ones, in three ranks, with a corresponding distance between them. Then, on command, the fourth mounted rank was formed up behind the dismounted ranks.[8]

Included in the Swedish cavalry, the irregular Valash Regiment served as Hungarian or Polish-Lithuanian light cavalry.

Grenadier Units Attached to Cavalry Regiments, and Their Action in Battle

In the dragoon regiments formed in the Baltic provinces, special units of grenadiers were officially introduced, it is possible to see this in surviving documents. For some of the regiments there is firm information about the presence of grenadiers, and maybe this was also the case in other dragoon regiments, information on which does not, sadly, survive. Thus, in V. A.

---

7   *Kungl. Lifregementets Till Häst Historia*, p.123.
8   *Kungl. Lifregementets Till Häst Historia*, p.125.

CHARLES XII'S KAROLINERS VOLUME 2

Portrait of Charles XII at Narva, artist unknown. In the background cavalry can be seen attacking, wearing cuirasses over their coats.

Shlippenbach's dragoon regiment, Livländskt Dragonregegemente W. A. Shlippenbach, there were grenadiers on the establishment of each company of the regiment.[9] 16 grenadiers were also part of A. J. Shlippenbach's Livländskt dragoon battalion, Livländskt Dragonskvadronen A. J. von Shlippenbach.[10] In 1704, there were also four grenadiers in the Öselska Lant dragoon squadron, Öselska Lant Dragonskvadronen.[11] Grenadiers in the dragoon regiments were trained in the same way as the grenadiers in infantry regiments. But even without officially having grenadiers on their establishment, sometimes dragoons of some regiments had to take on these functions. There are several interesting evidences of the use of grenadiers by Swedish cavalry both on foot and mounted. Thus, during the siege and storming of Lvov, the use of grenades by dragoon units is recorded when the city was taken by storm by only a few Swedish dragoon regiments.[12] A Bremiska dragoon regiment serving on foot distinguished itself during the storming of Lvov, throwing grenades at the fortifications and at the city's defenders and then went on the attack, breaking through the defences. In 1705, during the actions in Livonia, near Mitava, it was recorded that Swedish cavalrymen – grenadiers, in line of march, with hand mortars, threw grenades at the Russian cavalry from the saddle.[13] B. Megorsky found in the Russian archive of NIA SPbII RAS, a document, also recording the use of horse mortars in cavalry combat by the Swedish cavalry. The document will be published in detail by Megorsky but with his kind permission I want to describe this in outline and in brief. The Russian Cavalry's Colonel Murzenko describes the skirmishes of his regiment with the Swedish cavalry companies in Livonia in the summer of 1705, where the actions of the Swedish grenadiers are mentioned: 'the Swedes began to throw hand grenades and from the mortars, which are carried on the saddle.' This description also speaks about the use of hand mortars from saddles by units of Swedish grenadiers in with the cavalry regiments.

Arrangement of Musicians in Cavalry Formation

Musicians in the cavalry regiments were trumpeters, in dragoon regiments there were drummers, oboists, and musicians playing the shalmey and the dulcimer. In addition to the trumpeters assigned to each unit, there was a kettledrummer in each cavalry and dragoon regiment. During parades he would ride in front of the regiment and stand on the right flank, in battle he would be positioned on the right of the regiment or was placed at the

---

9 K. Kroon, Kolme lovi ja greifiall pohjasojas, (Tallin: 2007), p.95.
10 Lars-Eric Höglund, *The Great Northern War 1700–1721. Colours and Uniforms* (Karlstad: Acedia Press 2000) p.86.
11 K. Kroon, *Kolme Lovi ja Greifiall Pohjasojas* (Tallin: Argo, 2007), p.402.
12 Knut Lundblad, *Geschichte Karl des Zwölften Königs von Schweden*, Band 1 (Hamburg: Friedrich Derthes 1835), pp.301–305.
13 K. Tatarnikov, Officers' Tales of the First Quarter of the Eighteenth Century. *Ostavnye chiny i zapoloshchennye chiny* [Retired ranks and *zapoloshnye chiny*] (Moscow: 2017), T. 2. C. 2295.

rear. The rest of the musicians were also positioned on the right flank of the regiment. Musicians accompanied the regiment during ceremonies, parades, and religious ceremonies (*korum*). During battle, the musicians retreated back to behind the regiment, on the right flank, immediately behind the first company. In dragoon regiments the drummers stayed close to the guidon-bearer.[14] In the painting by D. Martin, 'The Battle of Poltava' in the collection of the Museum of the Battle of Poltava, at Poltava in Ukraine, the Swedish kettledrummers are clearly visible on the right flank of the cavalry companies, next to the trumpeters

Painting depicting the Battle of Poltava. Louis Caravacca, 1718, from the collection of the State Hermitage Museum

---

14 K. Tatarnikov, *Stroevye ustavs instructions and instructions of the Russian Army of the XVIII century*. Collection of materials, vol. I (Moscow: 2010), p.104.

2

Arms and Equipment of Troopers and NCOs of Cavalry and Dragoons

Cuirasses

The Swedish cavalry wore cuirasses, which had been taken into use in 1687, under Charles XI. They were made at the Norrköping factory from iron and painted black. As a rule, the cuirasses of privates consisted of a breastplate only and without backplate. They were lined with elk or buffalo leather of a pale yellow colour, and fastened with two straps which crossed at the back, and buckled at the side. The cuirasses were made in three sizes, and the thickness could also vary.

In the companies of 1700–1702, cuirasses were worn by all those who were entitled to them. From 1702, in the army under Charles XII, cuirasses were taken out of use, because the King believed that they only burdened the soldiers and tired the horses. But in some regiments they remained in use. Östgöta Kavalleriregegemente, for example, gave up its cuirasses only in 1705.[1] Regiments stationed in Sweden's German possessions, and the Finnish and Baltic provinces of Sweden continued to use cuirasses, but probably even in these regiments not everyone used cuirasses in battle. In the lists of trophies taken by Russian troops after the battles of Erestfer and Gummelhof, very few cuirasses were taken: '28 front plates, and 26 pairs of back and breast plates with one Swedish plate', and this despite the high losses among the Swedish cavalry regiments that took part in the battles – Karelska (Viborgs och Nyslotts län) Kavalleriregementet and Åbo och Björneborgs Läns Kavalleriregemente.[2] The small number of trophies taken confirms the idea that not all cavalrymen of the regiments participating in

---

1 Anders Larsson, *Karolinska Uniformer och Munderingar åren 1700 till 1721* (Tallinn: Jengel Förlag 2022), p.240.
2 V. Velikanov, 'Swedish Cavalry 1700–1709', in *Voin Magazine*, no. 6, p.27.

this battle used them, and it is possible that the trophies were primarily of non-commissioned officers' and officers' armour.

Later, in the Russian campaign, cuirasses were used by the cavalry regiments Åbo och Björneborgs Läns Kavalleriregemente, Nylands och Tavastahus Läns Kavalleriregemente, Karelska (Viborgs och Nyslotts län) Kavalleriregementet, and possibly the regiments Adelsfanan i Estland och Ingermanland, Adelsfanan i Livland och pä Ösel. In the Battle of Poltava, the cavalry of the regiments that were earlier part of the Livonian field corps of Count A. L. Levengaupt, who after the unsuccessful battle of Lesnaya brought the regiments to join the main army, may have worn cuirasses. Despite heavy battle losses, the Count managed to save and bring to the King about half of his original corps. Among them were several regiments armed with cuirasses, the men of Åbo och Björneborgs Läns Kavalleriregemente, Nylands och Tavastahus Läns Kavalleriregemente both took part in the battle.

The trophy collection of the Russian Armoury preserves several examples of Swedish cuirasses. A cuirass, inv No. Or-1554, 39 cm long and 35 cm wide; a cuirass inv No. Or-1552, is a breastplate 40 cm long and 34.5 cm wide; and a cuirass, inv No. Or-1551, is a breastplate 39.5 long and 37.6 cm wide.[3] In the Russian trophy collection Swedish cuirasses were preserved without their leather. It is likely that these cuirasses are from among those captured at Poltava and belonged to the above mentioned regiments. Initially there were many more captured cuirasses; the fact that only a small number have survived to today is explained by the fact that the captured Swedish cuirasses were used to equip Russian Cuirassier regiments Leib-Kurassier and Beverny, according to a Decree of 8 August 1733.[4]

From the time of Charles XI, all cavalry officers were required to purchase parade armour, which would serve for 13 years at training camps and parades. The fact that ceremonial cuirasses for officers were compulsory is evidenced by a Royal Decree until 1693.[5] Cavalry non-commissioned officers had the right to buy cuirasses, at their own expense. For example, from 1683 in regiments of the Noble Banner-Adelsfanan. Under Charles XII, the practice of wearing cuirasses by horse and officers of horse and some officers of dragoon regiments continued. The cuirasses were worn both over the coat and under it, over a leather jacket or waistcoat.

The supply of cuirasses to the regiments continued even during the period of active warfare. Thus in 1701, a lieutenant of the Nylands Kavalleriregemente, Gabriel Ridderkorp, had to provide cuirasses for officers and non-commissioned officers of this regiment. However, the cuirasses were not very popular, and there are known cases of refusal to wear them by cavalrymen of different regiments. Thus, after the Battle of Warsaw in 1705, the cavalrymen of the Östgöta Kavalleriregemente got rid of cuirasses.[6]

---

3   'Perfect Victoria' exhibition catalogue, C 274–277.
4   S. Letin and O. Leonov, *Russian Military Costume, from Peter I to Peter III* (Moscow: 2008), p.233.
5   Larsson, *Karolinska Uniformer*, p.238.
6   Larsson, *Karolinska Uniformer*, p.240.

ARMS AND EQUIPMENT OF TROOPERS AND NCOS OF CAVALRY AND DRAGOONS

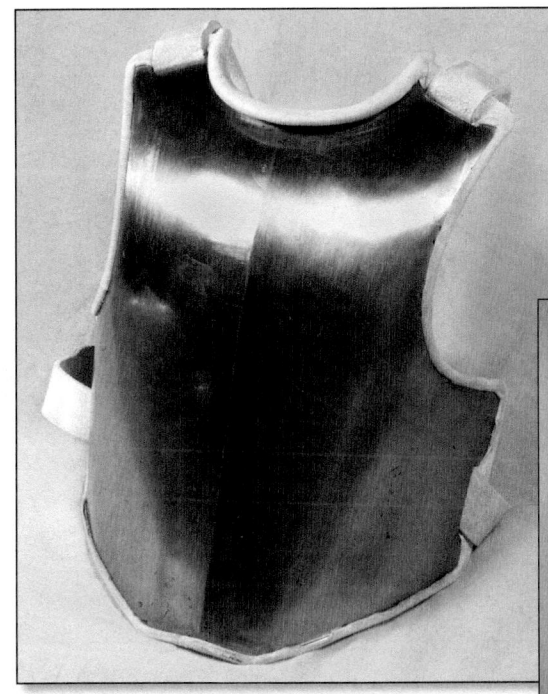

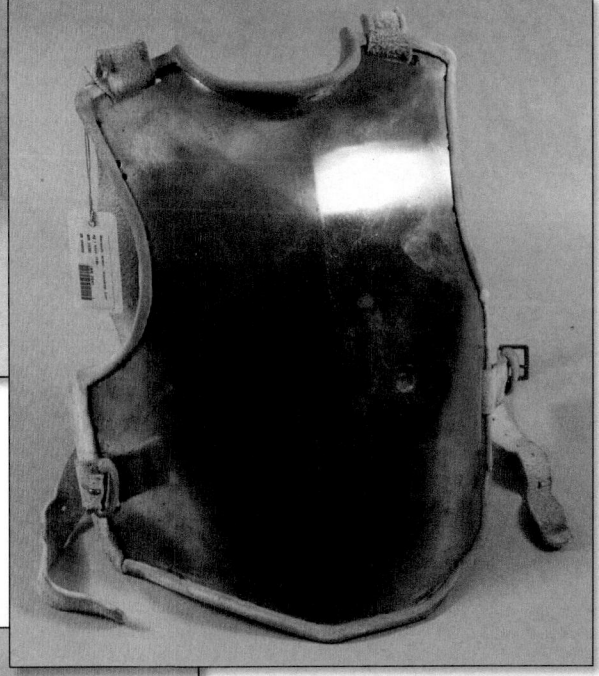

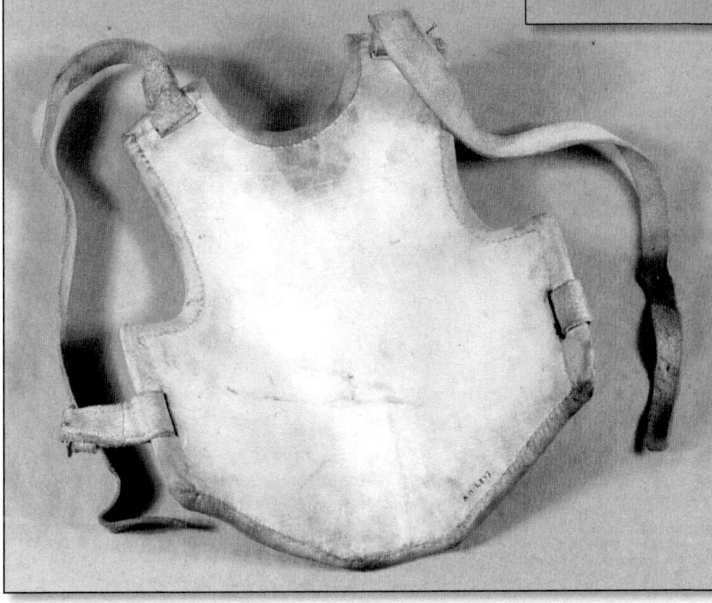

The collection of the Swedish Army Museum has preserved examples of the original cuirasses (AM.032357 and AM.032381) which show their original appearance.

CHARLES XII'S KAROLINERS VOLUME 2

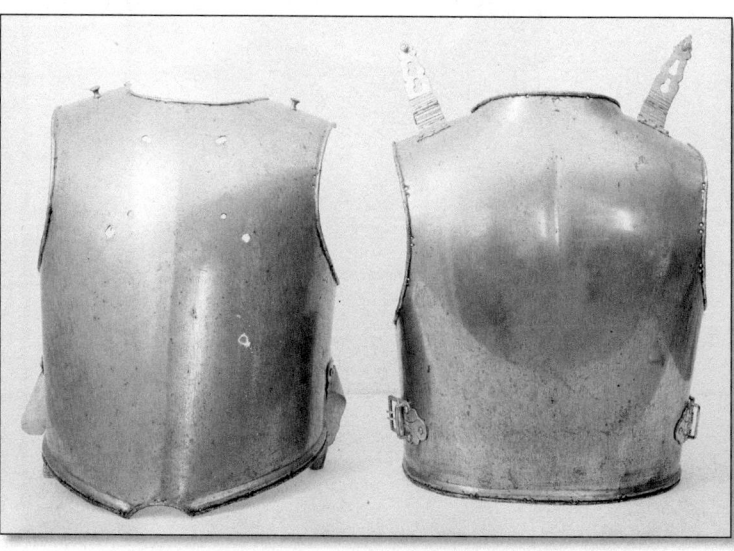

Clockwise from top left: Officers' and non-commissioned officers' cuirasses (Livrustkammaren 27720, 9459, 900; bottom left, cuirass bearing the monogram of Charles XI Livrustkammaren 106444).

ARMS AND EQUIPMENT OF TROOPERS AND NCOS OF CAVALRY AND DRAGOONS

The full back and breast cuirasses of cavalry officers and non-commissioned officers could be lined with a supravest with decorative edges along the armhole, around the neck and at the lower edge of the cuirass. It is clearly seen on some portraits of both Charles XII and cavalry officers of the period. A lining could also be directly attached to the inside of the cuirass. The shoulder straps on the full back and breast cuirass had, on top of the leather (to judge from contemporary portraits) rectangular plates attached to them. From a portrait of one of the Adelsphan officers, such plates could carry decorations in the form of royal monograms.

When cuirasses were abolished, they were still worn by non-commissioned officers and officers in the King's regiments. Officers, especially staff officers, could wear simple or ceremonial cuirasses. Officers' cuirasses were usually of full back and breast type and of polished steel. However, many portraits of cavalry officers show the use of blued cuirasses, and such (probably) ceremonial cuirasses were decorated in front with chased bronze overlayed decoration. Such armorial compositions were displayed at the front under the neck of the cuirass, or in the centre of the chest. The size of such decoration, as well as the actual design, were not to a set pattern; portraits of officers and preserved cuirasses show a great diversity of size, location and form. There were different versions of the royal monogram: shown below a crown, framed by palm branches, or either of these but with the addition of lion supporters at the sides. Probably, the officers who served under, and had cuirasses of the reign of, Charles XI continued to wear cuirasses with similar overlays, perhaps still with his monogram. After the death of Charles XII, the cuirasses were decorated with similar designs, but with the monogram of Queen Ulrika Eleonora, the sister of Charles XII, who became queen after his death but abdicated in 1721. Cuirasses were also decorated with the designs and monograms of Fredrik I (r. 1720–1751). The collection of the Livrustkammaren Museum preserves a number of examples of such cuirasses. One example of such a trophy cuirass, with the monogram of Ulrika Eleonora (MMK inv no. Or-1557/1-2) is in the collection of the Russian Museum, it is 43.7 cm along the breast ridge.

On one of the portraits of a dragoon officer the cuirass is decorated with the royal monogram.[7] The cuirasses of non-commissioned cavalry officers differed from those of troopers in that they were a full back and breast and, as a rule, not painted but polished.

Cuirasses for non-commissioned officers are recorded in Nylands och Tavastahus Läns Kavalleriregemente in 1701, And parade cuirasses for non-commissioned officers in Livregementet till Häst.[8]

---

7   Larsson, *Karolinska Uniformer*, p.109.
8   Larsson, *Karolinska Uniformer*, p.83.

Carbine/Musket Belts

A musket or a carbine was carried by troopers, non-commissioned officers of cavalry, and dragoon regiments, and in some cases by officers, on a special leather harness – a carbine belt (*karbinrem*). The belt was fastened by a large bronze buckle and studs and had a 'hook' also made of bronze (or the whole device was made of brass). The belt was usually made of elk or deer leather, and could be laced with braid. In the Armémuseum in Stockholm, and in the Livrustkammaren Museum there are several examples of such belts from the Great Northern War. The dimensions of one from the Livrustkammaren Museum, inventory no. 29335 (912:6),[9] are 1,750 mm long and 105 mm wide. A metal hook with a spring was attached to the belt, to which a carbine or musket was attached through a 'staple' embedded in the stock. For non-commissioned officers, the belt could be covered with silver galloon along the edge, as in the Bremiska Dragonregementet in 1700.[10] For officers who used a carbine, the belt with the hook to which the carbine could be attached, might be covered with cloth and galloon on the edges, as was done, for example, in the Verdiska Dragonregemente in 1703.[11]

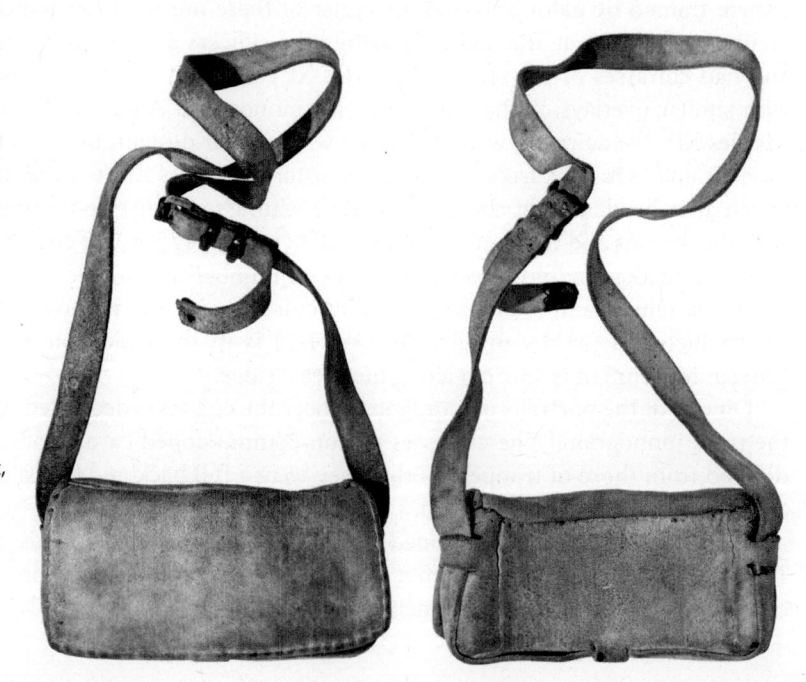

Above: Front and back view of a carbine belt, Livrustkammaren Museum collection.

Right: Front and back view of a cartridge Box (*patronväska*) and belt, c. 1700. Livrustkammaren Museum collection, inventory no. 18496 (15:155).

---

9 <https://samlingar.shm.se/object/F8E9A879-F1E9-4F64-96B3-A82352089BCC>
10 Lars-Eric Höglund, *The Great Northern War 1700–1721. Colours and Uniforms* (Karlstad: Acedia Press, 2000), p.84.
11 Höglund, *The Great Northern War 1700–1721*, p.87.

Cartridge Boxes

Cartridges for the musket or carbine were carried in a box slung over the right shoulder on a thin belt, a few surviving examples show their construction and dimensions – one, Kartuschväska inventory no. 32220 (913:20),[12] is 115 mm by 230 mm. Inside the cartridge box there were 12 tin tubes for the cartridges in a metal clip, although there are variants in the number of tubes, and a bag where there was a compartment for oiler. The lids of the ammunition boxes could be made of black or yellow leather, and in some cases the lids of the boxes had applied embossed or cast decorations in the form of crowned royal monograms, an example is in the Armémuseum in Stockholm, inventory no. AM.071208 *Kartuschväska för Kungliga Livdrabantkåren*. In this case, the overlay is in the form of a crown with four figural plates at the corners. But there could also have been overlays in the form of a royal monogram, for example, on the cartridge box inv. no. AM.070522. From the time of King Fredrik, there was customarily an applied crown and monogram. As a rule, another cover made of thinner leather was sewn on top of the main cover, with or without the monogram, to protect the metal overlays and the lid of the bag.

A variant of the black-coated cartridge pouch is known from the late seventeenth/early eighteenth century, in the Livrustkammaren inventory no. 18496 (15:155).[13] From the photo it can be seen that it is the same construction with tin tubes in one row, designed for 12 cartridges. This example also shows a variant whereby the cartridge box belt was equipped with a bronze buckle, a frame and a chape at the end of the belt in the form of a 'pelta'.

It is likely that in some cases, such as when the dragoons were committed to action in haste, the cartridge pouch could be worn around the waist. In order to put on and fasten the belt of the cartridge pouch on the waist, there were brass buckles, in some examples such buckles could be gold plated. There are no such buckles on the regular belts issued to the cavalry. Taking into account that belts on cartridge pouches of cavalry and dragoons were not wide, the buckles were smaller than those on the belt.

Non-commissioned officers also used ammunition boxes. They differed from regiment to regiment in terms of the colour of the leather on the lid and of the decoration. These differences are noted in the surviving descriptions below.

Livdragonregementet. In 1700, a cartridge box made of leather. The lid of the box is embroidered with gold thread (possibly a monogram or crown).

Pommerska Dragonregementet. In 1703, a black cartridge box with a yellow-tinted leather strap, buffalo skin colour with gilded buckles.

Taubes Dragonregemente. In 1704, black leather box on the same black belt.

---

12 <https://samlingar.shm.se/object/CAE48B6A-141D-4288-9A9E-ACF7E4383C36>
13 <https://samlingar.shm.se/object/8CC89DC7-67E9-46BA-9D7A-BD696AC3C885>

Dückers Dragonregemente. In 1705, a black leather box on the same black belt with two buckles.

Stenbocks Dragonregemente. In 1705, a black leather box on a same black belt with two buckles.

Schwerins Dragonregemente. In 1711, black cartridge box with yellow-tinted leather strap, buffalo leather colour with silver-plated buckles.[14]

Cartridge Boxes (*Amunitionstaska/patronkök*) of Troopers of Cavalry and Dragoon Regiments

Livdragonregementet. In 1700, black leather.

Taubes Dragonregemente. In 1704, a black leather ammunition box with two compartments inside, carried on a black leather strap.

Stenbocks Dragonregemente. In 1711, a black leather box.

Schwerins Dragonregemente. In 1711, a black cartridge box on a yellow strap with a buckle to fasten at the waist.

Upplands Ståndsdragoner. In 1716, black leather with a belt buckle.[15]

Bremiska Kavalleriregementet. in 1701, a yellow cartridge box with the royal monogram.

G. M. Lewenhaupts Värvade Kavalleriregemente. In 1696 a royal monogram with a brass crown was attached to the cartridge box.

Estländska Kavalleriregementet. In 1697 a royal monogram with a brass crown was attached to the cartridge box.

Adelsfanan. In 1709 a cartridge box made of elk leather, with a buff leather strap and brass buckle.

Riksänkedrottningens [The Queen Dowager's] Livregemente till Häst. In 1715, cartridge boxes with brass buckles.[16]

---

14 Larsson, *Karolinska Uniformer*, p.115.
15 Larsson, *Karolinska Uniformer*, p.123.
16 Larsson, *Karolinska Uniformer*, p.95.

ARMS AND EQUIPMENT OF TROOPERS AND NCOS OF CAVALRY AND DRAGOONS

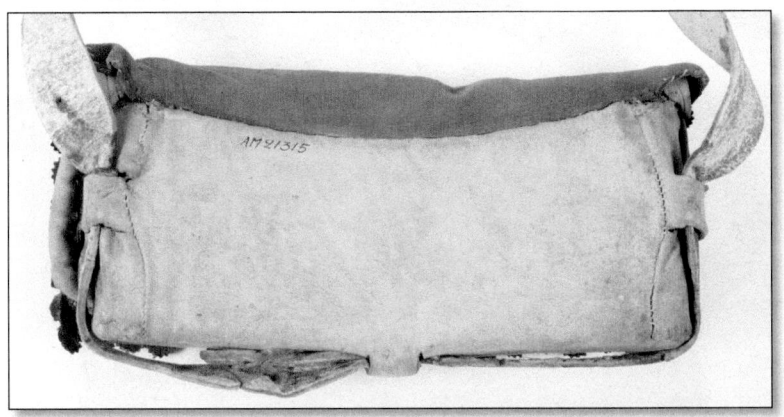

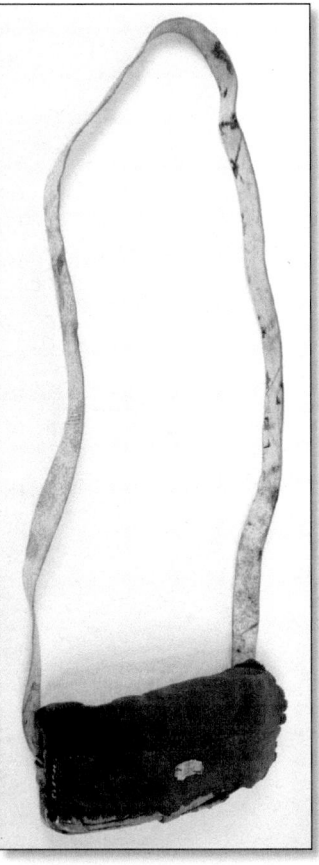

Top, centre, and above: Cartridge box from the collection of the Armémuseum in Stockholm, inventory no. AM.071208, *Kartuschväska för Kungliga Livdrabantkåren*.

Left: Internal view of a cartridge pouch showing the tinplate clip. Example from the Armémuseum in Stockholm, inventory no. AM.070522.

Grenadier Bags

Grenadier bags and information about grenadiers were examined in the first volume,[17] so this will only briefly cover them and in respect of the grenadiers in dragoon regiments. Sadly, it is not possible to trace the use of grenadiers by cavalry units, because of the loss of the archives and documentation at Perevolonchnaya in 1709. But some cases are recorded in surviving documents. For example, during the storming of Lvov in 1704. Bremiska Dragonregementet distinguished itself, including in its use of grenades. And in Livonia in 1705 grenadiers in a mounted formation fired grenades from hand mortars while they were mounted. The documents mention grenadier bags in several regiments. In Livländsk Dragonregemente in 1700 (50 pieces), and in 1705 at Stenbocks Dragonregemente grenadier bags, with bronze wick tubes with them.[18] Grenadier bags with fuse tubes fixed to them and a supply of grenades were kept in the stores and issued when needed, except probably for those units where grenadiers were on the staff of dragoon regiments. In this case the grenade bags and grenades were probably with the grenadiers at all times.

Grenadier bag. Collection of the Armémuseum, Stockholm, inventory no. AM.015481.

---

17   Sergey Shamenkov, *Charles XII's Karoliners, Volume 1: The Swedish Infantry & Artillery of the Great Northern War 1700–1721* (Warwick: Helion & Company 2022), p.26.
18   Larsson, *Karolinska Uniformer*, pp.124–125.

The ready-prepared grenades were stored in a special pouch. In the Swedish Army this was worn over the right shoulder on a narrow buckled belt, with a ring sewn to the belt from which grenade tubes and a spare fuse could be hung. The Swedish grenadier bags were made of black leather or unpainted leather with a natural ochre colour. The leather used was relatively soft, and in the middle of the bag it seems that the frame was not inserted for rigidity, and there is no information about the insertion of a wooden case. There were two compartments in the middle of the pouch bag, one of which was used to carry grenades. The lid of the grenade bag was decorated with the crowned royal monogram, in the form of a leather appliqué. It is possible that such appliqué could be coloured. In infantry regiments there are known cases of fabric applications on grenadier bags, and maybe something similar could be used on the bags of the dragoon regiments.

Sword Belt/Baldric (*Livgehäng*)

The trooper's shoulder belts were made of elk leather, with a yellow metal buckle and with a hook and a plate with a hole on the opposite side. It was sewn on the back side with braid. In those units where a wheelock carbine or wheelock pistols were in use, a spanner to prime the mechanism was attached to the belt on a separate leather strip. What this looked like is clearly visible on the preserved belt with such a strip from Livrustkammaren, Livrustkammaren 69435. The shoulder belts of non-commissioned officers could be lined with silver galloon around the edge, as for example was the case in the Bremiska Dragonregementet in 1700.[19]

Non-commissioned officers and corporals of dragoon regiments had gilded buckles on their belts. For example, in 1700 Livdragontegementet, a sword belt made of elk hide with a gilded buckle. In 1704 Taubes Dragonregegemente, a belt made of buffalo hide with a brass buckle.[20]

Dragoon Belts, with Bayonet

The dragoons' sword belt was similar in design to that of the cavalry, except when the dragoons were armed with bayonets. In this latter case, a scabbard for a bayonet was added to the belt. It is difficult to say whether all dragoons carried bayonets and used the appropriate belt during the Great Northern War. In the surviving records of some dragoon regiments, the following regiments are mentioned as having bayonets with scabbards:[21]

1704, Kunglig Majestäts Livregemente Dragoner and Livdragonregementet
1705, Stenbocks Dragonregemente

---

19 Höglund, *The Great Northern War 1700–1721*, p.84
20 Larsson, *Karolinska Uniformer*, p.114.
21 Larsson, *Karolinska Uniformer*, p.234.

1712, Bohus Dragonbataljon
1712, Västgöta Ståndsdragon Regemente
1714, Upplands Stånds Dragonregemente
1712, Jämtlands Dragonregemente

There is also a reference to bayonets with scabbards being carried by Södra Skånska Kavalleriregementet in 1720.[22]

During the Great Northern War the bayonets were carried in two different ways: separately, hanging on a loop from the belt harness, or on the belt next to the sword scabbard. A short bayonet may be more convenient to hang from the belt, but a long bayonet, such as that of all Swedish models of that time, seems unlikely to be hung from the belt in a mounted unit. The more logical choice is therefore the second option, when the scabbard with the bayonet was inserted into a loop on the belt harness. In this case, the belts of the dragoons, of at least these regiments above, was probably either similar to the infantry soldier's, or quite literally simply repeated its design.

The Standard/Guidon Belt

The standard belt was worn over the left shoulder and was made of elk leather with a metal hook. Such a belt could be covered with cloth and embroidered over with braid or galloon. An example of such a belt sewn with blue cloth with a galloon on the edge is recorded in the documents about the Swedish Adelsfan regiment.[23]

For dragoon regiments there is a mention of a standard belt of the Verdiska Dragonregemente in 1703 made of blue cloth with a wide silver galloon on the edge, and of the Pommerska Dragonregementet in 1703 made of blue cloth with two rows of gold galloon.[24] An example of the decoration of this late seventeenth century standard belt is preserved in the collection of the Livrustkammaren Museum.

A standard belt from Livrustkammaren, inventory no. N-241 A.

Standards of Cavalry and Dragoon Regiments

The standards and guidons of the Swedish cavalry have been described in detail many times, and both drawings of them and original watercolours have also been published a number of times, however this topic could not be skipped altogether. Therefore, in a few words the appearance and types

---

22 Larsson, *Karolinska Uniformer*, p.98.
23 Larsson, *Karolinska Uniformer*, p.80.
24 Larsson, *Karolinska Uniformer*, p.110.

of standard and dragoon flags used by the Swedish cavalry during the Great Northern War will be covered

The standard and guidon staff had a gilded bronze point in the form of a dart with a cut-out composition in the form of a royal monogram with a crown for regimental and company standards and guidons. The length of the staff of dragoons' guidons was about three metres, and to it, at the side, was nailed a metal staple with a ring on it, into which was inserted the clip attached to the guidon belt. The staff was usually of natural wood colour. The standard was nailed to the shaft with gilt nails through a braid. Two cords with tassels were fastened under the ferrule.[25]

Each cavalry regiment had its own standards with an armorial composition of the *länns* ('county' or 'province'), and royal monograms. For example, in Livregementet till Häst, all company standards were white with monograms, and the regimental standard displayed the royal coat of arms. In the other regiments, the regimental standard and dragoon guidons were also white with the royal coat of arms on them and with the regimental coat of arms in the canton. Company standards and guidons bore the royal monogram and the arms of the *länns*.

The standards made before the outbreak of war were more delicately decorated with paintings, later, in the restored regiments and regular regiments the decoration was simpler and more modest. The Adelphan standard has a silk damask cloth with the Royal Crown and CRS painted on it in gold and full colour. The edge was bordered with a gold fringe (Kompanistandar vid Adelsfanan, Livrustkammaren inventory no. 17526, 16983 (154)).[26]

The standards of the third-degree regiments were decorated even more modestly, with the coat of arms of the *län* painted on the in the upper corner of the red silk damask cloth – for example on the surviving standard of Karelens och Viborgs Läns Tremänningarregemente. This standard measures 220 mm high by 168 mm wide. In the dragoon regiments, under Charles XII, company guidons and the regimental guidon were made of white silk. In contrast to the cavalry standards, the dragoon flags were of the traditional 'split end' guidon shape. In the centre of the white damask was the Royal Coat of Arms with lion supporters, and with the inscription painted above the coat of arms in the centre 'CRS'. Along the edge was a border formed by gold palm branches and ornamentation similar to the double letter C, and at the corners small open crowns. An example of such a guidon is in Livrustkammaren collection, inventory no. 17076 (173).[27]

A leather cup, height 117 mm and diameter 66 mm, was attached to the outside of the right-hand stirrup of the standard-bearer in which the

---

25 <https://samlingar.shm.se/media/2BE79F1D-E15B-4FFC-863F-49F773EEFC02>

26 <https://samlingar.shm.se/media/CC161C4E-0FCA-4BA1-9A36-433FDEFD0496>, and <https://samlingar.shm.se/object/ADDF03C8-FD35-41F4-9DE1-EADFA0F13923>

27 <https://samlingar.shm.se/object/F6692C82-4DF1-4254-83A3-F86913509414>

butt of the standard or guidon staff was inserted.[28] FIL.30 Skoklosters slott no. 108893.

On the march the standard/guidon was put in a blue cloth cover, with leather stitched on top to protect the ferrule. The cover was decorated with a cloth or leather tassel.

Powder Horn

The cavalry also used powder flasks, horn containers in which gunpowder was kept. Powder was poured onto the pan of the lock of a flintlock pistol, carbine or musket. Sometimes soldiers carved designs on the powder horns, usually compositions with royal monograms and crowns. Powder horns were recorded in Adelsfana regiments in 1712, 1713 in Norra Skånska [North Scania] Kavalleriregementet – 980 pieces, in 1717 in Västgöta Kavalleriregemente.[29]

Olstro (Bucket) for Muskets

For convenience in a mounted formation, the musket butt could be inserted into a leather case, also known as a musket *olstro* (bucket), although it is difficult to say how widespread this practice was in the Swedish cavalry. The images of the first quarter of the eighteenth century, which have survived to us, do not show these buckets in use. The data on the use of the musket *olstro* which have come down to us are very fragmentary. In documents, the *olstro* for the musket is mentioned sporadically in some regiments. It seems that they were used in these regiments, and possibly in other regiments, from about 1704. From 1704 the *olstro* for the musket is mentioned in Livdragonregementet, in 1705 in Dückers Dragonregemente.[30] In use by Västgöta 3 Männingsregementet till Häst in 1704, and in Västgöta 3- and 5-Männingsregementet till Häst in the same year, in Adelsfanan in 1712, Södra Skånska [South Scanian] Kavalleriregementet in 1713, and Smålands Kavalleriregemente in 1714.[31]

Firearms

The musket was not only carried by ordinary cavalrymen, it was also recommended that officers should have carbines or muskets. In 1695 in Livregementet på Häst, officers were recommended to carry rifled carbines of musket calibre. In the records of some regiments there are surviving

---

28 <https://samlingar.shm.se/media/55C87308-CAF2-4C8C-8EC7-4C7771424C7D>
29 Larsson, *Karolinska Uniformer*, p.98.
30 Larsson, *Karolinska Uniformer*, p.124.
31 Larsson, *Karolinska Uniformer*, p.96.

references to carabineer haversacks. Officers' belts did not differ structurally from the belts of ordinary cavalrymen, but those of officers and non-commissioned officers could be covered with cloth and/or lace.

During the time of Charles XI, wheelock weapons were common, and at the beginning of the Great Northern War, some regiments still had wheelock carbines and pistols. This is certainly how the Leib Regiment went to war in 1700 – with wheelock carbines and wheelock pistols. The replacement of these with flintlock firearms did not take place until 1704.

The musket was carried by dragoons in the same way as by the horse, on a sling with a hook on the right-hand side, the musket could be carried with the butt down or the butt up, period images show both variants. It has also been suggested that dragoons may have carried muskets slung on their backs. 'The rider carried the carbine on his back,' is probably very similar to the musket that the dragoons had, 'hanging with the butt on his left knee and the muzzle over his right elbow.' These detailed rules are in *Ett Kortt Uttåg af … Konung Carl Den XII [:s] Exercitier til Häst*. When firing from horseback, the carbine was not unhooked from the belt.[32]

The horse and dragoons were armed, often in the same regiment, with different types and models of carbines, dragoon muskets, and cavalry muskets. In cavalry regiments there could also be dragoon model muskets in use.

Hand mortars firing 3-pound grenades were also in service with the Swedish cavalry, most likely in dragoon regiments or squadrons with grenadier units. We know little about the Swedish use of hand mortars on the battlefield. It is known that they were in service in the navy, and in the infantry, at least they are recorded in 1701 to the number of 144 examples in the Västgöta-Dals regemente.[33] What is even more interesting is that there are references to the use by Swedish cavalry of hand mortars for throwing grenades in battle against Russian cavalry. The first case, discovered by B. Megorsky, is briefly: in the summer of 1705 in Livonia, a Russian dragoon officer described a combat with Swedish cavalry and mentions the use of mortar bombs by the Swedes against them: 'they fought for a long time and began to throw hand grenades and from martirzers, which are carried on the saddle.' The second example of the use of mortar bombs by the Swedes described in contemporary documents refers to the same time and to the same company in Livonia. In describing his participation in the battles, a Russian dragoon mentioned an interesting detail about the circumstances of his wounding. In Courland, the Swedish mortars were faced by the dragoon sergeant Gavrila Nefedev, who in 1705 at Mitava was wounded, 'with a horse mortar in the left arm below the shoulder through and through.'[34] The text unambiguously speaks about the use of mortars from the saddle, meaning Swedish grenadiers fired mortars when in a mounted formation. For such a shot it was necessary to rest the butt of the mortar on the saddle, and for which

---

32 Tor Schreber von Schreeb, *Karolinska Förbundets Årsbok 1936: Kongl. Maij:tz Drabanter, 1695–1718: deras organisation, beväpning och mundering*, p.84.

33 Kfhc 68.

34 Tatarnikov, Officers' Tales.

CHARLES XII'S KAROLINERS VOLUME 2

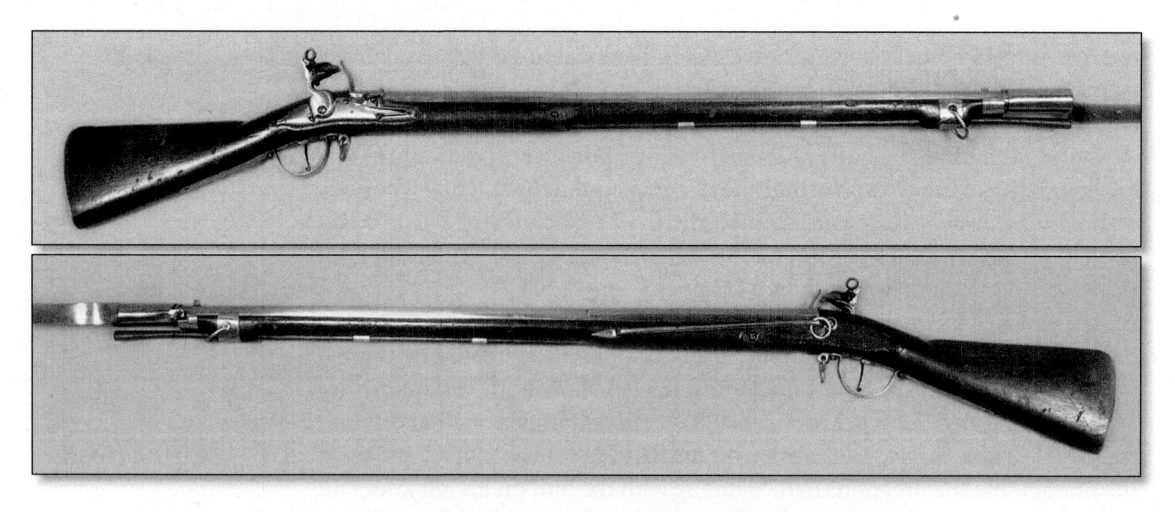

Above: AM.030768, Dragonmusköt model 1704 right- and left-hand side views.

Below: AM.031064, Carbine model 1699, right- and left-hand side views.

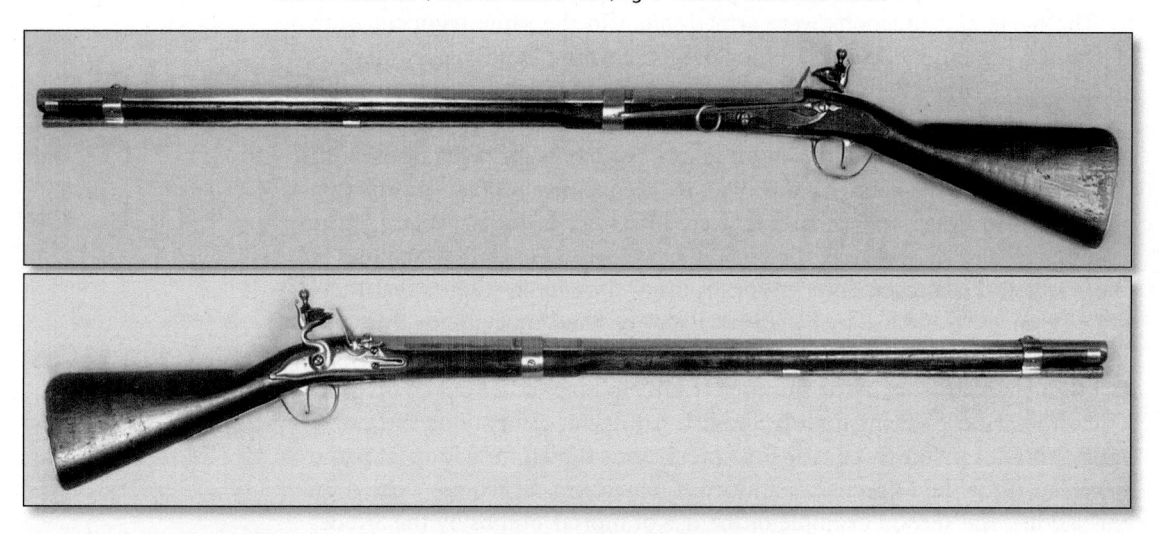

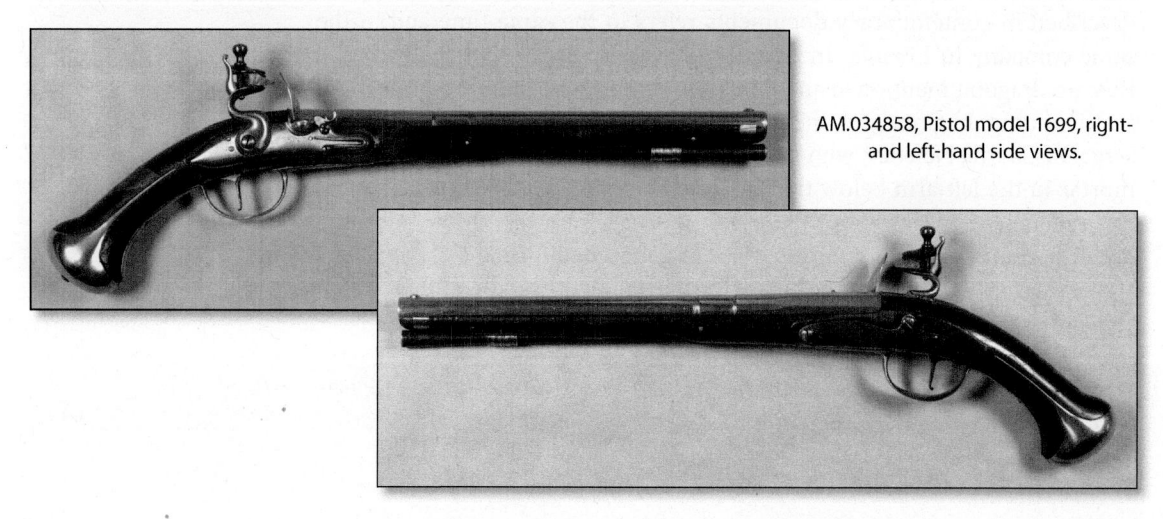

AM.034858, Pistol model 1699, right- and left-hand side views.

purpose there was a cut-out on the butt stock or a shaped convex metal part of the butt stock heel cover. An example of such a mortar is in the exhibition at the Poltava Battle Museum in Poltava, and also a mortar of 1700? There are several such mortars preserved in the Armémuseum in Stockholm, and in the Marinsmuseum in Karlskrova, inventory no. MM 02261.[35]

On one of the engravings from the library of Zurich, *Lebetes Pyroboli manuarii. Vulnificum ferrum torquent flammas que seguaces – Handmörser. Handmörser die werffen im Bogen zusammn. Zerspritzendes Eisen und Blitzende Flammen Meyer*, Johann [Zurich], 1711 Zentralbibliothek Zurich,[36] is shown cavalrymen with this type of weapon, and the method of firing it.[37]

In summary, we can say that there were not just grenadiers in the dragoon units, but also mounted grenadiers, although it is difficult to say in what numbers, and how widespread was the practice or their use. Probably, grenadiers with mortars were from the Livonian Dragoon regiments and squadrons, which, according to their establishment, had grenadiers. The Livländsk Dragoon Regiment took part in the battles near Mitava, and in the Battle of Gemäurtgof, and it is quite possible that the grenadiers of this regiment fired grenades from hand mortars while mounted within the formation. Indirectly in favour of this regiment is evidence that besides the above mentioned grenadier bags (50 of them), in 1700 there were also 600 grenades with all the necessary equipment for their use.[38]

Cavalry Officers' Swords, *Kavalleriofficersvärja*

There are quite a few examples of officers' swords from the Great Northern War period, one of them from inventory no.8 878 (15:150:a) Livrustkammaren,[39] of the characteristic form of the Walloon-type guard of the early model *Karolinska drabantvärjans fäste*. The sword has a length of 947 mm, and a width of 40 mm. The blade is straight, sharpened on both edges and tapering along its length to a point edges. On both sides of the blade are etched decorations consisting of a crowned monogram of Charles XII (double CXII), under which is *SOLI DEO GLORIA* (To God Alone be the Glory). The scabbard of the sword is also preserved in the collection.

Another example of a sword is in the Livrustkammaren, inventory no. 12352 (1888) Kommendervärja, Sverige 1715–1718,[40] traditionally carried by Charles XII at Fredrikshald in 1718. It has a total length of 1,193 mm, and a width of 138 mm. Additionally, privately commissioned swords with decorations added to suit the customer's taste were also carried.

---

35 Larsson, *Karolinska Uniformer*, p.172.
36 <https://doi.org/10.3931/e-rara-65892>
37 B. Megorsky, *Peter the Great's Revenge: The Capture of Narva and Ivangorod by Russian Troops in 1704* (Moscow: St Petersburg: 2016), p.129.
38 Larsson, *Karolinska Uniformer*, pp.124–125.
39 <https://samlingar.shm.se/object/ECAF8ED5-DB8C-440A-9C98-729F23C1275B>
40 < https://samlingar.shm.se/object/12F0823F-5208-497C-BB68-37F62AFCCA83>

CHARLES XII'S KAROLINERS VOLUME 2

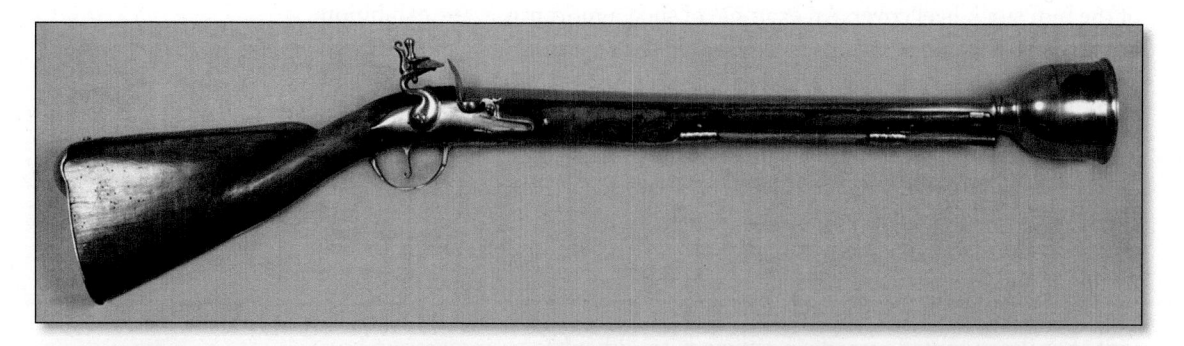

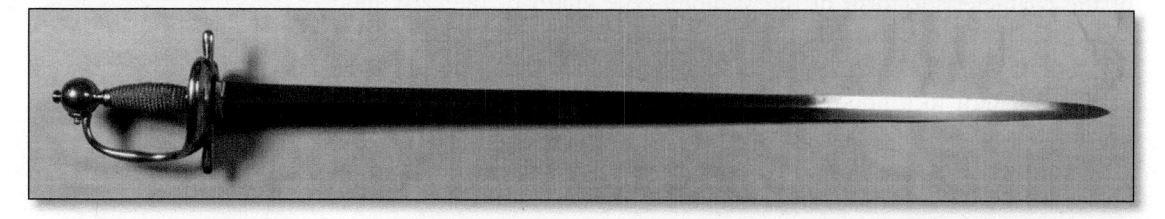

Top: Hand mortar from the Armémuseum in Stockholm, inventory no. AM.23478.

Centre: Detail showing from a Swiss engraving showing grenadiers using hand mortars.

Bottom: Kommendervärja, 1715–1718, Livrustkammaren 43299

Right: Sword, 1701. Armémuseum, Stockholm, inventory no. AM. 049921.

A large number of swords were deposited in the Russian State Trophy Collection and were shown at the exhibition in 2009. Among these are officers' swords from different years and with some differences in decoration. Cavalry swords differ in that they have a Walloon-type guard. To describe the decoration of some swords in more detail.

An example of an officer's sword from 1706, MMK, inventory no. Or-4025; the hilt is made of copper alloy and the Walloon-type guard is covered with gilding. Officer's sword MMK, inventory no. Or-4037/1, is similar to the sword example of 1706 – the blade is covered with gilt engraving, the bowl of the hilt both inside and outside are decorated with etching and engraving of a plant motif.[41] An officer's sword example of 1706 has a hilt of copper alloy with gilding, a Walloon-type guard. An award sword of 1710, MMK inventory no. Or-4386, has a hilt of copper alloy, a gilded grip, on both sides of the blade is the etched crowned monogram of Charles XII framed by palm branches. On the outer and inner surface of the bowl on both sides is also engraved the crowned monogram of Charles XII framed by palm branches. The date 1712 is engraved on the sides of the monogram on one side. A new model of Swedish award sword appeared in 1710, and the sword of 1706 was taken as a basis, it was intended for as an award to officers who distinguished themselves.[42] An officer's sword of 1710, MMK inventory no. Or-4385, is decorated with a similar ornamentation, with monograms on the blade and the guard as on the previous sample.

Swords of cavalry non-commissioned officers and troopers were used of different models, with iron or brass Walloon-type grip. Dragoons probably also used infantry style swords, with the corresponding form of hilt.

Cavalry Trooper Uniforms

The complete set of clothing and equipment of a Swedish cavalryman is described by the example of the trooper Livregementet till Häst during the restoration of the regiment in the autumn of 1709. Below is the complete list of the numerous items of uniform, equipment, armour, and horse furniture, all that has been omitted is the separate listing of the cost of the items. This list is of particulars interest given how few such detailed descriptions have survived. The text is given in the original Swedish, which is appropriate since this text occasionally uses names and terms in Swedish. In the following there are details the main items of clothing and equipment.

En blå kappa af godt inrikes tillverkadt och väl krympt kommiskläde, som bör vara 9 kvarter i bredden, 7½ alnar å 4 daler

Tre alnar dubbelbredt blått boy till foder å 2 daler

---

41 'Perfect Victoria' exhibition catalogue, C.296 & 297.
42 'Perfect Victoria' exhibition catalogue, C.305.

CHARLES XII'S KAROLINERS VOLUME 2

Above: Swedish and Saxon cavalry clash at the Battle of Düna, David von Krafft
Below: The Battle of Narva. Detail from a portrait of Charles XII, Narva Art Gallery.

ARMS AND EQUIPMENT OF TROOPERS AND NCOS OF CAVALRY AND DRAGOONS

En aln kanfas

Tvänne par kappspännen af mässing, ett större vid kragen och ett mindre neder på skörten, kosta ...

Skräddarearbetslön

En rock af lika kläde som i kappan med tvänne fållar i hvar sida samt krage och uppslag af kläde, hvartill erfordras 4¾ alnar, 4¾ alnar blått foder boy, och vikes fodret väl under knapphålen

Två dussin mässingsknappar, hvaraf ett dussin sättes framanför, ej längre ned än jämnt efter öfversta kanten af klappen, treneder på klappen och två ofvan, en vid hvart hörn och en i hvar sida efter modellen ä i daler En och en half aln kanfas Arbetslön

En skinntröja af bock-eller renläder med mässingsknappar samt

underfodrad med linneväf. Den som icke har reneller bockläder får i dess ställe taga godt baggeller getskinn till tröja.

Ett par goda bockhudsbyxor med klapp frampå och buldans-byxsäckar

En god svart kommishatt med svettrem samt galon och hatband af hvitt kamelhårsgarn

Ett par handskar med buffelhudskragar och bockskinnsgrepp

Ett par passer-eller smoriäderstöflar med helskurna kragar och sporrläder till

Ett par förtennta sporrar.

En halsduk af svart lärft om tio kvarters längd att hafva tvänne slag kring halsen

En skjorta af hemgjord grof lärft

Ett par goda ullstickade stöfvel strumpor

Ett buffelläders lifgehäng med helskuren taska och starkt raäs-smgsspänne uti ...

En värja af modellet

Ett värjeband af svart smorläder.

En karbinrem af sämskadt buffelläder med stark järnhake och mässingsbeslag

Detail from The Battle of Narva, Tallinn City Museum.

En karbin efter modellet

Ett patronkök med älghuds öfverdrag

En god stark sadel, väl gjord att han icke bryter, med mässingsknapp och allt tillbehör af bolster och godt remtyg, dock utan förbögel, med mässingsbeslag och söljor ...

Ett par stegböglar förtennta

Ett par betselstänger

Ett eschabrak af blått kläde, underfodradt med bzildan eller fyrskäftväf och med en svart läderkant omkring ...

Ett par flintlåspistoler

Ett par pistolstrumpor med blå ströflingar eller kappor af fint boy eller kjersingskläde.

En lodformare, dubbel till bägge skjutgevären, kostar 3 daler, af hvilken tvänne ryttare sig betjäna

En grimma med repskaft

En täckgjord med hästtäcke

En tvärsäck

En foderpåse

En viskduk

En skrapa förtennt

En ströborste

En gång hästskor och tvänne gånger som …

An som ryttaren själf plägar anskaffa

En halsduk

En skjorta

En bröstlapp

En nattmössa

En kam med foder

Ett par skor med spännen till

Ett par strumpor[43]

---

43 Kungl. Lifregementets Till Häst Historia, pp.115–116.

3

The Headwear of Troopers, Hat and *Karpus*

The primary headwear of officers and troopers of the cavalry was a broad-brimmed hat made black or dark grey felted wool.

The hats of troopers were trimmed with white woollen braid, camel yarn, silver or gold braid, sometimes with galloons. Non-commissioned officers had a hat of black felt with silver or gold lace, the hat brim was fastened with a silver button. Musicians had a hat covered with silver or gold braid, as well as woollen braid worked through with coloured thread, resulting in an ornamentation in regimental colours.

Hat of Charles XII

According to pictorial sources from before the Great Northern War, the brim of felt hats was pulled to the crown by a cord that was sewn around the brim and passed through the eye of a button that was inserted into the left crown of the hat. Depending on how tightly the cord was tied, dictated how tightly the hat brim was pulled to the crown. If the cord was tightly tied, the silhouette of a triangle was formed. At the beginning of the war another way was also practised – the brim loosely pulled, or pulled to the crown on one side only. Gradually, however, the fashion came in for hats to be more tightly drawn to brim to crown – the result was the well-known tricorne form. Often, sometimes in the same unit, some troopers wore *karpus* caps, and another part received hats, and both items appeared in use in the same unit at the same time. Sometimes, for marksmanship, a bundle of hay was inserted behind the drawn-up brim of the hat on the left side. This was an old tradition known from the modern Skanian War, and is in fact somewhat analogous of a cockade.

In addition to the hat, the *karpus* hat was quite common. The karpus was a cloth hat, the brim of which was sewn from several sections, for example four or six, the seams could be covered with woollen cord. In 1695 it was

THE HEADWEAR OF TROOPERS, HAT AND KARPUS

supposed to buy grey cloth (pre-washed, decorated), for 100 karpus, as well as blue cloth *blå boj*, as well as lining cloth for Smålands Kavalleriregemente.[1]

A 'cowl' and a visor were sewn to the body of the *karpus*, and could be buttoned to it. The visor could be of different shapes, a shaped cape or oval and large, as on the infantrymen from the equestrian portrait of Charles XII from the art gallery in Narva. The large cowl might have several buttons, which could be used to unfasten it at the chin, thus protecting the whole head and neck from the cold. The *karpus* was made taking into account the regimental colours. For example, a blue body combined with yellow or red cowl. The cowl could be small, or unfolded and buttoned at the chin, like montero caps. In making a *karpus*, at the end of the seventeenth century the following amounts of fabric were used: 1¼ aln red *walmar*, ⅛ aln *Dwalk*.[2]

In 1695, the Jämtlands Kavallerikompani used 3½ cubits of grey cloth, 1½ cubits of wool for lining, and seven pieces of cloth-covered buttons.[3]

The *karpus* could also be decorated in various ways, in the seams could be stitched in the release of dash colours, on top a woollen pompon could be added, an example of such a *karpus* can be seen on the equestrian portrait of Charles XII. The royal *karpus* shows a yellow-coloured brush or a bundle of hay. Fully furred *karpus* caps are also known.[4]

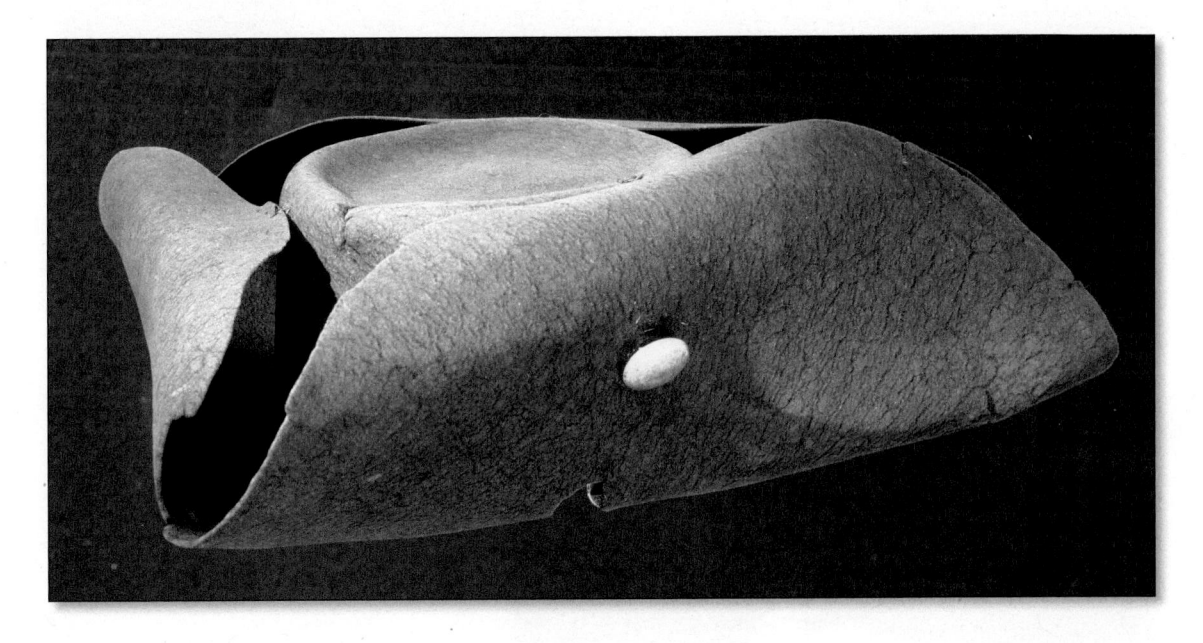

Hat of Charles XII

---

1 E. Bellander, *Dräkt och Uniform* (Stockholm, 1973), p 212.
2 Bellander, *Dräkt och Uniform*, p.154.
3 Larsson, *Karolinska Uniformer*, p.89.
4 L. Rangstöm, *Modelejon Manligt Mode 1600 -tal 1700-tal 1500-tal Livrustkammaren* (Stockholm, 2002), p.173.

CHARLES XII'S KAROLINERS VOLUME 2

Right: Detail from a portrait of Charles XII wearing a *karpus*.

Below: Portrait of Per Andersson Frestare, by David Klöcker. Ehrenstrahl NMStrh 22-Nationalmuseum.

4

The Uniform of the Cavalry and Dragoons

Cravat

Most men from cavalry and dragoon regiments wore a cravat (or stock) made of black cloth, of different variations. The fabrics used were wool, linen or silk. The length of the stock cravat varied; for example, a length of three alns (elbows) in 1719 in Västgöta 3-Männingsregementet till Häst,[1] or a length of 74 cm and a width of 23 cm of black cloth in Östgöta Kavalleriregemente in 1717. In some regiments the cravat may have been in other colours rather than black. Thus in Västgöta Kavalleriregegemente, and in Västgöta 3-Männingsregementet till Häst in 1704, it was white and black.[2] In Pommerska Dragonregementet in 1703, and in Stenbocks Dragonregemente in 1705, it was red.[3] The cravat could be tied in a knot in the front or tied with a lace, and there was also a variant of the cravat with two laces sewn into the edges, which were used to tie the cravat at the back of the neck.

Hair was gathered at the back of the head and was placed in a special pouch, black in colour and rectangular or trapezoidal in shape. This pouch was made of black cloth of various sorts, or in some cases of silk.

Cavalry Troopers' Coats

In the late 1680s and early 1690s, many cavalry regiments that had previously had leather coats and various colours of uniforms,[4] began to change in their majority to blue or grey uniforms with regimental facings. In some regiments the colour of the coats was grey, and the green Bohus Dragonskvadron coat looks quite exotic. In 1692 new uniforms in blue cloth with blue lining were

---

1 Larsson, *Karolinska Uniformer*, p.81.
2 Larsson, *Karolinska Uniformer*, p.81.
3 Larsson, *Karolinska Uniformer*, p.112.
4 A. Åberg, Göransson G., *Karoliner* (printed in Yugoslavia, 1989) pp. 31, 40.

ordered for the Södra Skånska (S. Scanian) Kavalleriregementet from a merchant in Malmö.[5]

During the Great Northern War, the cavalry used several patterns and variations of uniform that differed in cut, details, number of buttons, etc. The first – the 'Senior Model' was without a collar, or later similar but with a collar, was made during 1680s until about 1692. These coats were not generally used during the war, but judging by contemporary descriptions collars were not added to all coats until 1702. From about halfway through the 1690s, based on the 'Senior Model' and with changes according to royal edicts, several 'transitional' patterns appeared. These patterns were worn between 1694 and c. 1706. Sometimes they were already being made with collars and smaller cuffs. However, in a number of regiments collars on the coats of troopers are not mentioned in the patterns of the early period of the war (see below). In the infantry regiments there were different shapes of pocket flaps: horizontal, narrow, rectangular, any or all with rectangular or pentagonal flaps, with different number of buttons, etc.. In the cavalry, judging by the surviving sources, the most common preference was to have rectangular horizontal pocket flaps, with three buttons and buttonholes. But it is possible that non-commissioned officers and officers could have flaps with up to seven buttons and buttonholes. In the next version, called the 'newest pattern' of coat, approved in 1706 and which was worn from about 1707 (with some variations until the end of the war). The result was a coat whose design elements had previously been used, but which were now finally approved en masse. This 'new set pattern' was a coat with buttons and buttonholes reaching to the waist, with a collar, with small slit rectangular cuffs, and with horizontal pocket flaps, with three buttons.

The colour of the coat was most often blue, although of different shades, but there were also grey coats. In most regiments the facing colour was yellow, or light/ pale yellow. These new coats probably had the same number of buttons as on the surviving coat AM.015470, however by the 1690s there were already changes and variations, for example, from two narrow vertical flaps to horizontal – rectangular, with three buttons. Thus, judging by the surviving drawings and orders, three-button horizontal flaps were the most popular. The shape of the cavalry pocket flap was not the same for all of the regiments however, pocket flaps could be of different sizes, with flat edges, or with a curve at the bottom. Buttonholes, judging from the surviving drawings, were sewn with thread, less often with a reinforcing of cloth. The buttonholes could be sewn with threads of different colours, and white, yellow and blue threads are recorded. During the same period the cut of sleeves also changed; the sleeves narrowed, sleeves with a protruding visible part of a button cuff, and a wide high sewn on cuff were no longer manufactured. It was probably the same as with the Foot Guards and the rest of the infantry regiments. Changes in the uniforms of the cavalry also probably started with the Guard Cavalry Regiment, and then the innovations spread to the rest of the regiments.

---

5   Bellander, *Dräkt och Uniform*, p.210.

THE UNIFORM OF THE CAVALRY AND DRAGOONS

Early eighteenth-century drawing of a pocket flap and button design.

In 1695 Charles XI ordered that 'the clothing for all in Livregementet till Häst shall be blue, the coats will be cut tight around the waist, of proportionate width, with small square lapels. The uniform of the lieutenant colonel and the major are to have the same appearance as the uniform of troopers, the lieutenant and the cornet.'[6]

After these innovations, by 1700 the coat, as a result, became somewhat longer, and pleats were made on the skirt at the back and sides of the vent, which increased the amount of cloth used. According to the King's Decree, the coat was to be made with a collar, and small slit cuffs, with two pleats in the skirt at the sides. In the early years of the war the buttons on coats could still be placed all the way down the front. The coat and waistcoat buttons could be of simple cast pewter, of bronze, or of brass, and could be flat or convex. As a rule, coats were single-breasted, but in Verdiska Dragonregemente the coats of non-commissioned officers, corporals, and ordinary troopers were double-breasted.

Since the orders to introduce new uniforms in the army could not be executed at once for a number of reasons, the introduction and manufacture of the new uniforms in the cavalry regiments, as in infantry regiments, took a year, and some regiments a number of years. During this time cavalry regiments were wearing and patching and restitching the uniforms they had as necessary, only gradually receiving the new uniforms. The replacement of pieces for the new uniforms varied almost regiment to regiment. For many regiments the situation with clothing was concerning. Uniform items were worn out from the harsh conditions of military operations and of simply marching. There were examples when some units were given captured Saxon coats taken from the Saxon military stores during the campaigns of 1701, and from the battle of Kliszow. Many items of equipment and clothing were used from captured

---

6   Bellander, *Dräkt och Uniform*, p.210.

Swedish dragoon, from a ceiling painting in the Finnish Manor of Suur-Sarvilahden.

Saxon military stores, and on 16 September 1701 Charles XII ordered E. Dahlbergh to issue Saxon uniforms to Schlippenbach's Dragoons and to some other units. Apparently Saxon uniforms and other uniforms were received by the regiment in the last months of September 1701.[7] The Saxon uniforms of that period differed significantly in cut from the Swedish uniforms. Saxon uniforms were red, with a single row of buttons, with different coloured linings and with large round cuffs. From the early 1700s Saxon coats were made wide sleeves with wide stitched cuffs, rectangular pocket flaps positioned low in the skirts. One can imagine what a motley appearance of the cavalrymen of Schlippenbach's Dragoon Regiment, Livländskt Dragonregemente had as a result of these issues. However, even the use of captured uniform items did not solve the clothing problem. In January 1702, E. Dahlbergh called on the inhabitants of several Courland towns to urgently make uniforms for another dragoon regiment – Albedyls Dragoner. In April of the same year, the aforementioned dragoon regiment of W. A. Schlippenbach required a lot of uniforms, and by May Schlippenbach complained that the boots of dragoons and cavalry were completely worn out.[8]

In 1704 Karl Gustav Renscheld managed to order clothes and shoes from a number of merchants in Breslau for Livdragonerna, Adelsfanan, Södermanlands och Kronobergs Regementen and Upplands Kavalleriregemente. These clothes were to be delivered to stores in Poland.[9]

While the army was in Saxony, there was also a great deal of work going on at home to provide the troops with the necessary clothing. In 1704 contracts were made with tailors in Stockholm, to deliver 1,000 pieces of finished 'soldier's clothing' consisting of coats and breeches. The order used 5,750 cubits of good blue cloth, and 4,252 cubits of yellow wool for linings. In several instances, sources from this period contain information about contracts for headwear – hats and *karpuses*.[10]

At the end of 1706, Charles XII gave some general instructions regarding clothing for recruits arriving from Sweden. The changes mainly affected the uniform of the privates, the coat was now made narrow, but wider at the bottom, had pleats on the sides and lower tails at the back. The big change affecting all categories was that the buttonholes on the front, and the row of buttons

---

7   H. Palli, *Between the Two Battles for Narva. Estonia in the First Years of the Great Northern War 1701–1704* (Tallinn, 1966), p.99.
8   Palli, *Between the Two Battles for Narva*, p.100.
9   Bellander, *Dräkt och Uniform*, p.223.
10 Bellander, *Dräkt och Uniform*, p.225.

THE UNIFORM OF THE CAVALRY AND DRAGOONS

Detail from the 1717 painting, *The Battle of Lesnaya 1708* by Jean-Marc Nattier, showing a fallen Swedish cavalryman wearing a double-breasted coat.

themselves, now ended at the waist. This change gave a distinctive character to the new military uniform, which should perhaps be called the 'Young Carolingian Uniform'. It was probably influenced by the military fashions of Germany, particularly of Brandenburg-Prussia. The amount of cloth needed for coats increased from 4½ cubits to 5½ cubits, and the width at the hem of the coat was as much as eight cubits. The number of buttons was greatly reduced; on the front there were now no more than 11–12, one on each side at the top of the pleats, three for each pocket, and three small ones at the bottom of each sleeve.[11] Hooks were placed at the corners of the coat's tails, and the tails were turned up and fastened with hooks, creating the characteristic silhouette of the Caroline soldier. However, as various iconographic sources show, the tails were not always buttoned, or hooked, back. A further description of the new type of cavalry uniform is known from the example of a coat for Adelsfan Regiment in 1709. There is a drawing of the coat flap, with three buttons, and the amount of material needed for manufacture.[12]

Most Swedish cavalry and dragoon regiments wore single-breasted coats, but there is evidence that double-breasted coats were also used. Apart from the portraits of a number of Swedish cavalry officers posing in double-breasted coats; double-breasted coats were also worn, as mentioned above, by non-commissioned officers and troopers. A painting from 1717, *The Battle of Lesnoy 1708*, by Jean-Marc Nattier (see detail above), shows Swedish cavalry, and among them is the figure of a fallen Swedish cavalryman wearing a

---

11 Bellander, *Dräkt och Uniform*, p.228.
12 Larsson, *Karolinska Uniformer*, pp.216–217.

51

CHARLES XII'S KAROLINERS VOLUME 2

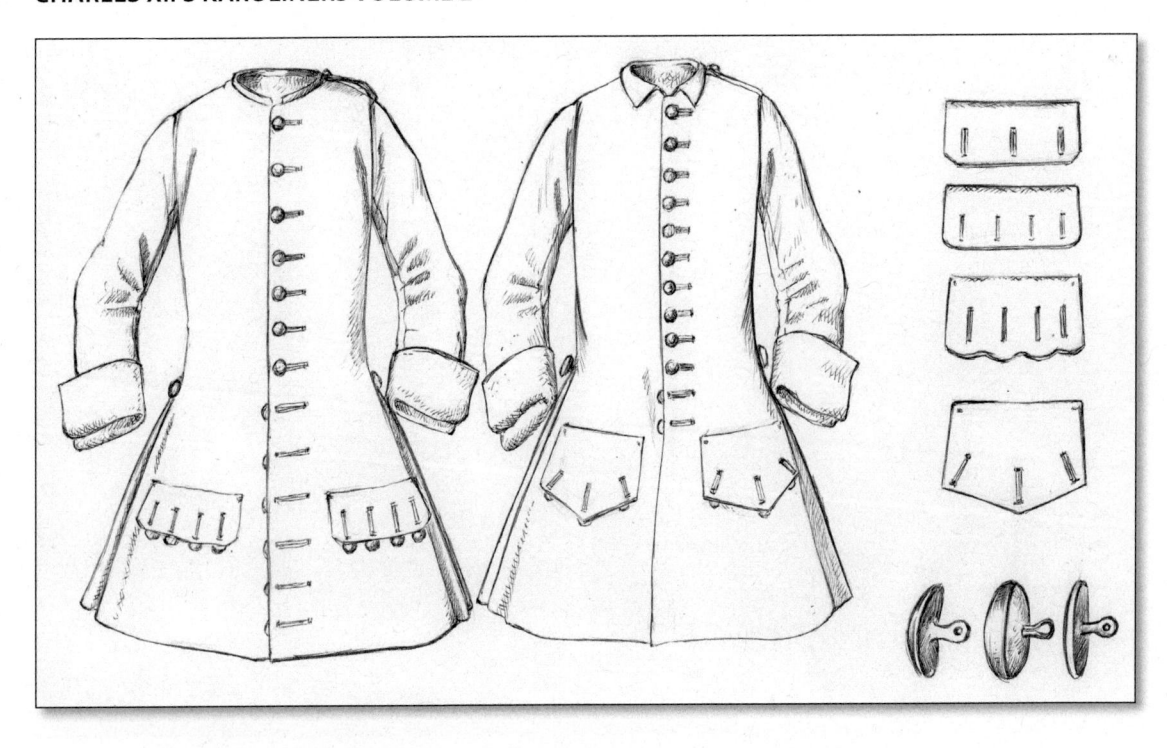

Above: Coats of a trooper of Swedish cavalry, note the form of pocket flaps and buttons. (Author's illustration)

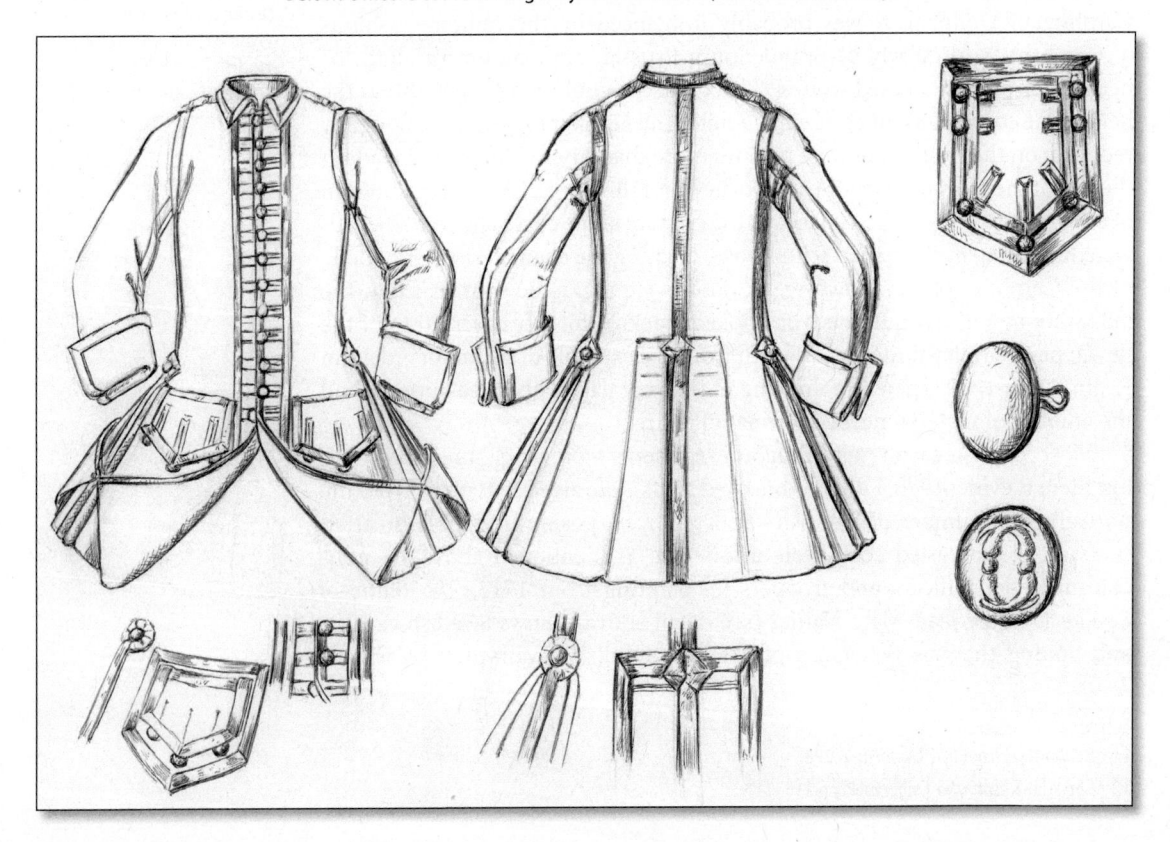

Below: Officer's coat showing a layout of the lace. (Author's illustration)

double-breasted blue uniform with a yellow lining and cuffs. According to the recollections of the artist's daughter, the painter worked under the direct supervision of Tsar Peter, which may well indicate that the details of armour and uniforms shown on the painting are quite accurate, and thus it is possible to exclude the possibility of this being a fantasy of the artist. Unfortunately, which specific Swedish regiment was intended by the artist is unknown, and remains in question.

Despite the fact that the majority of cavalry regiments switched to cloth coats as early as the end of the 1690s, some regiments continued to wear leather coats ('buff coats') made of buffalo or elk skin, *Elgshuds Köller*, instead of uniforms of cloth, even after the outbreak of the Great Northern War. Such *buff coats* were used in Riksänkedrottningens [Queen Dowager's] Livregemente till Häst, in Adelsfanan i Estland och Ingermanland, Drottningens [The Queen's] Livregemente till Häst, or Estniska Kavalleriregementet.

In the collection of the Armémuseum in Stockholm there are several of these buff coats preserved both complete and in fragments, which allows a detailed examination of the cut and of the small differences.

Buff Coats (*Kyller*)

By the beginning of 1700, almost all Swedish cavalry, following the Royal Decrees, had replaced the buff leather coat. The Royal Decree of 12 April 1700, for example, sets out that the troopers of the Noble Banner Regiment, Adelsfanan, are to be provided with good leather waistcoats, which they are to use in the field in place of the buff coats which are to be left at home.[13] Interestingly, later in the 1727, 1729 and 1756 regulations on cavalry clothing, in addition to waistcoats made of leather or cloth, Swedish *Elgshuds Köller* are also mentioned, with the proviso that they should be used only on parades. The *Köller kolettes* from the Great Northern War have survived to our time in quite a large number, at least three of them are in the collection of the Armémuseum in Stockholm (inventory nos AM.030912 and AM.030915 (see photos overleaf) and AM.032356).

In Livrustkammaren there are even more – about a dozen coats from the end of the seventeenth or the beginning of the eighteenth century. They are all of the same type, with hooks on the front, and buttons on the sleeves, on the edges of the inside of the front, and the hems are covered with a wide braid, or fabric. The buttonholes are finished with yellow thread. Inventory no. 20843 (911:4),[14] or 20842 (911:3),[15] are moose leather coats with long sleeves and a small, 20 mm wide collar. Fastening is at waist level with a 15 mm diameter fabric covered button. Coat with leather epaulettes, 230 mm long. Slits at the sides 580 mm high, and at the back 580 mm high. Back with a slit. Sleeves with slits at the bottom, 130 mm long with six round brass buttons.

---

13 Schreber von Schreeb, *Karolinska Förbundets Årsbok 1936*, p.101.
14 <https://samlingar.shm.se/media/DC90E0CA-2CE5-45E0-8679-C266CB066B6C>
15 <https://samlingar.shm.se/object/21B6D50C-65DD-4AA3-999B-DA6732211C92>

CHARLES XII'S KAROLINERS VOLUME 2

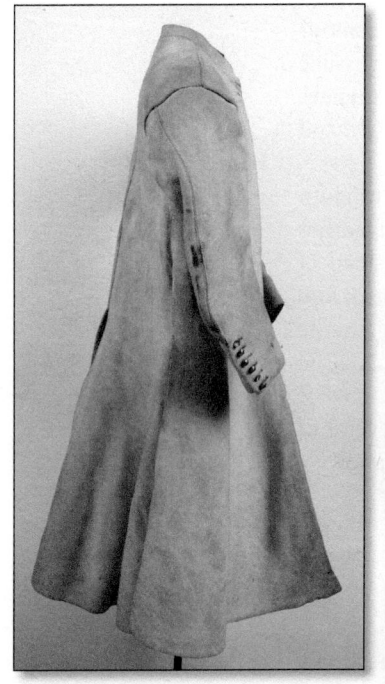

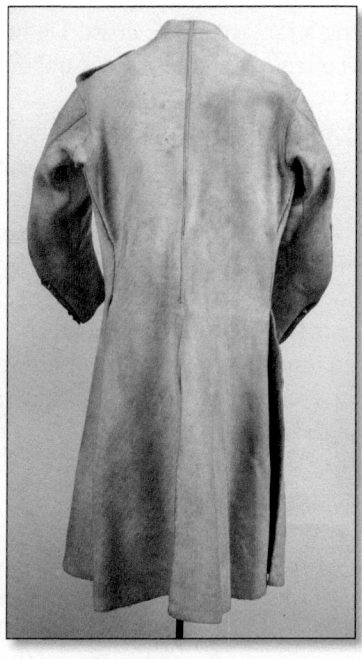

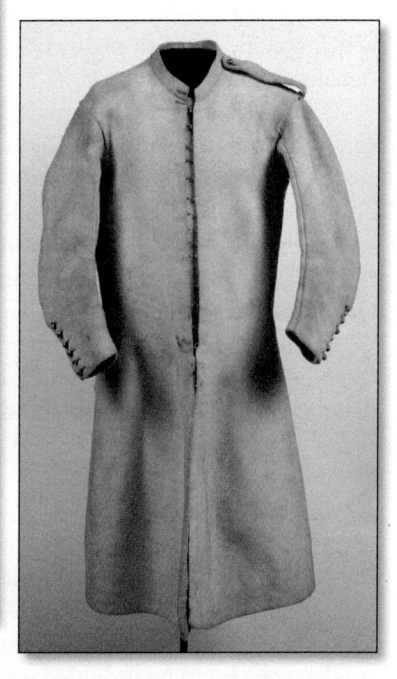

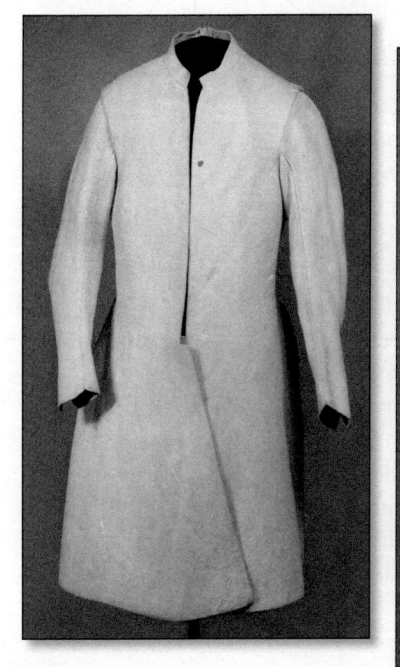

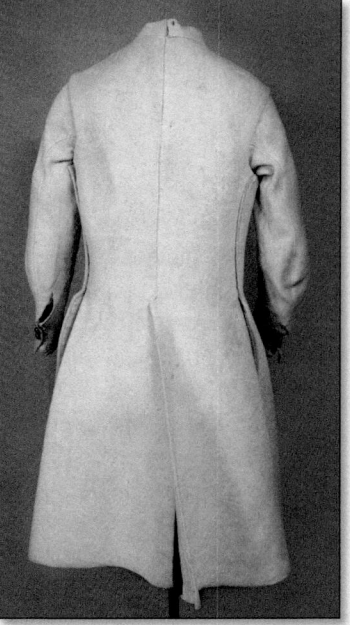

Leather buff coats at the Armémuseum in Stockholm (above, AM.030912; left, AM.030915).

The bottom of the sleeves are lined with brown cloth. A strip of fabric is sewn around the edges of the inside of the coat. Inventory number 20840 (911:1).[16], length at front 1,030 mm, at back 1,100 mm, sleeve 620 mm.

Pajrock

From 1702, in the descriptions of cavalrymen's clothing there was mention of an item that combined the function of a coat and a cloak – the *pajrock*. The *pajrock* is a type of clothing with an appearance closer to a coat, with a somewhat simplified, looser cut, which allowed it to put it on top of a coat. The *pajrock* was made of blue cloth or grey *vadmal*. It is probable that soldiers did not have pockets and flaps on the *pajrock*. The *pajrock* combined the function of a coat and a cloak, in fact it was the prototype of a modern overcoat and similar items of clothing are known ever since the seventeenth century. The sleeves of the *pajrock* had to be wide enough to be worn over the coat, and it also had to be wide enough in the body. The *pajrock* may have protected its wearer from the cold a little better than a cloak. For example in the Upplands Ståndsdragonregemente, five cubits of blue cloth, 11 cubits of lining cloth, and a dozen pewter buttons were needed to make a *pajrock*.[17]

Unfortunately, neither detailed descriptions, nor drawings, nor the cut of the *pajrock* are recorded in Swedish documents of the era. There are also no surviving *pajrocks* of this period in Sweden. The only specimens of European *pajrocks*, which can be used to give an idea of its appearance and construction during the Great Northern War period are in the St Petersburg Hermitage, in the wardrobe of Peter the Great. One example of a *pajrock* is inventory no. E/rt 8459, being single-breasted and of ochre-brown cloth, with ochre-greenish lining. A second is double-breasted, made of dense thick green cloth, without a lining, instead being painted in red and able to be turned inside out, and accordingly be red with green lining. Both examples are without pockets.

There are two collars sewn on the brown page-jacket, 18 buttons and buttonholes, the buttons are covered with cloth, and the buttonholes are stitched. There are two buttons on each of the cuffs, in the middle and on the back of the sleeve. Three more buttons and buttonholes are located on the collar, which is raised to cover the throat, the second collar, cape, covered the shoulders, like the cape of a cloak. In total there are 25 buttons on the *pajrock*. The cuffs are wide and sewn, and there was a slit in the back of the *pajrock*.

There were also two collars sewn onto the green *pajrock*: a small standing collar, and a second collar that could be raised to close at the neck, with buttonholes, in two rows of three, for a total of six buttons. Unbuttoned, the collar lay over the shoulders. The edges of the collar and the seams are piped with silk cord. Buttonholes are edged with silver thread, on both sides there are seven buttons covered with silver, three buttons on the round cuffs, one at each side, at the beginning of the side pleats and at the bottom of the side

---

16 <https://samlingar.shm.se/object/0D62A8BD-C061-46AE-9A10-3CC07FDFC861>
17 Larsson, *Karolinska Uniformer*, p.120.

CHARLES XII'S KAROLINERS VOLUME 2

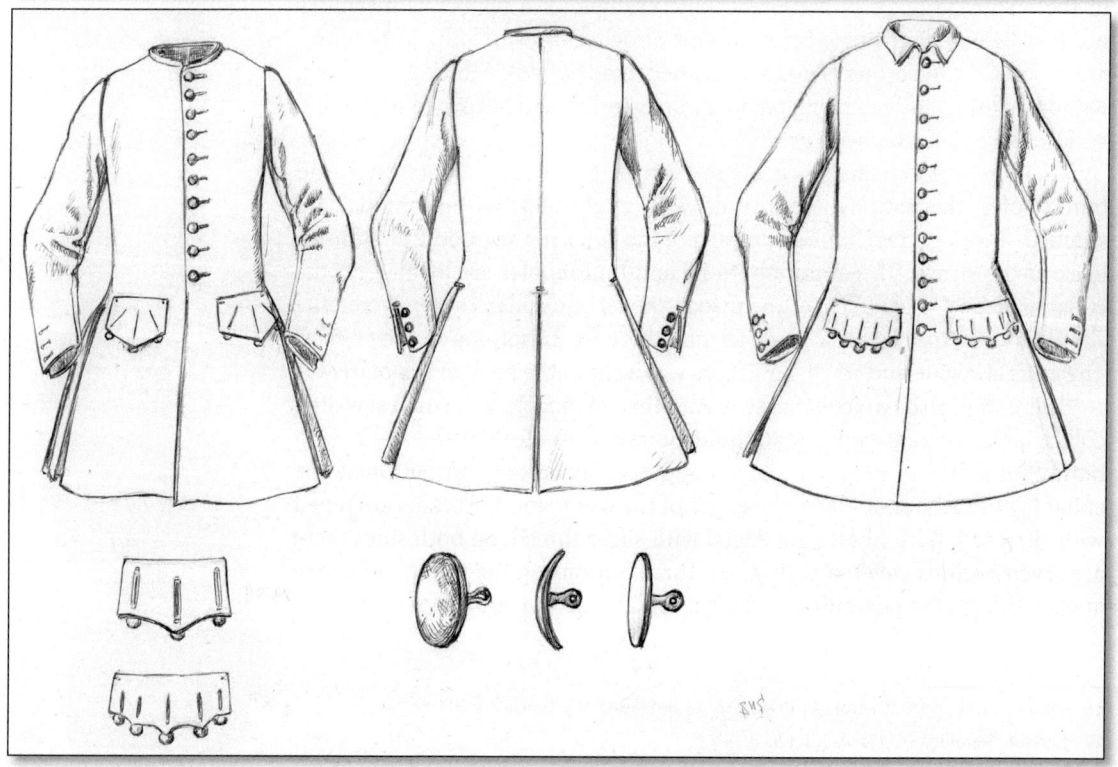

pleats. In total there are some 30 buttons. On the red side there are also 24 buttons, so that this *pajrock* could be worn with either side out, green or red.

The examples described above show the diversity in the cut of the *pajrock* coat. In the Swedish Army, judging from the scanty descriptions, it seems that the first coat – single-breasted with fewer buttons and a simpler, more spacious cut – was commonly used.

Facing page:
Top, cavalry troopers in a cape and *pajrock*.

Bottom, drawing of a waistcoat showing variations of pocket flaps and buttons.

(Author's illustrations)

Waistcoat

After the abolition of buff coats, the cavalry introduced leather or cloth waistcoats, worn under the cloth coat. The buff coat was replaced by a lighter leather *väst* (*tröja*), a piece of clothing that was also called a waistcoat (*kamisol*). The cavalrymen of the Södra Skånska cavalry received such waistcoats, made of deerskin, in 1694. According to the regimental commander, leather waistcoats were already used in all other cavalry regiments. In the Östergötlands Kavalleriregemente in 1695, both a buff coat and a leather waistcoat are mentioned. By the outbreak of war in 1700, the entire Swedish cavalry was equipped with leather waistcoats.[18]

Thus, what we call a waistcoat in documents can be called variously, *camisol*, *väst*, *skinntröjor*, but it is the same type of clothing, although the amount of material used is slightly different depending on the fabric or leather used. The waistcoat of troopers and non-commissioned officers was leather, or less commonly cloth, single-breasted and with sleeves, but it is possible that sleeveless waistcoats were also used. The preferred leather to be used was reindeer or moose made in such a way that it had a suede-like surface of different shades of yellow In the cases when it was not possible to find reindeer or moose leather, for manufacture of these waistcoats, a thinner goat leather could be used. The collar on waistcoats was most often in the form of a narrow standing design, but in portraits there are waistcoats with a small stand-up collar, as a rule, these are moose leather coats. We see such a collar on the portrait of Charles XII in the Tallinn City Museum, and on the portrait of Magnus Gabriel von Köhler, as well as on some other portraits. The waistcoat was lined with linen and fastened with cast bronze or pewter buttons. The waistcoat reached the middle of the thigh, but in the middle of the 1710s, began to become shorter. The front does not appear to close one side over the other. The buttonholes on the side and on the flaps of pockets were made in the same way as on the coats – in a frame – or were sewn over with thread. Buttons on leather and cloth waistcoats were not sewn on, but a hole was punched through, and through which the loop of the button was threaded and then fastened onto a leather cord on the inside. Buttons could also be placed on the sleeves. The images show waistcoats with pockets with flaps, fastened with three or four buttons. The flaps could be either rectangular or variously shaped along the lower edge. Troopers' leather waistcoats of the period of the Great Northern War have not survived, but a

---

18 Bellander, *Dräkt och Uniform*, p.211.

CHARLES XII'S KAROLINERS VOLUME 2

THE UNIFORM OF THE CAVALRY AND DRAGOONS

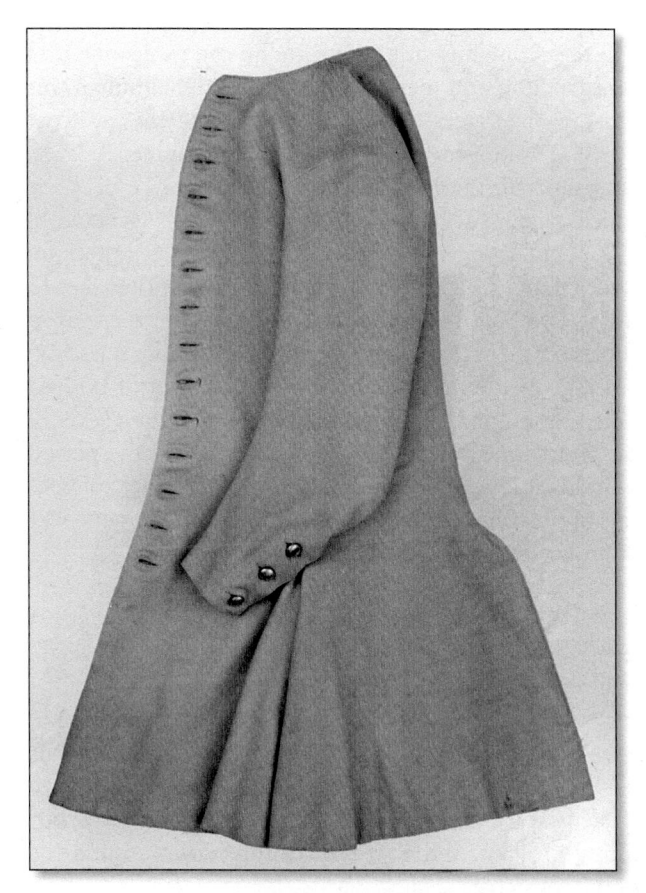

Left: Leather waistcoat. Livrustkammern inventory no. 20853 (42:153).

Below, and facing page: Waistcoat of Charles XII (Livrustkammaren collection)

preserved waistcoat in the Armémuseum in Stockholm can give some idea of the appearance, construction and method of manufacture, although this example is from a somewhat later period, c. 1730s–early 1740s. The waistcoat (inventory no.AM.022991) belonged to Kapten (Captain) Anders Rålamb, who fought in the campaigns of Charles XII.

The waistcoat which belonged to Kapten Anders Rålamb is made of yellow-coloured elk skin, cut, despite the fact that it is an officer's coat, not from solid sheets of leather, but assembled from smaller pieces. There are 13 flat pewter buttons on it, two buttons on the cuffs, and three on the shaped pockets. The buttonholes on the waistcoat are slit and hemmed with undyed silk thread. In the middle, on the front and back, it is lined with undyed canvas, but the sleeves are unlined. Taking into account a certain level of conservatism and the short time period between this coat and the period under consideration in this study, it is logical to assume that leather soldier's and officer's waistcoats of the time of Charles XII were sewn in the same way and of the same or approximately the same construction.

Another waistcoat which is in the collection of the Livrustkammaren, inventory no. 20853 (42:153),[19] looks very similar to a piece from the first quarter of the eighteenth century, but dates from the end of the seventeenth or beginning of the eighteenth century. It is thus another waistcoat from the Great Northern War. It is difficult to say whether this is civilian or military, but it still gives a good idea of the method of manufacture, and the proportions of leather waistcoats. It is made of elk leather, with long sleeves, and a 40 mm wide lapel collar. It fastens at the front with 15 hooks, the sleeves have four brass buttons, the lining in linen, and a strip of cloth is sewn around the edges of the inside of the waistcoat.

A surviving example of what the cloth waistcoats of troopers and officers might have looked like can be seen in a surviving examples of one that belonged to Charles XII. The waistcoat is made from yellow cloth, probably the colour of suede. It is fastened on the side with 14 gilded brass buttons, with three more buttons on the cuffs, the buttonholes are stitched around. The waistcoat is without pockets, lined with a plain weave yellow wool, the back and part of the shelves are lined with yellow baize (*ylle boj*). Inside, in the area of the buttonholes, a strip of cloth is sewn that closes the buttonholes about halfway. There is a cut-out in the armhole under the sleeve.

Breeches (*Byxor*)

During the Great Northern War, there were two variations of breeches (*byxor*) with a folding flap with three buttons of pewter or cast bronze, or breeches with a fly. In the cavalry regiments, breeches were made of leather – reindeer, elk, or goat. In a number of cases there are records of breeches made of blue factory cloth, or imitating the colour of suede. The breeches for the cavalry were also made of coarser, home-made cloth (*vadmal* literally homespun).

---

19 <https://samlingar.shm.se/object/493FB8D0-82ED-4C37-86FA-323938FB19E8>

THE UNIFORM OF THE CAVALRY AND DRAGOONS

Vadmal breeches were usually not dyed grey. By a royal decree, soldiers' breeches were supposed to be of good goat or deer skin.[20] No soldier's breeches of the period of the Great Northern War have not survived, but an idea of the appearance and method of manufacture can be gained from a somewhat later, about 1730s to early 1740s, example in the Armémuseum in Stockholm. These breeches (inventory no. AM.022993) belonged to Kapten (Captain) Anders Rålamb, who took part in the campaigns of Charles XII. The breeches are made of yellow leather (goatskin or elk skin), with three pewter buttons, and are fastened at the back with a cord. One button was fastened at the waist, and two buttons fastened a 'hinged' flap. The breeches were not sewn from a single piece of leather, but assembled from smaller pieces. Troopers' leather breeches were probably made in the same way and were of the same approximate design. Trooper's breeches were also fastened with three buttons, two on the flap and one on the belt. The length of the breeches was to come to just below the knee. Buttonholes on elk or goat skin breeches could be framed or threaded. Buttons on leather breeches were not sewn on, but a hole was punched through which the tang of the button was threaded and then attached to the leather cord on the inside. Sometimes pockets were put on soldiers' breeches, there could be several pockets, including the front of breeches with flaps.[21] On one of the preserved pairs of breeches of Charles XI (Lrk inventory no. 3347) there are four buttons on the fly and one on the waistband, and they have three pockets, one in the waistband in front and two in the sides.

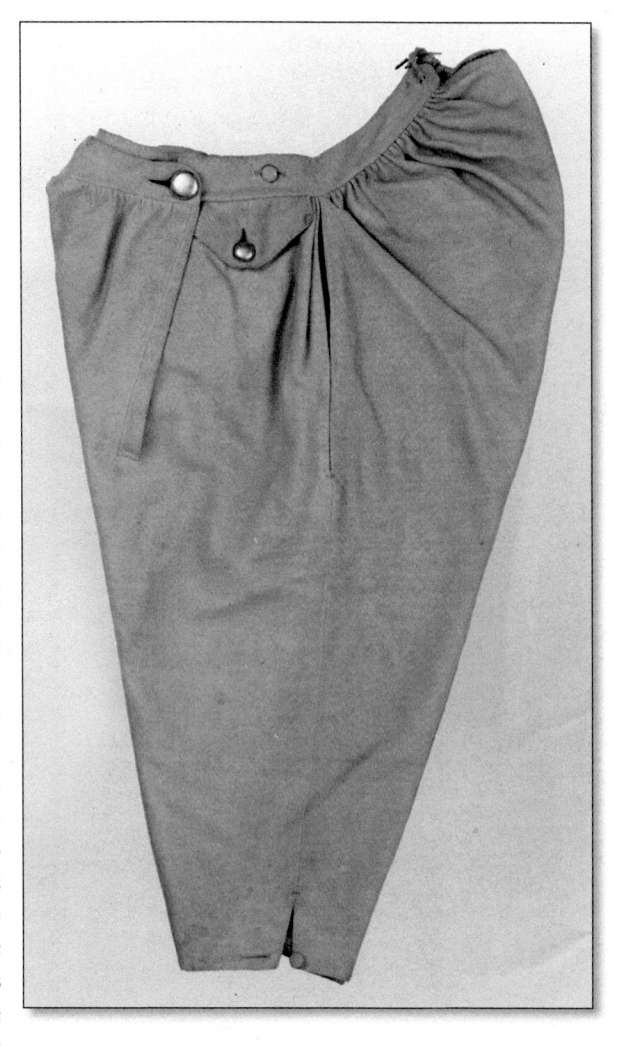

Breeches belonging to Charles XII.

Cloak

The cloak for the cavalry of the period was of cloth, cut semicircular or full round, and long enough to come to below the knee. It was made of blue or grey cloth – with a lining according to the facing colour of the regiment, and a collar that was also of a burgundy colour. The shape of the collar could be rounded and small, or with pronounced corners, as it can be seen on the surviving example of an officer's cloak belonging to Charles XII. The collars of non-commissioned

---

20 Bellander, *Dräkt och Uniform*.
21 T. Jakobsson, *Artilleriet under Karl XII:s-tiden*, Armemusei Skrifter I (Stockholm, 1943), p.275.

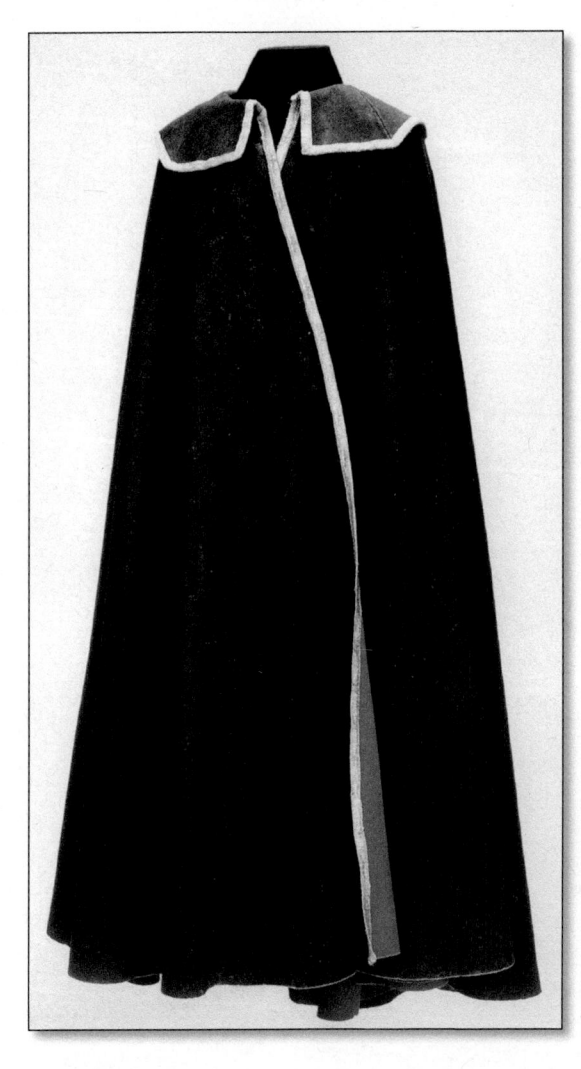

Swedish officer's cloak from the collection of the Hermitage, St Petersburg.

officers' and troopers' cloaks were often edged with white woollen or yellow braid, as well as with metallised silver or gold braid. The lining of the cloak was sewn on the front edges, from the collar to the bottom, also padded shoulders and part of the back part of the bottom of the cloak at the slit.

In 1716, the cloak of the private Tyska Dragonregementet was made of eight cubits of blue cloth, 1¾ cubits of lining wool, and had a pair of buckles. In 1717, the cloak of the Upplands Ståndsdragonregemente in 1717 used 7¼ cubits of blue cloth, two cubits of blue lining wool, one cubit of canvas, and one pair of bronze buckles.[22] In Nylands och Tavastahus Läns Kavalleriregegementet in 1703 the cloak took eight cubits of grey cloth, six cubits of grey lining wool, and a pair of buckles. In 1719 for a trooper of the same regiment the cloak used eight cubits of cloth two cubits wide, and 3½ cubits of woollen lining cloth.[23] In general, cloaks of troopers of cavalry regiments used approximately the same amount of cloth, the only difference appears to be in the amount of woollen lining fabric.

The cloak was fastened at the throat by a pair of brass or bronze buckles, which were shaped like a triliscus, one of the buckles had a hook. A second pair of smaller buckles also appear in the descriptions, these buckles, which were sewn on the front edges in the middle of the cloak and closed the front of the cloak preventing them from opening, and thus ensured the covering of the whole body. For convenience when travelling these small buckles could be fastened to the back of the cloak.[24] This is shown in the detail of a painting by Johan Filip Lemke (1631–1711), which shows soldiers walking with Stockholm in the background. The buckles of non-commissioned officers could be plates with silver. Examples of both large and small buckles are known from occasional finds in the Poltava region.

Uniform of the Troopers of Cavalry Regiments Recorded in Surviving Documents

Study of the **Livregementet till Häst** regiment shows how cavalry were supplied, and their clothing. In 1700, troopers wore hats with gold galloon

---

22 Larsson, *Karolinska Uniformer*, p.121.
23 Larsson, *Karolinska Uniformer*, p.93.
24 Bellander, *Dräkt och Uniform*, p.201.

THE UNIFORM OF THE CAVALRY AND DRAGOONS

lace. The coats were light blue with bronze buttons, the lining and cuffs were blue. Pocket flaps had three buttons. Leather waistcoat and breeches. The description does not mention a collar, and it is quite possible that in 1700 the model of coat without a lapel collar was still in use by this regiment.

In 1701 the Livregementet till Häst wore items such as:

> *Hatt svart, helt slät utan galon eller snören, med mässingsknapp. Rock av ljusblått kläde med boj av samma färg, med nedvikt krage och "svenska" ärmuppslag, smal i livet och med flata mässingsknappar. Väst av blått kläde med krage samt ärmar med uppslag, så att den skulle kunna användas vid rockens avtagning, mässingsknappar men mindre. Byxor av renhud eller bockskinn med klaff och fickor*[25]

Thus the regiment was using black hats without lace, with brass buttons, a coat with a collar and Swedish small cuffs, narrow in the waist and with flat brass buttons. Besides leather waistcoats, blue cloth examples with brass buttons of smaller size than on the coat are also mentioned. Leather breeches with a flap (*latsbant*) and pockets. All these clothes were worn out by 1701 and required replacement. Axel Spens reported this to the King in October 1701, and also that he had reached an agreement with a Riga merchant to purchase new coats and hats for non-commissioned officers and troopers. By the spring of 1702 the uniforms were again badly worn, as Spens wrote on 27 May, sending to Riga *Rotmistre* Lilljeström and Corporal Gyllenax to see if an order for new sets of clothes for the regiment was ready. New hats with gold and silver galloon and coats made of blue cloth, with new buttons, were being made. By 1703 the clothes and the rest of the order, were ready. The new items of clothing were to be stored in Marienburg.[26] But by 1706 all the hats and waistcoats in the regiment were again badly worn.

In 1703/06 cavalrymen wore a hat with gold galloon lace, a light blue coat with blue woollen lining. The woollen cloth waistcoat was light yellow, resembling the colour of an ox skin leather waistcoat (*baffle*). In November 1706, Kreutz wrote that hats, coats and waistcoats were badly worn. In 1706 for making new uniforms each trooper was allocated 5½ cubits of blue fabric, nine cubits of blue woollen fabric for the lining, 2¾ cubits of pale or light yellow cloth, two dozen pewter buttons, besides two dozen more buttons for the waistcoat, a hat with a leather band inside and 1¼ boats of gold galloon. '*5½ alnar blått kläde, 9 alnar blått boy, 2¾ alnar paillegult kläde, 2 dussin rockknappar af tenn, 2 dussin kamisollknappar, 1 hatt med lädersvettband uti och 1¼ lod guldgalon.*' Before leaving Saxony, the regiment was to receive this uniform and equipment.[27] In 1707 the troopers of the regiment wore a hat with gold galloon lace, a light blue coat with pewter buttons and a blue lining and cuffs, light or pale yellow waistcoat and leather breeches. The regiment fought in the uniform issued in 1706 until the Battle of Poltava.

---

25 Bellander, *Dräkt och Uniform*, p.222.
26 *Kungl. Lifregementets Till Häst Historia*, p.114.
27 *Kungl. Lifregementets Till Häst Historia*, p.114.

Engraving depicting a Swedish cavalryman, 1717. (Alf Åberg, *Fångars Elände, Karolinerna i Ryssland 1700–1723* (Stockholm: Natur och Kultur, 1991), p.9))

After the disaster at Poltava, in October 1709 the regiment was rebuilt, and a detailed list of everything necessary was drawn up. Here is a list of articles of clothing. The cloak was 7½ cubits of blue cloth, nine kvarter wide. Three cubits of double wide lining blue cloth (*blått boy*), one cubit of canvas (*kanfas*). Two pairs of brass buckles, one pair of larger buckles under the collar, the other pair of smaller buckles, which were on the cloak at about hip level. The coat, with collar, with two pleats in the skirt at the sides, was of the same blue cloth as the cloak. It was made of 4¾ cubits of cloth, 4¾ cubits of blue wool lining, of which the buttonholes were made. One and a half cubits of canvas. Two dozen brass buttons, of which one dozen are supplied on the side, the length reaching below the waist to the level of the pocket flaps. Three buttons were placed under each shoulder on the epaulettes and one button at each side closing the side vents.[28] In the company from Nerke in 1710, everything was made from *vadmal* – a cloth of home production and of poorer quality than that factory made, it was originally grey, but it could be dyed.[29]

A leather waistcoat of moose or reindeer skin with brass buttons, lined with linen cloth. If a has waistcoat of elk or reindeer could not be made then, in its place, a good lambskin or goatskin was acceptable. Goatskin breeches with a flap pin in front. A black hat with a braid woven from white camel yarn. A pair of gloves, with cuffs, of buffalo leather with the fingers of softer

---

28 *Kungl. Lifregementets Till Häst Historia*, p.115.
29 Höglund, *The Great Northern War 1700–1721*, p.51

THE UNIFORM OF THE CAVALRY AND DRAGOONS

goatskin. A pair of boots. A cravat of black cloth about 10 kvarters long, suitable as to be able to wrap round the neck twice. A pair of stockings.[30]

In 1718, the regiment received new hats, cloaks, leather waistcoats, and in 1720, new coats. At the end of the war in 1722, troopers of the Livregementet till Häst had hats with gold galloon (probably those issued in 1718), a coat with bronze buttons, a cloak with two pairs of buckles, leather breeches, a leather waistcoat without buttons, or leather coats.[31]

Adelsfanan i Sverige och Finland. Until 1704 the regiment wore grey hats with blue-yellow tape, and a grey cloth coat, with yellow lining and cuffs. The waistcoat and breeches were leather. They had a cloak of grey cloth with yellow lining and collar. In 1704 the hats were changed to black with silver galloon lace and new coats of blue with blue lining and cuffs, silver lace on the collar and bronze buttons were issued. The breeches and waistcoat were leather. In 1705 recruits received hats with a wide white braid and blue coats with bronze buttons. Instead of cloaks they were issued grey *Pajrocks*. In 1708 they had grey coats. In 1710 the regiment had hats with silver galloon lace, blue cloaks with bronze buckles, a blue lining and galloon lace on the collar. Blue coats with bronze buttons, blue lining and cuffs. Waistcoat and breeches of leather.[32] In 1709 a black cravat.[33]

The new coats issued in 1709 were blue, with pleats on the sides, and had a blue lining. The collar and cuffs were of blue cloth, the buttonholes were made of blue camel-wool yarn. Brass cast buttons with lowered edges. There were no buttons on the sleeves. Pocket flaps with three buttons and buttonholes. On the shoulder a strap with a button to support a sling for the carbine, the button was the same as those on the front of the coat.[34]

Västgöta Kavalleriregemente. In 1700 cavalrymen of this regiment wore the new uniform received earlier. Hats with silver galloon, a blue coat with bronze buttons and yellow lining, and a yellow leather waistcoat and breeches. This uniform was worn until 1708. New items such as hats, coats and cloaks were issued in 1710 and 1712. By 1715, the regiment had hats with a wide white braid, a blue coat with yellow lining, cuffs, blue cloaks with yellow lining, and leather waistcoats and breeches.

Åbo och Björneborgs Läns Kavalleriregegemente. In 1701, the cavalrymen of this regiment had hats and *karpuses*, grey cloth coats with grey lining and cuffs and pewter buttons. The cloak was also grey with grey lining. The breeches and waistcoat were leather. In 1708 new hats and new blue uniforms were received. In 1712 the re-raised regiment wore hats and clothing of grey *vadmal*. In 1718–1719 hats, *pajrocks*, waistcoats and breeches were of grey *vadmal*.[35]

---

30 *Kungl. Lifregementets Till Häst Historia*, p.115.
31 Höglund, *The Great Northern War 1700–1721*, p.51.
32 Höglund, *The Great Northern War 1700–1721*, pp.51–52.
33 Larsson, *Karolinska Uniformer*, pp.89–90.
34 Larsson, *Karolinska Uniformer*, p.90.
35 Höglund, *The Great Northern War 1700–1721*, p.52.

Smålands Kavalleriregemente. In 1700–1704, the troopers of this regiment had hats with wide gold galloon lace, a blue coat with a blue lining and blue cuffs and bronze buttons. Grey coat with bronze buttons and a yellow collar and lining. Leather waistcoat and breeches. In 1710–1712 they had hats with white braid, blue coats with blue lining and cuffs.[36] In 1714, blue coats with blue lining and bronze buttons.[37]

Nylands och Tavastahus Läns Kavalleriregegemente. From 1696, the troopers of this regiment had hats, a grey coat with a red lining and cuffs and pewter buttons. A leather waistcoat and breeches. In 1701 they were issued hats and grey *karpus*, a grey coat with grey lining and cuffs and pewter buttons. A grey cloak with grey lining. The breeches and waistcoat were leather.

In 1702 making a *raitarsky* cloak used eight cubits of grey cloth, six cubits of grey lining wool and a pair of buckles.[38] In 1702, 900 grey coats, and for each another one cubit of *caniface* and ¾ measure of silk.[39] In 1708 recruits wearing grey *vadmal*. In the period 1712–1718 they wore hats, grey and blue coats, and waistcoats and breeches made of leather and of *vadmal*.[40] In 1719 the coat used five cubits of cloth, 6½ cubits of woollen lining cloth, two dozen large buttons, and seven small pewter buttons.[41]

Östgöta kavalleriregemente. In 1700, the troopers of this regiment had hats with silver braid, blue coat with yellow lining and cuffs and with bronze buttons. Leather waistcoat and breeches. In 1706 new hats also with silver braid were issued. In 1709/10 the hats had white woollen braid.[42] In 1717, coats required five cubits of blue cloth, 4¾ cubits of yellow woollen cloth for the lining, 1½ dozen bronze buttons, and half a dozen bronze buttons for sleeves.[43]

Karelska (Viborgs och Nyslotts län) Kavalleriregementet. In 1702, the troopers of this regiment had grey coats with pewter buttons.[44] The new uniform of 1702 included a grey *karpus* with blue lining, a grey cloth coat with blue lining and blue cuffs and with pewter buttons. Leather waistcoat and breeches. In 1708 the regiment had blue coats, and in 1710 *karpus*, cloak and waistcoat of *vadmal*. In 1713 the regiment had a new uniform – blue *karpus* and a blue coat. In 1718 recruits were in *vadmal* clothing.[45] In 1719, a coat required four cubits of blue cloth, four cubits of lining cloth, and English pewter buttons.[46]

In 1702, the cavalrymen of the **Norra Skånska [North Scania] Kavalleriregementet** were issued new uniforms, which included hats with

---

36 Höglund, *The Great Northern War 1700–1721*, p.53.
37 Larsson, *Karolinska Uniformer*, p.90.
38 Larsson, *Karolinska Uniformer*, p.92.
39 Larsson, *Karolinska Uniformer*, p.90.
40 Höglund, *The Great Northern War 1700–1721*, p.53.
41 Larsson, *Karolinska Uniformer*, p.92.
42 Höglund, *The Great Northern War 1700–1721*, p.54.
43 Larsson, *Karolinska Uniformer*, p.91.
44 Larsson, *Karolinska Uniformer*, p.91.
45 Höglund, *The Great Northern War 1700–1721*, p.54.
46 Larsson, *Karolinska Uniformer*, p.92.

silver braid. A blue coat with silver-plated pewter buttons, the buttonholes lined with blue camel's hair thread. The cuffs are blue, as is the collar. There is silver braid on the collar and the lining of the coat is yellow. On the coat went five cubits of good cloth and seven cubits of yellow lining wool. In 1710, hats with white woollen braid, blue coats, new blue coats, leather waistcoats and breeches, some cavalrymen use items of grey vadmal. From 1713 onwards, hats with white braid, blue coats with yellow lining and cuffs. Blue coats, breeches and waistcoats made of leather.

Södra Skånska [South Scania] Kavalleriregementet. In 1701 a new uniform was issued of hats, blue cloaks with s blue lining and with bronze buckles. Light blue coats lined in the same light blue and with bronze buttons, blue cloth waistcoats and leather breeches. In 1703 new blue coats were issued, and new waistcoats made from the old coats. In 1704, new hats with a wide silver galloon. Recruits were issued with leather waistcoats and breeches. In 1705 coats and breeches were made of blue cloth. The regiments received new uniforms in 1706/07. In 1711 the troopers had blue cloaks, blue coats, leather waistcoats and breeches.[47]

Riksänkedrottningens [Queen Dowager's] Livregemente till Häst. In 1702–1708 cavalrymen of this regiment wore hats with a wide silver galloon. They continued to use leather buff coats, blue coats with brass buttons, the coats were lined with blue, the cuffs were also blue. A blue cloak lined blue. In 1715 they wore old hats of 1701 with gold braid, blue coats with buff leather coats, and leather breeches. Blue cloaks lined blue and with bronze buckles.[48]

Bohus Dragonskvadron. In 1702 cavalrymen of this regiment wore hats with silver braid. Green coats with yellow lining and cuffs and with bronze buttons. Green cloak with yellow lining, waistcoat and breeches of leather. In 1712 new hats with silver braid, new cloaks in the same colouring as earlier.[49]

Jämtlands Kavallerikompani. From 1695 the troopers of this regiment wore grey *karpus*, grey coats lined blue, grey cloth coats with blue lining and blue cuffs. Waistcoats and breeches of leather. In 1695 the old clothes for Jämtlands Kavallerikompani are listed, for example grey cloak, grey *karpus*, buff coat, old hat, grey cloth coat, leather waistcoat, goatskin breeches, black ribbon for tying hair, and a cuirass.[50]

Adelsfanan i Estland och Ingermanland. The troopers of this regiment wore dark grey hats with blue and yellow braid. At the beginning of the war leather *buff coats* were used instead of coats. A grey coat with yellow lining and cuffs. Grey cloak with yellow lining, leather waistcoat and breeches. In 1708/9, hats, blue coat, leather waistcoat and breeches.

Adelsfanan i Livland och pä Ösel. The troopers of this regiment had a dark grey hat with yellow braid. A grey coat with yellow lining and yellow cuffs. Leather waistcoat and breeches.

---

47 Höglund, *The Great Northern War 1700–1721*, pp.55–56.
48 Höglund, *The Great Northern War 1700–1721*, p.56.
49 Höglund, *The Great Northern War 1700–1721*, p.65.
50 Bellander, *Dräkt och Uniform*, p.212.

Cavalrymen, detail from a Nationalmuseum engraving – Tribute to Charles XII, dated 1697. The proportions of the uniforms and the rectangular small pocket flap are clearly visible.

Upplands 3-männingsregementet till Häst. In 1700 cavalrymen had hats with white braid, corporals had silver braid on their hats. Blue coat with blue lining and blue cuffs and with bronze buttons and. Cloak, blue with bronze buckles and blue lining. Cravats white and black. Waistcoat and breeches of leather. In 1719 a new uniform was issued: hats with braid, black cravat, *pajrock*, coat, waistcoat and breeches of *vadmal*.

Upplands Femänningsregementet till Häst. In 1710–13, the cavalrymen of this regiment had blue coats with yellow lining and cuffs, black cravat, leather waistcoat and breeches. In 1715 they were issued coats of infantry colour blue with blue collar and cuffs, and with a yellow lining, and 552 yellow woollen cloth waistcoats.

Västgöta 3-Männingsregementet till Häst. In 1704, the cavalrymen of this regiment had hats, coat and a cloak of *vadmal*. The waistcoat and breeches were made of leather, with a black or blue cravat. In 1716 hats with bronze buttons, a blue cloak with bronze buckles and yellow lining, blue coat with blue lining and cuffs and bronze buttons, black cravat, leather waistcoat and breeches.

Skånska 3-Männingsregementet till Häst. In 1700–1, the cavalrymen of this regiment had hats, blue coat with red lining and cuffs – old uniforms inherited from Södra Skånska [South Scania] Kavalleriregementet waistcoat and leather breeches. In 1711 a new uniform was received: hats with silver braid, coat, cloak, waistcoat and breeches of blue cloth. Blue cravat and blue stockings.[51]

Bremiska Kavalleriregementet. From 1696, the troopers of this regiment had their hats edged with silver braid. Blue coat with white lining and cuffs. Blue cloak with blue lining and silver braid on the collar. Leather breeches and waistcoat. From 1701 hats with gold braid, blue coat with blue lining and cuffs and bronze buttons, buttonholes sewn with blue thread.

The Uniform of the Private Dragoon Regiments

Kunglig Majestäts Livregemente Dragoner Livdragonregementet. In 1700, the dragoons of this regiment wore hats with camelot braid. The cravat was black. A blue coat with a blue lining, blue cuffs and bronze buttons. The cloak was blue, the waistcoat and breeches were of leather.

Drottningens [The Queen's] Livregemente till Häst or Estniska Kavalleriregementet. In 1699 the troopers of this regiment wore hats with gold braid. A white cloak with bronze buckles a cravat tied with a red or blue bow. Leather buff coat, leather breeches. In 1703 the regiment had blue cloaks; in 1708 blue cloth coats.

Pommerska Kavalleriregementet. In 1702, the troopers of this regiment had hats with white braid; blue coats lined with red and with red cuffs and a red collar, with tin buttons and buttonholes sewn with white thread; leather breeches.

Bremiska Dragonregementet. In 1700, the dragoons of this regiment had hats with silver braid; blue coats with suede-coloured lining and cuffs and buttons of tin, the buttonholes were sewn with blue thread; a black cravat, a leather waistcoat with tin buttons and leather breeches. Blue cloak with suede-coloured lining and silver braid on the collar.

Karelska Lantdragonskvadronen. From 1696, dragoons of this regiment had a grey coat of *vadmal*. In 1701 they had new coats, waistcoat and breeches of *vadmal*. From 1712, hats had yellow braid, and the coat, cloak, waistcoat and breeches of *vadmal*.

Livländskt Dragonregemente. In 1701–1702 the regiment used captured Saxon uniforms. In 1703–08, the regiment's dragoons had hats with yellow braid, blue coats with bronze buttons, blue cloth waistcoats, and leather breeches.

Ingermanländska Dragonregementet. In 1700 presumably *karpus*, coat, cloak, waistcoat and breeches of grey *vadmal*. In 1702, blue coats with yellow

---

51 Höglund, *The Great Northern War 1700–1721*, p.116.

lining and cuffs, breeches presumably also blue. From 1708, a new uniform which included a *karpus* hat, blue coat and waistcoat. From 1713 coat and breeches made of *vadmal*, leather waistcoat, yellow stockings.

Pommerska Dragonregementet. In 1703, the dragoons of this regiment had a hat with gold and yellow braid, a blue cloak lined blue, a blue coat with blue lining and cuffs and bronze buttons. And with the buttonholes panelled in gold and yellow and the collar, pocket flaps and cuffs edged with gold and yellow braid. The waistcoat and breeches were of leather.

Verdiska Dragonregemente. In 1703, the dragoons of this regiment had hats with white braid, a blue double-breasted coat lined blue with blue collar and cuffs, and with pewter buttons and the buttonholes sewn with white thread, the collar and the pocket flaps were edged with white braid. The waistcoat and breeches were of leather. Corporals had a hat, collar and coat flaps edged with silver braid.

Meierfelts Dragonregemente. In 1703 the dragoons had hats with yellow braid, a blue coat with yellow lining and cuffs and bronze buttons, a blue cloak with yellow lining and collar, and leather waistcoat and breeches. In 1706 cloaks with silver braid, coats blue with cuffs and lining of aurore colour, waistcoat and breeches of pale yellow colour under 'buff'.

Stenbocks Dragonregemente. In 1705, the dragoons of this regiment had hats with yellow braid, blue cloak with yellow lining, a blue coat with yellow lining, cuffs and collar and pewter buttons. Red cravat. The waistcoat was of leather-coloured woollen cloth, with stamped pewter buttons, and buttonholes edged with yellow cord. In 1705 the leather breeches had a linen lining and three pewter buttons.[52]

Taubes or **Schlesiska Dragonregementet.** Dragoons of this regiment in 1704/5 wore hats with silver braid, a black cravat, a blue cloak with yellow lining and bronze buckles. The coat was blue with a blue lining and blue cuffs and bronze buttons. The waistcoat and breeches were of leather.

Dückers or **Preussiska Dragonregementet.** In 1704/5 the regiment had hats with silver braid, as well as blue *karpus* with yellow braid. The cloak was blue with blue lining and bronze buckles. The coat was blue with yellow lining and cuffs and bronze buttons. The cravat was black. The waistcoat and breeches were made of leather. In 1705 blue wool lined in linen was used for the breeches which had three buttons.

Bassewitz Dragonregemente or **Dragonregemente i Wismar.** Dragoons of this regiment in 1711 wore hats with silver braid, a cloak with a blue lining and collar, a blue coat with blue lining and cuffs and with pewter buttons, a black cravat, a blue cloth waistcoat and leather breeches.

Schwerins Dragonregemente. Dragoons of this regiment in 1711 wore hats with silver braid, a blue cloak with a blue lining, a blue coat lined blue with blue cuffs and with pewter buttons, a red cloth waistcoat and leather breeches.

Vietinghoff's or **Barthska Dragonregementet.** Dragoons of this regiment in 1714 wore hats with white braid, a blue cloak with a white lining and

---

52 Larsson, *Karolinska Uniformer*, p.121.

THE UNIFORM OF THE CAVALRY AND DRAGOONS

collar, a blue coat with white lining and cuffs and with pewter buttons. White cloth waistcoat and blue cloth breeches.

Tyska Dragonregementet, 1716. The dragoons of this regiment had 4½ cubits of blue cloth for a coat, including collar and cuffs, 4¼ cubits of wool for its lining, two dozen brass buttons and 1½ skeins of camel yarn for buttonholes.[53] Making a waistcoat needed 2½ cubits of blue cloth, five cubits of canvas for lining, 1½ dozen bronze buttons, one skein of camel yarn for buttonholes. For making breeches, in 1716, 1⅜ of blue cloth, four cubits of lining cloth and three bronze buttons.[54]

Upplands Ståndsdragonregemente. In 1703, the dragoons of this regiment had *pajrock* and blue coats. In 1704, a hat with silver braid, a *pajrock* of blue cloth, a blue coat with yellow lining and cuffs and bronze buttons and a blue and white cravat. The breeches and waistcoat were of leather. In 1714 a surtout *pajrock*. In 1717 making a *pajrock* used five cubits of blue cloth, 11 cubits of lining fabric and one dozen buttons. In 1717 making a coat took 4½ cubits of blue cloth, four cubits of blue woollen cloth, 1½ cubits of canvas and two dozen pewter buttons.[55] For making a cloak, in 1717, 7¼ cubits of blue cloth, two cubits of blue lining wool, one cubit of canvas, and one pair of bronze buckles were used. For the manufacture of the waistcoat it took 2½ cubits of suede-coloured cloth, five cubits of lining cloth and two dozen pewter buttons.[56]

Skånska Ståndsdragonregemente. In 1702 the dragoons of this regiment had hats with braid, blue *pajrock*, blue coat with yellow lining and cuffs and bronze buttons, black cravat. Waistcoats and breeches were of leather. In 1704 the regiment had blue cloth breeches and yellow stockings. In 1707 a new uniform was issued – hat with silver braid, blue coat with lining and cuffs in blue, and bronze buttons, waistcoat and breeches of pale yellow colour woollen cloth. The 1716 issue of new uniforms was a hat with silver braid, a blue cloak with blue lining, blue coat with blue lining and cuff and pewter buttons, a blue cloth waistcoat and leather breeches.

Västgöta Ståndsdragonregemente. In 1704, the dragoons of this regiment had hats with white braid. A grey *pajrock* of *vadmal*. Blue coat with lining and cuffs in yellow and with bronze buttons. Waistcoat and breeches of leather. In 1709 the regiment had: hat with braid, blue *pajrock*, a blue coat with pewter buttons, yellow braid on the shoulder and three buttons on the sleeves. The waistcoat and breeches were of leather. In 1712 hats had yellow braid, the coat was blue with lining and cuffs in yellow and with bronze buttons. Waistcoat and breeches of leather.

Öselska Lantddragonskvadrone. In 1703/04–08 an ordinary cavalryman had a hat, a blue cloak with yellow lining and bronze buckles, a blue coat with yellow lining and cuffs and bronze buttons, leather breeches and waistcoat.

---

53 Larsson, *Karolinska Uniformer*, pp.91, 120.
54 Larsson, *Karolinska Uniformer*, p.121.
55 Larsson, *Karolinska Uniformer*, p.120.
56 Larsson, *Karolinska Uniformer*, p.121.

Apart from the abovementioned regiments and squadrons, there were several other recruited companies and formations in the Swedish cavalry, but no data on their uniforms have been preserved. One of them (the Valash Regiment) is interesting however, and unusual for the Swedish Army of the period, and is worth looking at in more detail. The regular regiments of the Swedish Army, their actions in combat and general information about their uniforms are well enough reflected in various works, but the Western European reader is probably unfamiliar with the actions, uniforms and equipment of the irregular Valash Regiment. For example, Lars Erik Höglund wrote only a few sentences in his book, but there is some information to perhaps fill this gap.

The main protagonists in the Great Northern War actively used irregular cavalry. In the army of Peter the Great this role was played by Cossack regiments, consisting of controlled Ukrainian regiments, and various Asian Kalmuk formations. In the armies of the Polish-Lithuanian Commonwealth this function was performed by the Shlekhet militia, and regular light units. In the Swedish Army there were no such regiments and in battle this function was taken over by Polish-Lithuanian light units allied to the Swedes, as was the case in the battle of Jakobstadt in 1704. Later, Charles XII realised that he needed his own light cavalry to operate in such a vast territory. Light cavalry was much better compared to regular 'battle' cavalry for guarding communications, foraging and, most importantly, for reconnaissance. The Valash Regiment was just such a formation in the Swedish Army. Around the end of 1702, in the Swedish Army there appeared recruited light cavalry units headed by an Överste (colonel), K. Urbanovich, a Pole in Swedish service. Two Volokh squadrons took part in the Battle of Fraustadt in 1706.

In the Volokhsky Regiment of the Swedish Army, there were about 2,000 men – it is clear from their names and surnames that most of them were Poles and Ukrainians. The regiment was commanded by an officer of Moldavian (Volokh) origin, Sandul Koltu. Elements of the Voloshsky Regiment were taking part in reconnaissance skirmishes with Russian troops as early as 1708.

The first skirmishes with the Voloshsky cavalry of the Russians, were unsuccessful. But in the summer of 1708 fortune and skill were on the side of the Swedish Volokhs, they skilfully covered the march of the Swedish troops and prevented the Russians from taking prisoners.[57] However, in turn, the Swedish Volokhs conducted active reconnaissance and did take prisoners, as happened on 20 June 1708. After the victory at Golovchino, before the beginning of the Dnieper crossing, Charles XII sent light cavalry detachments to the north and south of Mogilev to distract the enemy. One such detachment successfully made a raid on the enemy and the actions of this detachment even forced the Tsar to change the route of his retreat of the defeated Russian troops. In the southern direction, the Swedish detachment, which included the Voloshsky Regiment, managed to blockade the garrison of Bykhov. But there were also failures, thus a small detachment under the command of Major M. Kanifer, numbering 40 men, was captured after an unexpected attack by Russian cavalry in Smoliany. The rest of the Volokhs of this company had

---

57 *Letters and Papers of Peter the Great*, T.VII, Vyp.2 (Moscow; Leningrad: 1946), p.901.

THE UNIFORM OF THE CAVALRY AND DRAGOONS

time to rejoin the regiment. In general, the actions of the different Volokh units in this operation were quite successful. By their actions Volokhs managed to mislead the Russian commanders, and gave Charles XII and the Swedish Army the opportunity, without enemy interference, to carry out the crossing to the left bank of the Dnieper on 4–5 August.

In the autumn of 1708, the Voloshsky Regiment numbered 10 companies each of between 60 and 100 men. Joining the King, the Ukrainian Hetman I. Mazepa, brought another 300 of his own Volokhs as part of his detachment. The Ukrainian Volokh remained with the Swedish Army, and shared the campaigns in the winter of 1708–1709. Charles XII had complete trust in Sandul Koltza, and in April 1709 'Överste' Sandul Koltza was sent to negotiate with the Silistrian Seraskir Pasha.[58]

At the Battle of Poltava, the Voloshsky Regiment carried out the task of diverting the Russians from the main Swedish column by moving behind the right flank. The regiment consisting of 11–12 companies had to pass through the Yakovetsky forest and act near the main Russian entrenchments. Exact information about the Regiment's actions in the battle have not survived, but it is known that it, having lost only one standard, was able to withdraw from the battlefield in an organised manner. Under Perevolochnaya, the Volosh horsemen scouted places for a crossing, and managed to cross the Dnieper. On 7/8 July, together with Zaporozhian Cossacks, the regiment covered the crossing of the Swedish detachment into Turkish territory. The Voloshsky Regiment continued their service in the King's headquarters at Bender.[59]

The complexity of the clothing of the Voloshsky Regiment is not recorded in the sources but we can safely assume that they wore similar clothing to other Voloshshy formations in the Polish and Russian Armies at the beginning of the Great Northern War.

One of the surviving paintings from the Great Northern War period from the National Museum in Warsaw (facing page, top) shows a skirmish

A cavalryman of the Voloshsky regiment. (Author's illustration)

---

58 O. Voloski Slisarenko, 'Polks Of The Armies of Karl XII, Peter I in the Campaigns of 1708–1709', in *Ukrainian Historical Journal 2017*, no. 1, p.36.

59 P. A. Krotov, *The Battle of Poltava* (for the 300th Anniversary), p.397.

Above: A skirmish between Wolosz light cavalry and Swedish cavalry. (National Museum, Warsaw, MNK (MP3284 MNW))

Below: Fragment of a standard. (Hermitage, St Petersburg, inventory no. ZN-3838)

between Volosh light cavalry and Swedish cavalry. The painting clearly shows short dolmans and narrow breeches tucked into yellow boots. On their head the cavalrymen are depicted wearing fur hats with cloth tops and with white rosette-like cockades. The cavalrymen are shown in red, blue and ochre dolmans and breeches. They are armed with sabres, pistols in holsters and carbines on slings. The cavalryman in the centre is depicted wearing a tashka (sabretache) embroidered with the arms of the Polish-Lithuanian Commonwealth. Such tashkas, as well as the whole costume, were characteristic of the Transylvanian, partly Volosh, and more widely the Hungarian national cavalry of the, and by the end of the seventeenth century they had spread, as well as the whole complexity of the clothing into many European armies. Later this complex of clothing was gradually transformed into the costume of the hussar formations of the European armies.

There is another little-known source, this time a Swedish painting on a Swedish standard, possibly showing Volokhs in Swedish service, or at least Swedish cavalrymen dressed in a similar style. This is a painted standard from the Hermitage collection (facing page, bottom). This was probably produced no later than in 1718–20, judging by the monogram of Eleonora Ulrika on one of the sides of the cloth. The painting, according to experts, was probably made in the earlier period.[60] In the catalogue of trophy items this standard is listed as belonging to Eleonora Ulrika and is described thus: 'a Swedish silk standard with the image on one side of fighting soldiers, some of whom are dressed in red and others in blue, and on the other side between two golden branches a double monogram [of Eleonora Ulrike].'[61] The painting on the standard shows a battle between grenadiers in red, (possibly Russian), and cavalry with sabres in their hands, wearing fur hats with white tops, blue dolmans and breeches, red boots; several figures are portrayed wearing white mantles. It is difficult to assert unequivocally that it is the Voloshsky Regiment in the Swedish service that is depicted, but, this is definitely a strong viability since this is a captured Swedish standard from the Great Northern War. In favour of the possibility that this does show Volokhs, is the style of the clothing. The figures show the same familiar set of clothes, which in the early eighteenth century were worn by light cavalry Volokh formations.

Service Personnel

In each regiment there were various non-uniformed ranks, workmen and artisans. They also wore uniforms, but slightly different ones, for some regiments.

---

60 V. Danchenko, *Swedish Banners and Flags*, exhibition catalogue (St Petersburg: State Hermitage Museum, 2021), p.144.

61 I. D. Talyzin, *Description of the Artillery Hall of Memorable and Unmemorable Objects 1862* (St Petersburg, 2006) p.76.

Adelsfanan: in 1717 blue coats with blue lining and two dozen brass buttons. *Pajrock* which used eight cubits of grey *vadmal*, one cubit of blue cloth for the cuffs, eight cubits of lining cloth and one dozen brass or bronze buttons.[62]

Norra Skånska [North Scania] Kavalleriregementet. In 1702 wore hats with a white cord, blue coats with yellow lining and cuffs. Leather waistcoat and breeches. Instead of leather boots, boots made of linen, probably something similar to 'German boots'.[63]

Stenbocks Dragonregemente. In 1705, hats with white cord, blue coat with a yellow lining and pewter buttons, leather waistcoat, leather breeches with three buttons, grey stockings, boots.[64]

Dückers or Preussiska Dragonregementet. In 1705 black hat with yellow and blue cord, blue cloak with yellow lining and bronze buckles.

Västgöta Kavalleriregementet. In 1717 a hat, grey *vadmal pajrock*, grey stockings, and boots.[65]

Smålands Kavalleriregemente. In 1714 a grey *vadmal karpus* with blue lapets of lined wool, grey coat with brass buttons, boots.[66]

Gauntlets (*Handskar*)

Gauntlets could be made entirely from moose leather, but could also be combined with buffalo leather, the softer moose leather being put on the finger and/or hand part of the gauntlets, the thicker buffalo leather forming the cuff covering part of the forearm.

In 1700 Livdragonregementet wore gauntlets made of moose skin. In 1703 Pommerska Dragonregementet, wore large yellow leather gauntlets with a deerskin hand and buffalo cuffs. In 1704 Taubes Dragonregemente had deerskin gauntlets with buffalo-skin cuffs.[67] The shape of the cuffs could vary, sometimes rounded, but most often of angled shapes.

Stockings and Leggings (*Stevels*)

Cavalrymen and dragoons had two pairs of stockings as a part of their clothing. Stockings could be knitted or made from yellow, blue or undyed *vadmal* wool. It took 1½ cubits of fabric to make stockings from woollen cloth.

Stenbocks Dragonregemente in 1705 had grey stockings made of *vadmal*, and in 1717 Västgöta Kavalleriregemente troopers were issued with two pairs of stockings.[68] In the dragoon battalion from Bohus, each dragoon had

---

62 Larsson, *Karolinska Uniformer*, p.145.
63 Höglund, *The Great Northern War 1700–1721*, p.55.
64 Larsson, *Karolinska Uniformer*, pp.145–146.
65 Larsson, *Karolinska Uniformer*, pp.144–145.
66 Larsson, *Karolinska Uniformer*, p.144–145.
67 Larsson, *Karolinska Uniformer*, p.114.
68 Larsson, *Karolinska Uniformer*, p.146.

THE UNIFORM OF THE CAVALRY AND DRAGOONS

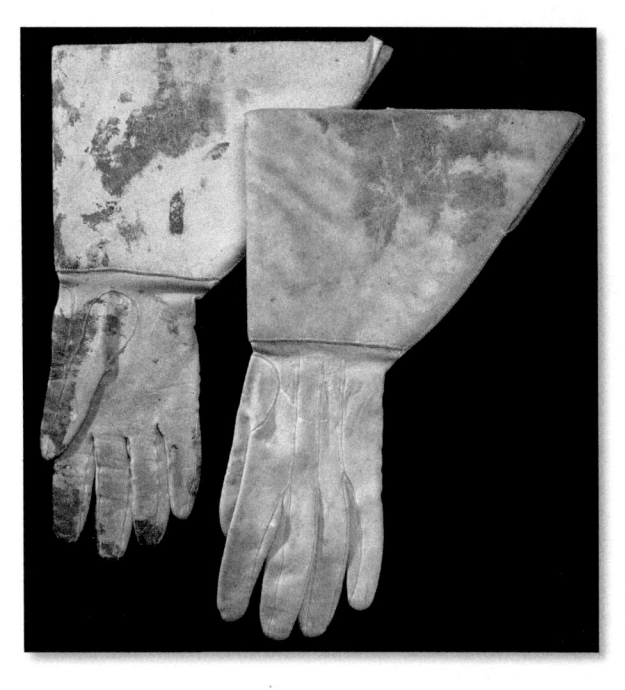

Above: Gauntlets of Charles XII. Livrustkammaren inventory no. 56413.

Right and below: Boots of the early eighteenth century, Armémuseum, Stockholm inventory nos AM.087198, AM.031214.

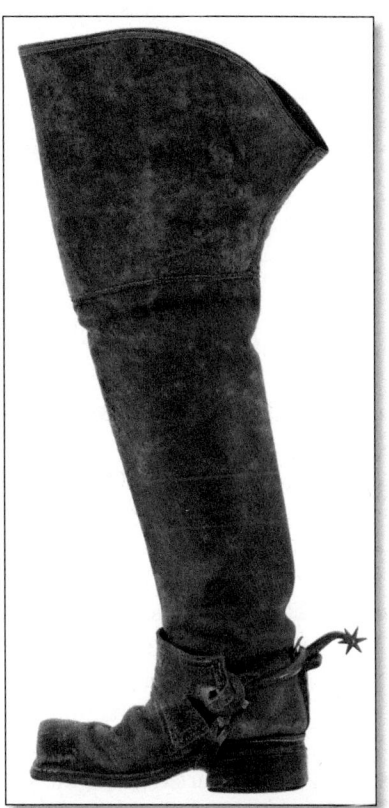

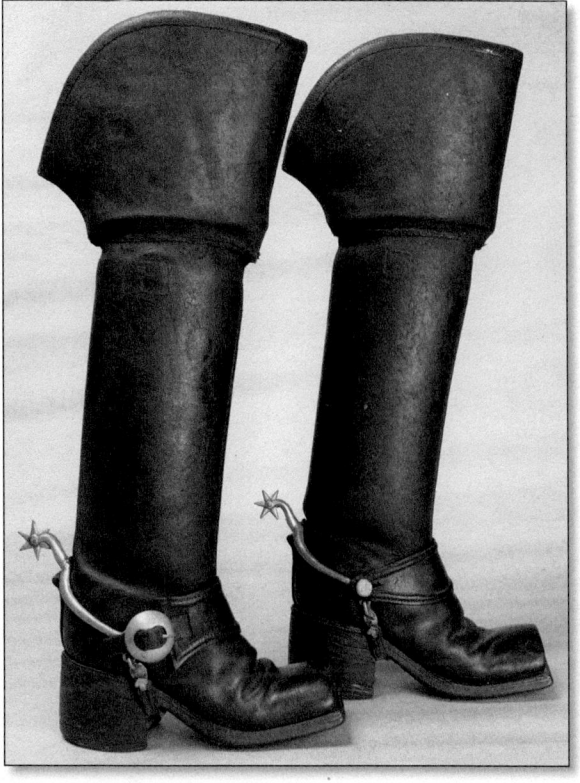

one pair of grey woollen stockings in 1712. In 1704 Taubes or Schlesiska Dragonregementet had grey stockings made of *vadmal*. In Upplands Ståndsdragonregemente in 1716 each dragoon had one pair of grey woollen stockings, and in Tyska Dragonregementet a dragoon had one pair of blue stockings in 1716.[69]

Linen leggings (*stevels*) are recorded in 1705 in the Stenbocks Dragonregemente – two pairs of linen leggings. The Drabants in 1695 had leather *stevels*.[70] The Dückers or Preussiska Dragonregementet in 1705 had one pair of linen *stevels*. The non-commissioned officers of the Pommerska Dragonregementet in 1703 had leather *stevels* stirrups.[71]

Boots and Shoes (*Stövlar*)

In 1700 Livdragonregementet dragoons had boots of oiled leather with spur flap, buckle, and steel spurs. In 1704 in the Taubes Dragonregemente the dragoons had boots with leather spur flaps and tinned spurs, and the same in 1705 in the Stenbocks Dragonregemente and the Dückers or Preussiska Dragonregemente. In 1716 Upplands Ståndsdragoner dragoons had boots, spurs, straps, and a pair of tinned spurs. Several surviving examples of the boots are preserved at the Armémuseum in Stockholm and at Livrustkammaren, e.g. artefact inventory no. AM.031214. The shape of the boots was generally the same for all regiments, although there could be some variations in the shape of the spur flaps.

The boots used by cavalrymen were of the same model as those used by infantrymen, with brass buckles.

---

69 Larsson, *Karolinska Uniformer*, p.116.
70 Larsson, *Karolinska Uniformer*, p.137.
71 Larsson, *Karolinska Uniformer*, p.114.

5

The Uniform of Cavalry and Dragoon NCOs

The hat of non-commissioned officers of cavalry and dragoon regiments was usually black with silver or gold galloon lace edging. Hair bags were made of black silk or *kalmuk*.

Coats, Waistcoats, and Cloaks of Non-Commissioned Officers, and Provosts of the Cavalry

Unfortunately, detailed information about the decoration of non-commissioned officers' coats does not survive for all regiments, therefore, this can only cover the little that is known. Coats of non-commissioned officers were made in three sizes. In general, the coat was of the same cut as that of the rank and file, but it was made of better quality cloth. Additionally, the collar, cuffs and pocket flaps were covered with silver or gold galloon lace. The buttons on the coats and waistcoats of non-commissioned officers could be simple pewter, but in most cases they were bronze (or brass), and covered with silver or were even gilt. Buttons as with as those of the troopers could be cast of pewter or bronze, somewhat domed; in some cases they were soldered from two pieces of brass or tin. Provosts monitored order in the units, combining the functions of military police with economic ones.

Adelsfanan i Sverige och Finland. In 1697, a black hat with gold galloon lace. The coat was blue.

Nylands och Tavastahus Läns Kavalleriregemente. It is very rare to find a metre-by-metre layout of the fabric for a uniform, thus it is well worthwhile to give this information in full: For making the uniform of a non-commissioned officer: '5 aln blått kommisskläde. 5⅓ aln blå foderboj, 2 dussin rockknappar, oblekt väv och blått silke' (five cubits of blue cloth, 5⅓ cubits of wool for lining, two dozen buttons, an unspecified amount of cloth, probably linen, for lining and blue silk).[1] The non-commissioned

---

1   Larsson, *Karolinska Uniformer*, p.81.

officers' waistcoat took 2½ blue non-commissioned officers' cloth, blue silk, two dozen buttons.

Smålands Kavalleriregemente. In 1714 non-commissioned officers had hats with silver galloon lace, and gilt buttons.[2] The coat was blue with gilt bronze buttons, the lining and cuffs were blue. The waistcoat was also blue with the same buttons and the same lining as on the coat. The cloak was blue.

Bohus Dragonbatalion. The 1715 the provost had a coat of green cloth with yellow lining collar and cuffs with flat brass buttons, with epaulettes and buttons on them.

Kunglig Majestäts Livregemente Dragoner; Livdragonregementet. In the 1700s, non-commissioned officers wore hats with gold galloon and gilt buttons. The coat was blue with gilded buttons, the button loops were sewn with gold thread, the lining and cuffs of the coat were blue and there was gold galloon goes on the collar. It should be noted that the collar was already on the coat by 1700. The waistcoat in 1700 was made of 'good deerskin' with gilt buttons, the buttonholes were edged with gold galloon. The breeches were also made of deerskin and had gilt buttons. The cloak was blue with gilt buckles.

The provost's cap was made of bear fur with a long top.[3] The description of the cap corresponds exactly to the description of the caps of the grenadiers, and to the preserved copy in the collection of the Armémuseum in Stockholm. The cap belonged to the provost of the Helsingland Infantry Regiment. The provost's coat was made of blue cloth and had a blue lining and brass buttons. The waistcoat was made of leather with brass buttons.

Pommerska Kavalleriregementet. In 1702 non-commissioned officers had a hat with a silver galloon lave. The blue coat had red lining and cuffs, the waistcoat was leather, and the breeches were blue. In 1702 they had a leather waistcoat and breeches of light blue cloth.

Bremiska Kavalleriregementet. In 1701 a hat with a gold galloon lace two fingers wide. A blue coat with blue lining and cuffs and bronze buttons. The buttonholes were edged with gold lace. The pocket flaps and cuffs were also edged with gold lace. The waistcoat and breeches were made of leather.

Bremiska Dragonregementet. In 1700 hats had wide gold galloon edged brim. The cravat was black. The coat was blue with silver-plated buttons, the collar, cuffs, and lining were suede-coloured. The collar and the pocket flaps were edged with silver galloon. Leather waistcoat with silvered buttons, leather breeches. Blue cloak with suede-coloured lining and silver-plated buckles.

Pommerska Dragonregementet. In 1703/07 non-commissioned officers had hats with silver galloon. A red silk cravat. A blue coat with gilt copper buttons. The description mentions blue buttonholes on both sides – thus suggesting that this was a double-breasted coat.[4] The collar, cuffs and pocket flaps were decorated with gold galloon. The waistcoat and breeches were of deerskin leather. The cloak was blue with a blue lining and bronze buckles.

---

2 Larsson, *Karolinska Uniformer*, p.81.
3 Larsson, *Karolinska Uniformer*, p.119.
4 Larsson, *Karolinska Uniformer*, p.112.

In 1703, the provost's coat was of the double-breasted pattern with brass buttons and buttonholes of yellow wool, cuffs and pockets were edged with golden yellow braid of the width of a finger.[5]

Stenbocks Dragonregemente. In 1705, hats with silver galloon, red silk cravat. A blue coat with pewter buttons, and buttonholes panelled in blue, the coat lining, collar and cuffs were yellow. The waistcoat and breeches were leather. The waistcoat had flat pewter buttons and buttonholes sewn around with yellow thread. The waistcoat was lined with white linen. There were three buttons on the breeches. The blue cloak had a yellow lining and bronze buckles.

A blue coat with yellow lining, yellow collar and cuffs, with pewter buttons and yellow loops. A waistcoat made of light yellow fabric, under leather, with flat pewter buttons, the buttonholes were edged with yellow cord. The cloak was blue lined yellow and had brass buckles.

Taubes or **Schlesiska Dragonregementet.** In 1704/05, a hat with a silver galloon lace three fingers wide. The coat was blue with blue lining and cuffs, buttons gilded. The collar and pocket flaps were edged with gold galloon. The waistcoat and breeches were leather with brass buttons. Provost, a blue coat with blue lining and with brass buttons.

Dückers or **Preussiska Dragonregementet.** In 1705 hats with gold galloon lace, blue silk cravat. The coat was blue, the buttons were bronze, the buttonholes were panelled in yellow. The cuffs and pocket flaps were edged with gold galloon. In 1704 the waistcoat had brass buttons and a linen lining. In 1705 the waistcoat was blue with gilt brass buttons, the breeches were also blue, with three buttons.

Tyska Dragonregementet, 1716. The coat required 4½ cubits of blue cloth, and the same amount for the lining, with two dozen brass buttons. Two measures of camel yarn thread (*4½ aln blått kläde. 4½ aln boj, 1 aln lärft 5/4 aln brett till stoffering och rocksäckar. 2 dussin mässingsknappar. 2 lod kamelgarn*).[6] In 1716, 2½ cubits of blue cloth five cubits of linen, and 1½ dozen brass buttons were used to make the waistcoat.

The provost had 4½ cubits of blue cloth (*blått kläde*) for the coat, and 4¼ cubits for the lining, two dozen brass buttons, and 1½ lod of camel's hair for the panelling of the buttonholes. The cloth waistcoat was made of 2½ cubits of blue cloth, five cubits of lining cloth, 1½ dozen brass buttons, one lod of camel hair for the buttonholes. Breeches were of blue cloth, and used 1⅜ cubits of cloth and three brass buttons. A cloak of blue cloth with brass buckles.

Skånska Tremänningsregementet. In 1719 hats with silver galloon lace.

Västgöta (och Bohus läns) Tremänningsregemente till Häst. In 1719 hats with silver galloon and English pewter buttons. Blue coat with blue lining and English pewter buttons.[7] Leather waistcoat with pewter buttons. A blue lined cloak with two pairs of silver-plated buckles.

Verdiska Dragonregemente. In 1700–1703, hat with silver galloon. The blue coat was made of English cloth with a blue lining, and with a double row

---

5   Larsson, *Karolinska Uniformer*, p.120.
6   Larsson, *Karolinska Uniformer*, p.81.
7   Larsson, *Karolinska Uniformer*, p.81.

A non-commissioned officer (provost) from Kunglig Majestäts Livregemente Dragoner in a hat similar to a grenadier's. (Author's illustration)

blue, covered buttons, the buttonholes were edged with light blue linen silk. The collar and pocket flaps were edged with silver galloon lace. The waistcoat and breeches were leather, the corporal's coat was made on the same principle, but with narrower silver galloons on the collar and pocket flaps.

The coat was made of grey cloth with a blue lining covered with twisted white-blue cord on the collar, pocket flaps and cuffs.

Upplands Ståndsdragonregemente. In 1717, making a coat took five cubits of blue cloth, 4½ cubits of blue wool for lining, 1½ cubits of canvas, 1½ cubits of lining cloth, 1½ cubits of camel hair thread and two dozen English pewter buttons. In the same year, 2½ cubits of suede-coloured cloth, six cubits of cloth, two dozen small stamped buttons, and ¾ yard of camel hair threads were used to make a non-commissioned officer's waistcoat.

Provosts in 1717 wore a *pajrock*, into which went five cubits of blue cloth, 11 cubits of lining cloth and one dozen pewter buttons.

6

Officers' Uniform of the Cavalry and Dragoons

Hat

Hats of dark grey or black felt, usually edged with galloon lace, most commonly gold, but sometimes of silver. Judging by the portraits, the amount of galloon used was based on the rank, financial assets and taste of the customer (officer). The lace could be smooth or with floral ornamentation. The hat was lined with black canvas. A cord attached to a button on the left side of the brim was used to pull it up. Extant descriptions record these hats for cavalry officers:

Livregementet till Häst in 1700. Hat (grey) with gold galloon.

Adelsfanan i Sverige och Finland. Black hat with gold decoration (1696).

Ostgotaregemente. Hat with gold galloon lace (1697).

In the dragoon regiments:

Verdiska dragonregementet. In 1703, a black hat with silver galloon.

Pommerska dragonregementet. 1703, black hat with narrow gold galloon.

Taubes Dragonregementet. 1704–05, hat with gold galloon.

Stenbocks Dragonregemente. In 1705, a hat with a broad gold galloon.

Schwerins Dragonregemente. In 1711, black hat with wide silver galloon.

Bremiska dragonregementet. In 1700, hat with a wide silver galloon.

CHARLES XII'S KAROLINERS VOLUME 2

Left: Hat and other clothing of Charles XII.

Below: THe hat and coat of Kapten (Captain) Carl Vilhelm Drakenhielm.

Plate 1

A trooper from the reign of Charles XI
(Illustration by Sergey Shamenkov © Helion & Company 2023)
See Colour Plate Commentaries for further information

Plate 2

Trooper, Riksänkedrottningens Livregemente till Häst (Hedvig Eleonora) [Queen Dowager's Regiment], and Estniska Kavalleriregemente. The two looked similar.

(Illustration by Sergey Shamenkov © Helion & Company 2023)

See Colour Plate Commentaries for further information

Plate 3

Trooper of the Västgöta Kavalleriregemente *c.* **1700**

(Illustration by Sergey Shamenkov © Helion & Company 2023)

See Colour Plate Commentaries for further information

Plate 4

Trooper of the Östgöta Kavalleriregemente *c.* **1700**

(Illustration by Sergey Shamenkov
© Helion & Company 2023)

See Colour Plate Commentaries for further information

Plate 5

Trooper of the Smålands Kavalleriregegemente 1700–1704

(Illustration by Sergey Shamenkov
© Helion & Company 2023)

See Colour Plate Commentaries for further information

Plate 6

Trooper of the Adelsfanan of Estonia, Ingria, Livonia and Ösel (Saaremaa)
(Illustration by Sergey Shamenkov © Helion & Company 2023)
See Colour Plate Commentaries for further information

Plate 7

Trooper of Livregementet till Häst, 1706–1709

(Illustration by Sergey Shamenkov
© Helion & Company 2023)

See Colour Plate Commentaries for further information

Plate 8

Trooper of Nylands Kavalleriregemente, 1696–1701

(Illustration by Sergey Shamenkov
© Helion & Company 2023)

See Colour Plate Commentaries for further information

Plate 9

Dragoon trooper, Livonian Dragonregemente W. Shlippenbach 1702–1703

Illustration by Sergey Shamenkov
© Helion & Company 2023)

See Colour Plate Commentaries for further information

Plate 10

Dragoon of the Livonian Dragonregemente W. Shlippenbach, 1703–1707

(Illustration by Sergey Shamenkov © Helion & Company 2023)

See Colour Plate Commentaries for further information

Plate 11

Corporal of the Verdiska Dragonregementet, 1703

(Illustration by Sergey Shamenkov
© Helion & Company 2023)

See Colour Plate Commentaries for further information

Plate 12

Trooper of Dückers or Preussiska Dragonregementet, 1705

(Illustration by Sergey Shamenkov
© Helion & Company 2023)

See Colour Plate Commentaries for further information

Plate 13

Colonel (Överste) A. G. Muhl Karelska (Viborgs Län) Double Regiment of Horse, 1703

(Illustration by Sergey Shamenkov © Helion & Company 2023)

See Colour Plate Commentaries for further information

Plate 14

Staff officer, Adelsfanan of Estonia and Ingermanland (Swedish Ingria), 1700

(Illustration by Sergey Shamenkov © Helion & Company 2023)
See Colour Plate Commentaries for further information

Plate 15

Second Cornet, Adelsfanan of Sweden and Finland, 1700

(Illustration by Sergey Shamenkov
© Helion & Company 2023)

See Colour Plate Commentaries for further information

Plate 16

Staff officer of a cavalry regiment in a ceremonial coat worn over a double-sided ceremonial cuirass, with decoration
(Illustration by Sergey Shamenkov © Helion & Company 2023)

See Colour Plate Commentaries for further information

Plate 17

Officer, Adelsfanan of Sweden and Finland, 1700

(Illustration by Sergey Shamenkov © Helion & Company 2023)

See Colour Plate Commentaries for further information

xvii

Plate 18

Cavalry officer in an unadorned service coat and wearing a leather waistcoat and breeches

(Illustration by Sergey Shamenkov © Helion & Company 2023)

See Colour Plate Commentaries for further information

Plate 19

Officer of Livregementet till Häst in a non-regulation service coat with additional decoration
(Illustration by Sergey Shamenkov
© Helion & Company 2023)
See Colour Plate Commentaries for further information

Plate 20

A cavalry officer in a service coat with buttonholes edged in gold galloon lace over a breastplate
(Illustration by Sergey Shamenkov © Helion & Company 2023)
See Colour Plate Commentaries for further information

Plate 21

Officer, Kunglig Majestäts Livregemente Dragoner; Livdragonregementet, 1700
(Illustration by Sergey Shamenkov
© Helion & Company 2023)
See Colour Plate Commentaries for further information

Plate 22

Officer, Verdiska Dragonregementet, 1703

(Illustration by Sergey Shamenkov
© Helion & Company 2023)

See Colour Plate Commentaries for further information

Plate 23

Non-commissioned officer, Bremiska Kavalleriregementet, 1701

(Illustration by Sergey Shamenkov
© Helion & Company 2023)

See Colour Plate Commentaries for further information

Plate 24

Non-commissioned officer, Bremiska Dragonregementet, 1700

(Illustration by Sergey Shamenkov
© Helion & Company 2023)

See Colour Plate Commentaries for further information

Plate 25

Drabant, 1701
(Illustration by Sergey Shamenkov
© Helion & Company 2023)
See Colour Plate Commentaries for further information

Plate 26

Trumpeter, Adelsfanan of Sweden and Finland 1700

(Illustration by Sergey Shamenkov
© Helion & Company 2023)

See Colour Plate Commentaries for further information

Plate 27

Drummer, Stenbocks Dragonregemente 1705
(Illustration by Sergey Shamenkov
© Helion & Company 2023)
See Colour Plate Commentaries for further information

Plate 28

Pommerska Dragonregementet kettledrummer, 1703–07

(Illustration by Sergey Shamenkov
© Helion & Company 2023)

See Colour Plate Commentaries for further information

Plate 29

Musician of the Stenbocks Dragonregemente playing the hautbois, 1705

(Illustration by Sergey Shamenkov
© Helion & Company 2023)

See Colour Plate Commentaries for further information

Plate 30

Cavalry staff officer in double-breasted service coat

(Illustration by Sergey Shamenkov
© Helion & Company 2023)
See Colour Plate Commentaries for further information

Kettledrummer of the Drabant Corps, 1700

(Illustration by Sergey Shamenkov
© Helion & Company 2023)

See Colour Plate Commentaries for further information

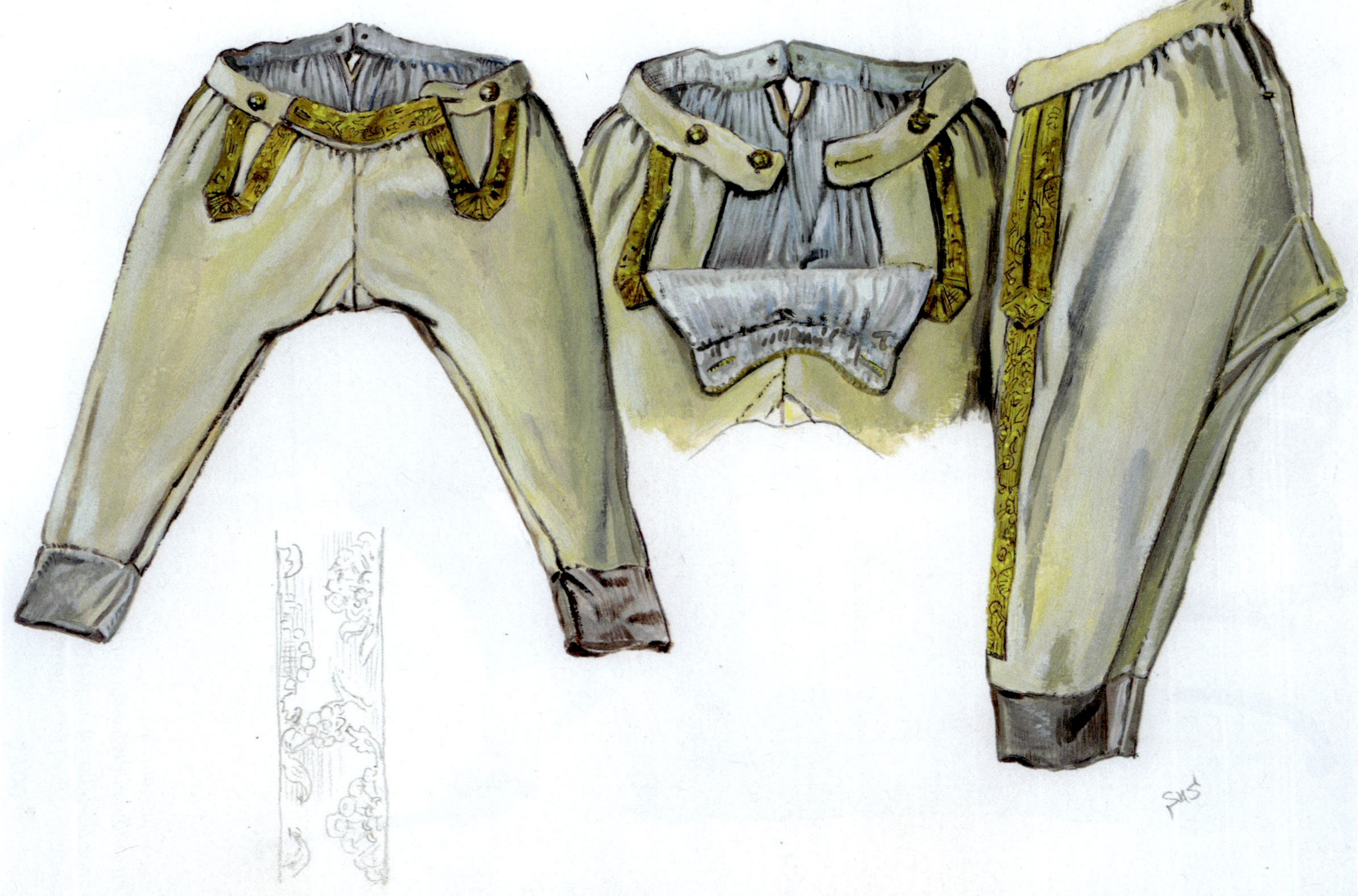

Plate 32

Breeches from the Hermitage, St Petersburg, G. E. inventory no. ERT-8458 (author's illustration). (Illustration by Sergey Shamenkov © Helion & Company 2023) See main text pp.101–102 for further information

xxxii

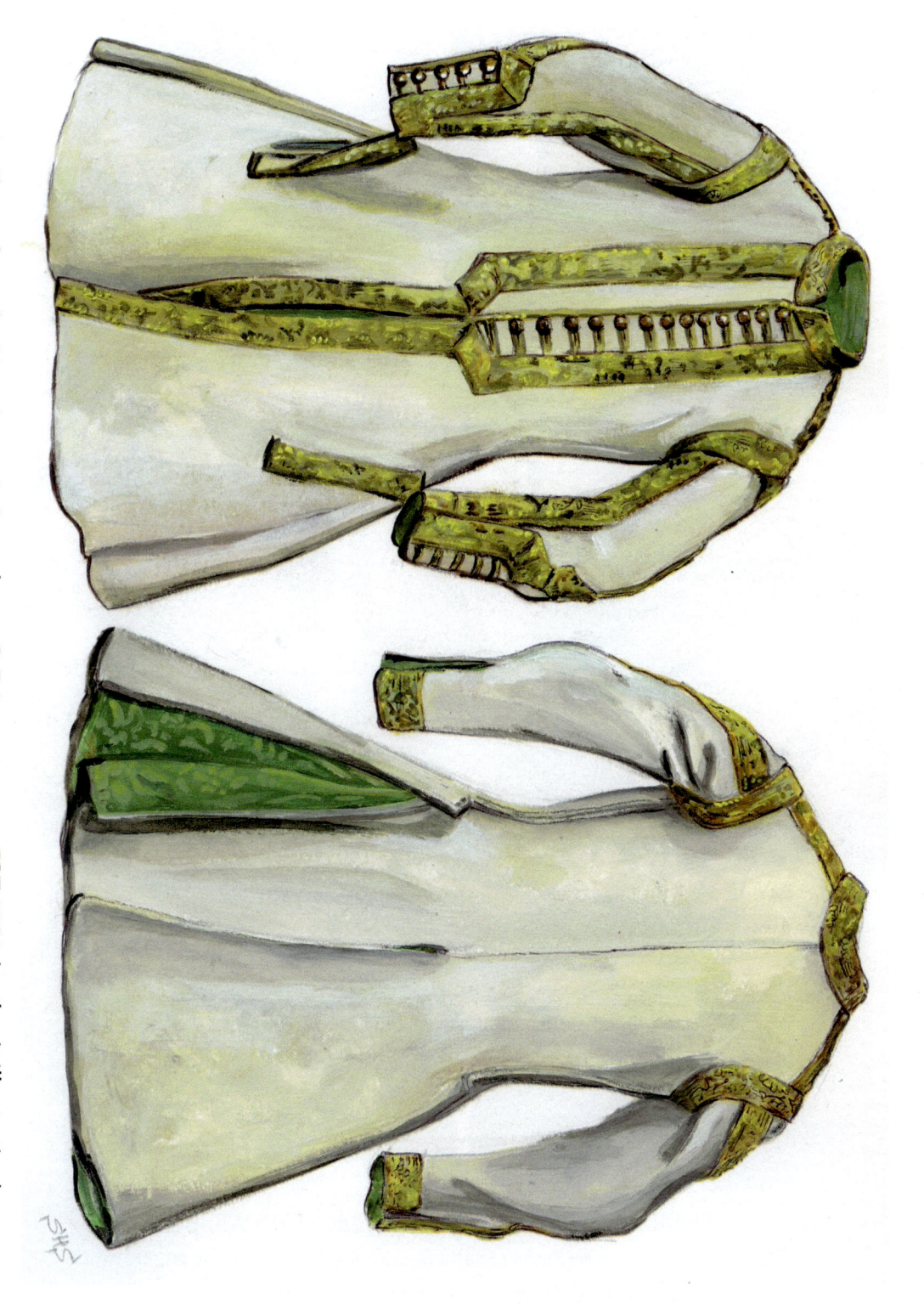

Plate 33

A buff coat from the Hermitage, St Petersburg, G. E. inventory no. ERT-8521 (author's illustration)
(Illustration by Sergey Shamenkov © Helion & Company 2023)
See main text p.98 for further information

xxxiii

Plate 34

Details of sword belts of the Great North War period
(Illustration by Sergey Shamenkov © Helion & Company 2023)
See Colour Plate Commentaries for further information

Cravat

The cravat of cavalry and dragoon officers could be white or black and either short, with ties at the back, or long, 74 cm in length and 26 cm wide, which could be tied at the front.

Livrock and *Paradrock*

The first volume of this study described in some detail how uniforms were introduced in the infantry, and the peculiarities of the cut. This section will clarify the peculiarities of cavalry uniforms – horse and dragoons – and how the uniforms of officers, non-commissioned officers, troopers, and musicians differed.

The coat of the officers of cavalry regiments existed in two forms: the simple everyday, the *livrock*, and the ceremonial, the *paradrock*.

In 1695 Charles XII ordered the introduction of the same simple *livrock* uniforms for cavalry officers: 'They were all to be cut to the same pattern. These uniforms, fitted with small slit cuffs, without decorations, blue buttonholes, and buttons, were to be worn by all officers from the captain to the fenrik on guard duty, and on campaign.'[1] This ruling was generally preserved throughout the subsequent war. The preserved examples of officers' uniforms and the images on portraits are an example of this. The colour and shade of blue were not specified, and it was impossible to actually ensure this was uniform throughout the army. The contemporary portraits and surviving items show that the uniform could be of many different shades of blue, from dark to almost black-blue. The lining of uniforms could be either blue or of a regimental colour, and there could be combinations of both whereby the collar and cuffs were blue and the lining of the regimental colour.

The surviving descriptions of materials help show how much, and of what, material was required to make an officer's coat. The making of an officer's coat (*officersrockarna*) in 1712 required: '5½ aln blått kläde, 5 aln gul boj, 1 lod blå kamelhårstråd, 1½ aln lärft till stoffering samt hade 3 dussin mässingsknappar.'[2]

The number of buttons on an officer's uniform could vary. Portraits show variations, there could be 12 or 14 buttons from the beginning to the bottom of the coat, and thus up to the belt fastened with six or seven buttons. Later buttons were more often simply 12 buttons reaching the level of pocket flaps, but at the same time some coats continued to have a lot of buttons to the hem. In some cases there could be less than 12, and they went only to the level of the flaps. Judging from images of the period, and the surviving examples

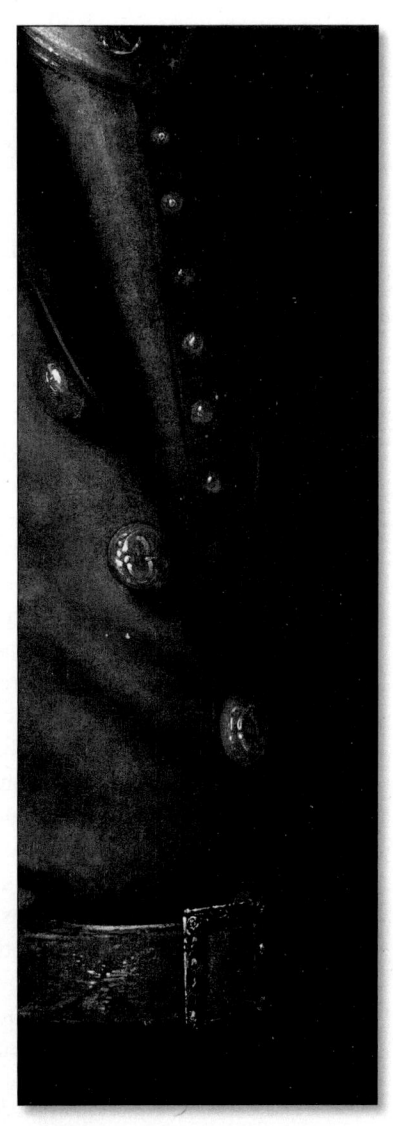

Buttons from the portrait of Axel Sparre.

---

1 Larsson, *Karolinska Uniformer*, p.76.
2 Larsson, *Karolinska Uniformer*, p.78.

of coats, cavalry officers sometimes had up to seven buttons on the pocket flaps of their coats, and often more than three. The buttons on officers' coats could be brass, lenticular in shape and hollow inside, soldered from two halves, stamped. Sometimes they were covered with gilding or silver. On many portraits are examples of buttons covered with gold galloon. On portraits of Swedish officers the buttons are in the form of a cone, known from archaeological finds with geometric ornaments imitating a galloon lace, these could be made by stamping and soldering and then gilding. The buttons shown on the coat on the portrait of A. Sparre have the royal monogram embossed on them.

The surviving coats of Charles XII, Fredrik I, and Löjtnant Drakenhielm are good examples of the cut of line officers' coats.

Charles XII's Coat, Worn at his Death at the Siege of Friedriksten[3]

The coat is fitted, and made of thin blue cloth, probably of English manufacture. The collar is placketed, eight centimetres wide, with about five centimetres in the centre at the back. The length of the coat is to below the knee, considering the height of Charles XII. It fastens with 12 gilded lenticular buttons, which are fixed on a vertically running leather cord hidden between the lining and the outer cloth of the coat. Two more buttons are placed at the waist, at the top of the side pleats. On the inside of the lining, at the top of the side pleats, the position of these buttons is echoed with triangle-shaped cloth overlays. The buttonholes of the coat are framed on the side, six centimetres long. The sleeve narrows to the cuffs, which are small and slit eight centimetres wide, there are three buttons on each cuff. The front cloth has an open edge, the lining is also blue wool although the sleeves are lined with waxed linen. The pocket flaps start at the level of the eleventh buttonhole and are fastened with seven buttons, the buttonholes are small, the pocket itself is in the form of a triangle and is made of fine leather. Pocket flap: width 16.5 cm at the top, 25 cm at the bottom, length in the centre to the central cape 24 cm.

The coat belonging to Prince Fredrik (Fredrik I av Sverige) and dated to 1716 has its own peculiarities of cut.[4] The coat, with a collar, is made of dark blue cloth, reminiscent of the so-called 'Prussian Blue' hue, with a red lining. The shoulder seam is angled backward. The coat is 111 cm long. There are 12 slit buttonholes on the front, and six buttonholes on the back, in the slit area, swatched with grey-blue silk thread. The length of the buttonholes on the front is about eight centimetres, vertical on the flap 9.5 cm. The beginning of the side folds and the button sewn at the top of the side folds are at the level between the tenth and eleventh buttons on the front, similar to the coat of Löjtnant Drakenhielm. The top of the pocket flap is at the level of the twelfth button, on the front. The pocket flap has seven buttons and false, non-

---

[3] *The Royal Facade. Charles XII in the Armoury* (Stockholm: 1998).

[4] Bellander, *Dräkt och Uniform*, p.254. Kept in Stockholm's Livrustkammaren, inventory no. Lrk 20754.

functional buttonholes. The three lower buttons are sewn to the cloth of the coat, four buttons in the corners of the buttonholes. At the top of the flap are two fastenings of the same silk as the buttonholes. The lining of the flap is red, the pocket itself is in the form of a triangle and is made of red silk. The size of the flap: 15 cm wide at the top, length in the centre to the end of the central cape 20 cm, width at the bottom 20 cm. The sleeves have blue cuffs, with a tack at the top of the cut and slit buttonholes. As on Löjtnant Drakenhielm's coat, two buttonholes are hidden. The cuff is slit, blue, with fastenings to the sleeve, at the centre and at the side of the top, at the edge of the cuff.

The surviving coat of Löjtnant Carl Vilhelm Drakenhielm of the Södermanland regiment, preserved in the Lungo Kirche in Södermanland, differs slightly from the royal example of Prince Fredrik. It is made of blue cloth, slightly lighter in colour that that of Fredrik. The shoulder seam is dropped back, and the lining is of woollen twill weave. There is no collar, and instead there is a narrow 1.5 cm wide lace sewn in place, there are 12 buttonholes 8–10 cm long on the front, and there are also two false loops on the back, on above the slit. At the waist, at the beginning of the side pleats, there is a single one button. The pocket flap is at the level of the twelfth buttonhole, it is 19.5 cm wide at the top, approximately 22 cm long from the top at the centre, and approximately 20.5 cm long to the central promontory. The hinges on the flap are false, framed, and the lining of the flap is yellow wool. The pocket is in the form of a triangle and is made of canvas. The three lower buttons are sewn onto the cloth of the coat, four buttons are in the corners of the flap buttonholes. The peculiarity of the sleeve cut is that it is made of one piece of fabric. There are three buttons and buttonholes cut through on the sleeve cuff, the lapel of the cuff overlaps two loops, thus leaving 12–13 cm. The buttons are lenticular, soldered, and gilded. The side folds are fixed with thread in three places – at the top, middle and bottom. The coat presumably follows the features of the 1706 model.[5]

Paradrock

The parade uniform was also blue, but with a galloon lace trim on the seams varying with the officer's rank:

> The parade uniform of the Lieutenant Colonel and the Major will be equally decorated with galloon lace. Parade uniforms of cavalry captains should be decorated with buttons and buttonholes of gold thread, and with gold galloon on the sleeves [apparently on the seams and around the armhole] and on the uniform hem. Parade uniforms of lieutenants, and cornets should also be equal to each other in form and appearance, but without galloons on the armholes of

---

5   Lars Ericson Wolke, *The Swedish Army of the Great Northern War, 1700–1721* (Warwick: Helion & Company 2018), p.24.

CHARLES XII'S KAROLINERS VOLUME 2

Above and facing page: Coat of Fredrik I, and Fredrik's complete suit of coat, waistcoat and breeches.

OFFICERS' UNIFORM OF THE CAVALRY AND DRAGOONS

Portrait of General Carl Gustaf Armfeldt, *c.* 1718–1719, David von Krafft.

OFFICERS' UNIFORM OF THE CAVALRY AND DRAGOONS

the uniform, but only buttons and buttonholes decorated with gold thread, and otherwise the same as those of Rothmisters.[6]

The dress uniform of lieutenant colonels and majors, judging by the arrangement of the lace on the portraits, must have looked lavish. Galloon lace was sewn on the front along the edge of the cloth, around or on buttonholes, and if the uniform was double-breasted, on the buttonholes on the right hand side of the coat. Galloon also went around the sleeve armholes on the sleeve seams and the cuffs, on the shoulder seams, and along and slits in the skirt, on the back of the slit, on the edges of the pockets, and possibly also around them. Also the galloon could go down the middle of the back of the coat to the slit, and could be laid out around the buttons inserted at the beginning of the side folds. A portrait of an unidentified officer from the early eighteenth century in the Nordiska Museet shows an example of how the galloons could have been sewn onto a ceremonial uniform.

Officer's uniform, Östergötlands Kavalleriregemente in 1697, described with gilded buttons, buttonholes decorated with gold thread, pockets edged with gold lace.[7]

Officers of Adelsfanan i Sverige och Finland had a blue uniform embroidered with gold galloon.[8]

Extant portraits of cavalry officers show both versions of uniforms, everyday and ceremonial.

On the portrait of General Carl Gustaf Armfeldt, painted *c.* 1718–1719 by David von Krafft, shows a uniform with buttons to the level of the pocket flaps. The portrait of Ture Gabriel Bielke (Livregementet till Häst) 1703, and a portrait of Colonel of Adelsfan, Alexander Magnus Hummerhielm, both by David von Krafft, show examples of such regimental undecorated uniforms. Some uniforms shown in the portraits record a non-standard pattern in cut and/or decoration. Thus, there are not only the traditional Swedish Army single-breasted everyday uniforms, with narrow standing collar, but also double-breasted versions of everyday uniforms. There are also varying sizes of cuffs, sometimes not even slit but round. On the cuffs of coats in some portraits there are three buttons. Three buttons on the cuffs of everyday uniforms are shown in a portrait of an officer who served in the Pomeranian Adelsfan regiment, after serving in the Rommerske Adelsfanen, as a captain, rittmester Dronningens Livregement 1715.

Detail of a portrait of Carl Gustav Spens.

---

6 Larsson, *Karolinska Uniformer*, p.78.
7 Höglund, *The Great Northern War 1700–1721*, p.54.
8 Höglund, *The Great Northern War 1700–1721*, p.51.

Above: Portrait of Carl Gustaf Dahlbergh, an officer of the Västgöta Kavalleriregemente, by David von Krafft.

Below: Portrait of an officer of the Estonian Adelsfan, Fritz Wachtmeister.

The decoration of the uniform on the portrait of Carl Gustav Spens is unusual for a Swedish officer. Spens took part in a number of battles, including the Battle of Dvina and Klishov, and by 1703 was captain in the Livregementet till Häst. Note the absence of a collar, the lace on the shoulders and armhole and on the front, instead on the edge of the front is a braided gold cord, and the same braided of gold cord with tassels, the so-called Brandenburgs. In this case it is probably a somewhat more decorated everyday uniform than it might usually be.

The everyday uniform of Johan von Schaar, in 1708 a Kapten, in 1720 Överstelöjtnant of the same Livregementet till Häst. The portrait shows that the uniform is lined with a narrow galloon lace on the edges of the collar and cuff, the buttons are positioned widely spaced from each other, about six buttons to the waist. Buttonholes are symmetrically cut on the left and right sides, lined with patches of galloon and sewing on the ends, two buttons are on the cuff, but there is probably additionally a third one as well. According to the fashion of coat decoration of the period, the same galloons should also be on the pocket flaps. In general, this uniform is something between a simple everyday uniform and a ceremonial one.

In the wardrobe of staff officers and generals there could be coats with trimming on the sides and hinges with braided cords, brand burgs, bastions or sections of floral ornament resembling figure eights. Examples of such decorations are found on several portraits of senior officers of the Swedish Guards Cavalry and of generals.

The number of buttons on the uniform was also unregulated. For example, on the portrait of Löjtnant Conrad Gustaf von Siegroth in 1712, wearing a simple uniform, up to the waist, there are only four buttons, but large silver buttons, so there could be six or seven buttons on the front.

In portraits of Charles XII, the coats have 13–14 buttons along the front (for example, *Karl XII till Häst* by David von Krafft). Buttons and buttonholes could be placed, equidistant, in pairs with a large distance between each pair, so that a total of three pairs of buttons could be placed on the front. In the portrait of C. H. d'Albedyhll, colonel and later major general of cavalry (*överste*

OFFICERS' UNIFORM OF THE CAVALRY AND DRAGOONS

för skånska tremänningskavalleriregementet 1712, överste för Skånska ståndsdragonerna och generalmajor av kavalleriet 1717) the uniform is shown with eight buttons, two at the top, and with a large distance between them two sets of three buttons. The classic version of an officer's everyday uniform is shown in the portrait of Stanisław Leszczyński, King of Poland, in the uniform of a Swedish officer.

Judging by the portraits, the already mentioned double-breasted coats were popular among officers. This fashion can be traced throughout the war. A variant of the double-breasted uniform is shown in the portrait of the officer of the Västgöta Kavalleriregemente, Carl Gustaf Dahlbergh, by David von Krafft.[9] The coat is lined with a narrow galloon lace on the collar, front and cuffs, the buttonholes on both sides are edged with galloon, the buttons are cone-shaped, the buttonholes are widely spaced, probably for six buttons. On a portrait of Carl Gustaf Morne, by David von Krafft in the Livrustkammaren in Stockholm and dated to 1705, Morne is shown wearing a double-breasted coat, probably a service uniform, which has large gilded buttons, five on front to the waist, widely spaced, the buttonholes are edged with galloon. Until 1704 Morne was colonel of the Ostgoth Cavalry Regiment, by 1711 he was a general. Another variant of the double-breasted coat is shown on the portrait of the Estonian officer, Adelsfan Fritz Wachtmeister.

In the cold season, coats could be lined with fur; fur was used for the lining of both single-breasted and double-breasted coats and such coats are shown on many royal portraits.

Above: Stanisław Leszczyński, King of Poland, in the uniform of a Swedish officer.

Below: One of a number of portraits of King Charles XII, wearing a fur-lined coat. (Tallinn Museum)

---

9 Carl Gustaf Dahlbergh, f 1691: volontär vid artilleriet 1708; korpral vid ett stånddragonreg. 1709; furir därst. 1711; sergeant vid livdragonreg. 1712; konrett vid Vestgöta kav.-reg 14/5; löjtn därst. Lewenhaupt, Adam: Karl XII's officerare. Biografiska anteckningar. 1920. s 131 <http://runeberg.org/karlxiioff/0145.html>.

CHARLES XII'S KAROLINERS VOLUME 2

Right: Portrait of Magnus Gabriel von Köhler, Kapten (Captain) of the Livdragonregementet, 1700s, by J. H. Wedekind.

Below: Detail from the Köhler portrait. The galloon on the hat is clearly visible.

OFFICERS' UNIFORM OF THE CAVALRY AND DRAGOONS

Officers' Uniforms of the Dragoon Regiments

Dragoon officers' uniforms also existed as both an everyday coat, *livrock*, and a parade coat, *paradrock*. According to the description, the service coat had no lace: 'Blue cloth uniforms with blue buttons and button loops, with small cuffs, which captains, lieutenants and warrant officers wear on guard duty or on campaigns, and have no galloons.'[10] The blue buttons in the description draws attention and this is probably an economy version envisaged to cover buttons with fabric, which was cheaper.

From Charles XII's order of 1695, *paradrock* for the officers of dragoon regiments was distinguished:

> The parade uniforms of Lieutenant Colonel and Major shall be in all things equally decorated with galloons. Parade uniforms of captains and captains-in-command must be equal to what was said before, decorated with buttons and buttonholes of gold thread and with gold galloon around the arm [the seams and the armhole] and the hem of the uniform. Parade uniforms of lieutenants, warrant officers, cornet officers shall also be equal to each other in shape and cut, but without galloons, and without galloon buttons of the uniform, but only buttons and buttonholes decorated with gold thread, and otherwise similar to those of captains.[11]

The uniform of an officer of the Livdragonregementet (Guard Dragoon Regiment) in 1700 is described as: 'Blue coat with blue lining, and cuffs, gold galloons, gilt buttons, buttonholes embroidered with gold threads.'[12]

The portrait of Schering Rosenhane (right), an officer who served in the Guards Dragoon Regiment in 1719 and later in the Ostgoth Cavalry Regiment in 1720, shows an everyday single-breasted uniform in light blue with six large gilt buttons and the buttonholes edged with floral ornamentation of silk or gold thread.

A service uniform, with five buttons on the front to the waist, and three buttons on the small cuffs, is shown in a portrait of Magnus Gabriel von Köhler (facing page), captain of the Livdragonregementet, dated to the early 1700s, by J. H. Wedekind. A captain of the Bochus Dragoon Regiment who served in the Livdragonregementet and returned back to the Bochus Regiment, H. J. Kruuse af Verhou,[13]

Portrait of Schering Rosenhane.

---

10 Larsson, *Karolinska Uniformer*, p.107.
11 Larsson, *Karolinska Uniformer*, p.108.
12 Höglund, *The Great Northern War 1700–1721*, p.82.
13 <http://runeberg.org/karlxiioff/0376.htm>

shows a dark blue everyday uniform, although interestingly a double-breasted coat, with six gilt buttons to the waist, the cuff is small, the lining of the uniform is light blue.[14]

The ceremonial uniform of the Leib-Dragoon Regiment is shown in the portrait (left) of Philip Hening Rothleib (Löjtnant 14 July 1702 Regementskvartermästare 3 May 1704, Kapten 5 August 1704). The portrait probably shows a captain's ceremonial uniform, covered with heavy galloon lace on the collar, on the front, and on the sleeves – front and back seams, armholes and cuffs. What is interesting is that the buttonholes are cut directly into the wide ribbon of the galloon.

For several regiments some information about the uniforms of officers at different points in the period has been preserved.

Officers of the **Livdragonregementet** have a blue coat with gilded buttons, buttonholes marked with gold thread, lining of the cuffs of naked silk (velvet).[15]

Bremiska Dragonregementet. Officers in 1700 had a blue coat with silver buttons and silver galloons corresponding to their rank, the lining was of a suede colour.[16]

Verdiska Dragonregementet. In 1703, blue coat with blue lining, blue buttons (buttons obviously covered with blue cloth) and blue buttonholes. There was a narrow gold lace along the edge of the collar.

Pommerska dragonregementet. In 1703, blue coat with blue lining, blue buttons and buttonholes.

Taubes Dragonregemente. In 1704–05, blue coat with blue lining, blue cuffs, gilt buttons. The edge, collar, pocket flaps, cuffs and buttonholes are edged with gold galloon.[17]

Stenbocks Dragonregemente. In 1705 a blue coat with yellow velvet collar and cuffs, flat brass gilt buttons, buttonholes panelled with gold galloon.

Schwerins Dragonregemente. In 1711 a blue coat with red lining and silvered buttons.[18] For making an officer's dragoon coat in 1712: '5½ aln blått kläde, 5 aln gul boj, 1 lod blå kamelhårstråd, 1½ aln lärft till stoffering samt hade 3 dussin mässings knappar.'[19]

Portrait of Philip Hening Rothleib.

---

14 Larsson, *Karolinska Uniformer*, p.109.
15 Höglund, *The Great Northern War 1700–1721*, p.82.
16 Höglund, *The Great Northern War 1700–1721*, p.84.
17 Höglund, *The Great Northern War 1700–1721*, p.97.
18 Larsson, *Karolinska Uniformer*, p.108.
19 Larsson, *Karolinska Uniformer*, p.108.

Waistcoats

Cavalry officers wore an elk leather waistcoat, varying in length from mid-thigh to knee length, under the coat. The peculiarity of leather dressing allowed the waistcoat to be soft, dense and durable. According to portraits, the leather waistcoat could have a small collar, as on the portrait of Charles XII from the Tallinn City Museum, and on the portrait of Magnus Gabriel von Köhler.

The officer's waistcoat was made either of cloth or moose leather. It was single-breasted, with or without sleeves, lined with canvas, wool, or silk, and fastened with buttons. Some portraits show small lapel collars. The waistcoat could be edged with galloon lace. The buttonholes and the flaps of the pockets were sewn with silk or metal thread, or sewn in a frame, and could be edged with galloon lace. Waistcoats had pockets with flaps that fastened with three, five, or, less often, seven buttons, the flaps were sometimes edged with narrow gold lace. The shape and location of the buttonholes could vary, for example on the portrait of Charles XII (SKANM.0019316) the buttonholes are placed at an angle, as it was also sometimes done on coats. The buttons were usually brass and gilded, but there were exceptions to this, for example, on the 1712 portrait of Conrad Gustaf von Siegroth, a löjtnant of the Livregementet till Häst, he is shown wearing a moose leather waistcoat with silver-plated buttons. Portraits of sitters only in a waistcoat are extremely rare, but one there is one of these rare works of art in the Collection of the Kuskovo Estate Museum in Russia. This portrait, from the 1690s, shows how leather waistcoats could be sheathed and decorated with galloon lace. The portrait, according to the modern revised attribution, depicts an unknown Western European officer, but there is also an opinion that it is a Swedish officer.[20] Galloon lace on the waistcoat of the officer in the portrait is everywhere along the edges, on the front, along the edge of the sleeve and on the front seam, and probably on the back as well. The buff coat is probably made of elk or bull leather, fastened in front with hooks. On the seams of the waistcoat connecting the back and the front and on the armholes of the sleeves it is stitched with gold thread. A similarly decorated buff coat, or waistcoat, is shown on the portrait of the young Charles XII by D. K. Ehrenstal (dated to 1697) in the collection of the Swedish Nationalmuseum in Stockholm, inventory no. Grh 2266.[21]

Some information on the differences in the waistcoats of officers of several regiments across the period has been preserved.

Kunglig Majestäts Livregemente Dragoner (Livdragonregementet). A leather waistcoat panelled with gold galloon.[22]

Verdiska Dragonregementet. In 1703, a blue cloth waistcoat, with blue buttons and silver galloon on the front.

Pommerska Dragonregementet. In 1703, a blue cloth waistcoat.

---

20 Peter the First and his entourage. Almanac vol. 465, SPb, 2015, p.103.
21 Lena Rangström (ed.), *Modelejon: Manligt Mode, 1500-Tal, 1600-Tal, 1700-Tal* (Stockholm: Livrustkammaren, 2002), pp.171–172.
22 Höglund, *The Great Northern War 1700–1721*, pp.82–83.

Taubes Dragonregemente. In 1704–05, a pale waistcoat with gilt buttons, buttonholes, and gold galloon panelled edge.

Stenbocks Dragonregemente. In 1705, a leather waistcoat.

Buff Coats

In 1700, the King ordered that buff coats, made of ox and elk leather, were to be replaced by leather waistcoats.[23] In some cases, cavalry officers continued to use leather buff coats instead of waistcoats. Such knee-length buff coats made of thick and dense elk or ox leather were fastened at the front with hooks. A wide silk braid was sewn along the edges and bottom of the coat, along the sides, on the back. Officers' coats could be embroidered with metal thread in foliate baroque ornament, or laid out with galloon lace. An officer's buff coat, as it appears from the signature, was preserved in Livrustkammaren, inventory number 15249 (3083). It belonged to an officer who fought at the Battle of Narva, judging by the inscription: '*Denna Kyller har använts af M …. holk … // som var General Major och Chef för Dalregt // vid Narva år 1700*.'[24] It is a buff coat, made of elk leather, with long sleeves and a narrow stand-up collar. The fastening is by hooks and eyes, eight and seven on each side respectively, arranged one after another. The cuffs of the buff coat are lined with red silk, and the sleeves are turned back as small cuffs. There are pockets in the side seams of the buff coat, sewn in red silk. The length of the coat is 1,065 mm at the front, 980 mm at the back and 595 mm at the sleeve.

In Swedish museums only simple buff coats have been preserved, but there is a similar coat edged with galloon in the Hermitage G. E. inventory no. ERT-8521.[25] The preserved European buff coat (from the wardrobe of Tsar Peter the Great) gives the opportunity to perhaps see how a staff or general officer's buff coat edged with galloon lace was like. Buff coats in the portraits are usually hidden under a cuirass or under the uniform, so that only the lower part is visible. Thanks to this preserved Western European, and possibly Swedish, coat it is possible to see the features of cut and decoration. Unlike other buff coats, this buff coat is fastened on the chest not with hooks, but with 14 buttons. The buttonholes and the edge of the front are covered with a narrow galloon lace. There are five buttons on the sleeves, the buttonholes are embroidered with a similar narrow galloon lace. On the edges of the buttonholes and around the buttons are edged with wide galloon lace from top to bottom on both sides of the coat. The collar, shoulder seams, armholes, sleeves front and back seams and around the buttons on the sleeves are also edged with wide galloon lace. The buff coat has a green silk lining with floral style design, slit vertical pockets, lined with a wide gold galloon on top. The buttons are soldered brass; the gold galloon is patterned with vegetation-style ornamentation.

---

23 Larsson, *Karolinska Uniformer*, p.221.
24 <https://samlingar.shm.se/object/CEB4D806-9874-4E5B-8A3D-C3FAF1D9D1A8>
25 'Perfect Victoria' exhibition catalogue, illustration 303.

OFFICERS' UNIFORM OF THE CAVALRY AND DRAGOONS

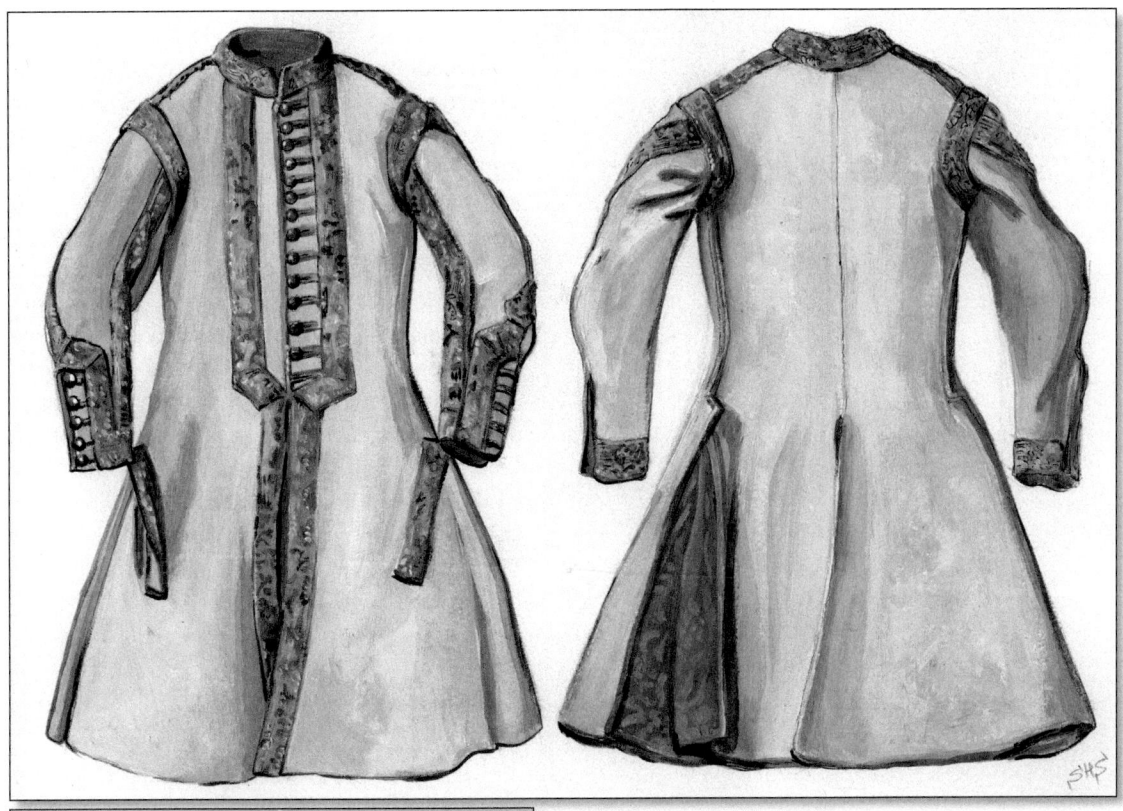

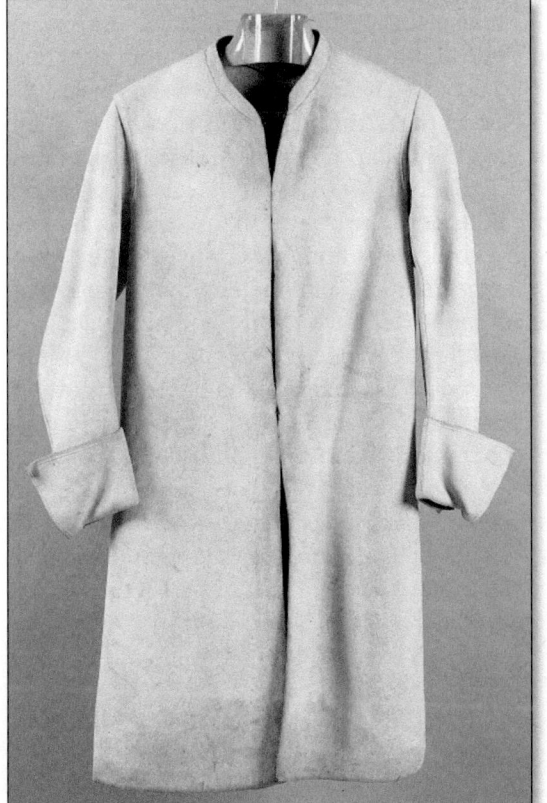

Above: Author's drawing of a buff coat from the Hermitage, G. E. inventory no. ERT-8521. See also colour section plate 33.

Left: Officer's buff coat, Livrustkammaren, inventory no. 15249 (3083). It is interesting that in this case the coat has a turned back cuff.

Buff coats, instead of leather waistcoats, decorated with galloon lace, or simple undecorated ones are shown together with cloth coats in a number of portraits. King Charles XII himself is shown wearing such coats in portraits, and more than once in a portrait from 1714 by Michael Dahl (Nationalmuseum, Stockholm). Many Swedish generals and senior officers are also depicted in similar buff coats. For example, such coats with uniform coats and cuirasses are shown on the portrait of General Carl Gustaf Armfeldt of 1718–1719, by David von Krafft, and the portrait of Kapten-Löjtnant (Captain-Lieutenant) Carl Gustaf Hård, by David von Krafft.[26] A buff coat decorated with galloon lace is shown in the portrait (left) of Amiral Hans Wachtmeister (1641–1714) in the Marinmuseum in Karlskrona.

Admiral Hans Wachtmeister

Breeches

The breeches of cavalry officers were usually also made of moose leather, in some cases with a side seam and front lapband, and more rarely of blue or leather-coloured cloth. Leather cavalry breeches from the Great Northern War have not survived, but there are some from a somewhat later period, 1730s to the early 1740s, in the Armémuseum in Stockholm. These breeches (AM.022993) belonged to Kapten (Captain) Anders Rålamb, who fought in the campaigns of Charles XII. The breeches are made of yellow leather (goatskin or elk skin), fastened at the front with three pewter buttons and fastened at the back with a cord. One button was fastened at the waist, and two buttons fastened a hinged flap. Despite the fact that these are an officer's breeches, they are cut and made of a number of small pieces of leather, which is certainly not aesthetic to modern eyes, but it is obvious that the attitude to the material was somewhat different in the eighteenth century.

Charles XII's breeches are made of a pale yellow cloth, probably what might be called 'suede-coloured,' unlined and thus most likely worn over linen pantaloons. The breeches are cut wide at the top and narrow at the bottom. In the front there is a flap, the *latsbant*, and in the back there is a slit from the waist, which allows for the adjustment of the waist of breeches with the help of a cord. There is a single button fastening at the cuff at the bottom. The breeches have 10 pockets of different sizes, sewn from thin soft leather.

---

26 M. Olin, *Det Karolinska Porträttet Ideologi, Ikonografi, Identitet* (Stockholm: Raster, 2000) – S. 27, 65, 237.

OFFICERS' UNIFORM OF THE CAVALRY AND DRAGOONS

The breeches are fastened with a front flap, the buttonholes are made in a 'framed' way. Buttons are made of gilded brass.

Fredrik I's breeches are 77 cm long, made of blue cloth, with a gold silk lining, also with a lapel pin, but slightly different in cut, number and location of the four pockets. The waist fastens on two buttons, there are two pockets in it, and also two pockets are located under the lapel. The buttonholes are slit and worked with silk thread. Unlike the King's breeches, there is no button fastening at the bottom of the leg and they are not gathered into a cuff.

All these subjects are presented in detail in the first volume of this work.[27]

Unfortunately, no other breeches from the Great Northern War have survived in Swedish museums. While there is a clear understanding of the cut and materials of cloth breeches, there are some problems with leather breeches. Leather breeches were the main type of leg clothing for soldiers and officers of the Swedish Army, but there are no leather breeches confidently attributed to the period. The above described breeches of Kapten Anders Rålamb, although retaining the main features of the cut, are somewhat later in period. But, there are other leather breeches from the beginning of the eighteenth century in the Hermitage, G. E. inventory no. ERT-8458. The surviving moose leather breeches are from the same suit as a European coat and from the wardrobe of Tsar Peter the Great. They are in very good condition and give an opportunity to understand how the leather breeches of officers of cavalry and dragoon regiments may looked like. The breeches on the portraits, as a rule, are hidden under the coat, and the details of their cut and decoration are thus not visible. Thanks to these preserved Western European breeches made by European tailors, it is possible to see the cut and decoration of officers' breeches.

Moose leather breeches from the Hermitage are, in general, of a similar cut to cloth breeches, lined with undyed canvas. They were fastened in the front with four small galloon buttons, fastened on a lapel pin. Button loops are edged with yellow silk. The flap as well as the breeches are both lined with unpainted canvas. The breeches have 4 vertically arranged pockets, two on the sides of the lapel and one more in the each of the side seams. In the front on the edge of the flap, around the pockets, and on the side seams from top to bottom (in the form of a lambassa) the breeches are edged with a wide galloon lace. The bottom of the breeches is lined with unpainted canvas (shown on the colour illustration). This canvas cuff could be lowered or could be raised upwards to protect the breeches from rubbing against the boots, functionally like the later stevel-stibbettes. The length of the breeches is 87 cm.

Extant descriptions of the breeches of officers of dragoon regiments show that there may have been variants of cloth breeches, but in suede colour, similar to the surviving breeches of Charles XII. The blue cloth breeches may have been of the same type and cut as Fredrik I's breeches:

Bremiska Dragonregementet. In 1700, suede-coloured cloth breeches, edged with silver galloon.

---

27 Sergey Shamenkov, *Charles XII's Karoliners, Volume 1: The Swedish Infantry & Artillery of the Great Northern War 1700–1721* (Warwick: Helion & Company 2022) pp.96, 121.

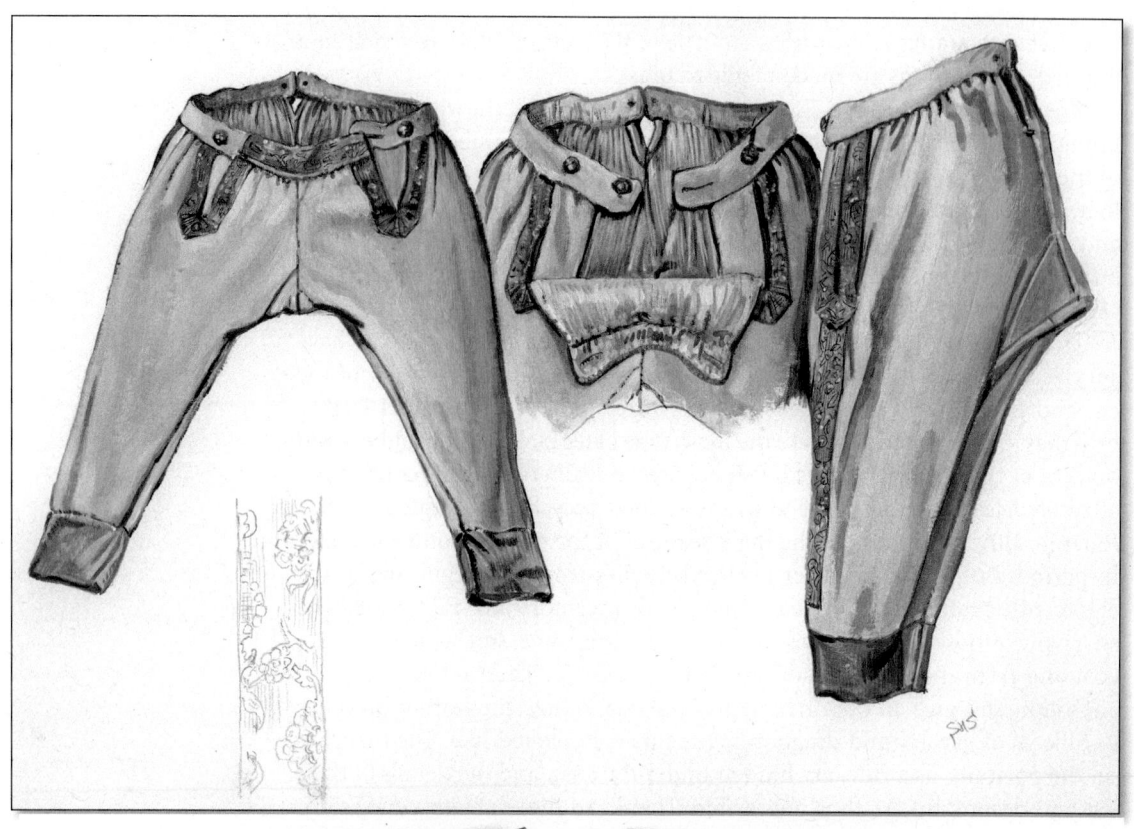

CHARLES XII'S KAROLINERS VOLUME 2

102

OFFICERS' UNIFORM OF THE CAVALRY AND DRAGOONS

Pommerska Dragonregementet. In 1700, leather breeches edged with gold lace.

Taubes Dragonregemente. In 1704, leather breeches with gilt brass buttons and gold embroidered buttonholes.

Schwerins Dragonregemente. In 1711, blue cloth breeches.[28]

Cloak

In inclement or cold weather, cavalry officers wore a cloth cloak with a collar. There are several authentic examples of such cloaks in museum collections in Sweden and Russia.

The officer's cloak was made of a thicker, heavier cloth than the coat; blue in colour, it had a round cut of about eight metres in circumference (the cloak of Charles XII), and fell to around the middle of the calf. The material needed for sewing a cloak is known: *8 aln kommiskläde* (eight cubits of cloth), two cubits wide, 3½ cubits of plain weave woollen lining cloth (*3½ aln boj*), and one cubit of canvas.[29] In the middle of the back of the cloak, at the bottom, a slit was made. On the surviving cloak of Charles XII the stitching is in the middle of the back, a wide collar with shaped cut-outs is attached at the neck.[30] The collar could be embroidered on the edges, could be made of cloth of regimental colour, or could be blue – the colour of the cloak. Along the edge along the side could also be put a pozument (as for example on the cloak from the State Hermitage Museum inventory no. ERT-8555). The cloak was lined with cloth or flannel,[31] the lining was sewn completely over the entire area of the cloak. Another variant made use of a particularly thick cloth, one side of which was blue, and the other was dyed (literally 'painted') in the regiment's facing colour, imitating a coloured lining. The officer's cloak was fastened or stitched or attached by wire under the throat by bronze, gilded or silvered buckles, cast or chased (cf. AM.015490).[32] The right buckle had a hook, the left buckle had a catch for it. One buckle with a hook is preserved on the cloak of Charles XII, it is an undecorated, simple model, perhaps closer to the soldier's than that of an officer. Preserved in museums, and also found on battlefields, officers' buckles are decorated with relief images. The motif for this decoration was the crowned royal monogram, in various stylistic variants. The shape of the buckles also varied, with round, oval, drop-shaped and trilice shape all being popular. In some

Example of a cloak buckle. (Photo from the author's archive)

Facing page:
Top, breeches from the Hermitage, St Petersburg. G. E. inventory no. ERT-8458. (Author's illustration. See also colour section plate 32)

Bottom: Fredrik I's cloth breeches, with unbuttoned waist.

---

28 Larsson, *Karolinska Uniformer*, p.110.
29 Larsson, *Karolinska Uniformer*, p.223.
30 *The Royal Facade*, p.10.
31 'Perfect Victoria', exhibition catalogue, p.345.
32 <https://digitaltmuseum.se/011024369885/kappa>

103

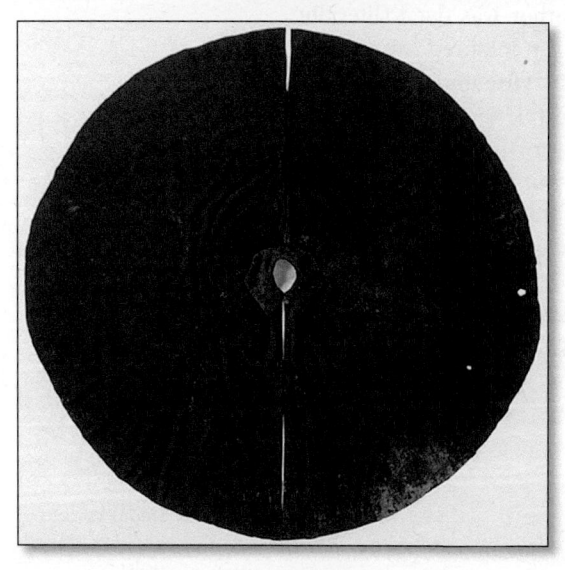

known examples, the monograms and subjects on the buckles of officers and staff officers repeated motifs from the officers' gorgets, showing the Crown and the Royal Monogram. On the gorgets of staff officers the monogram with the crown was surrounded by sprigs of laurel, similar decorations are found on some cloak buckles.[33] It is probable that cloak buckles were not regulated, and were ordered by officers privately, made in accordance with individual taste, available material, rank and type of service. Additionally, approximately in the middle of the front edge were attached two smaller buckles smaller without monograms, which made it possible to fasten the cloak to close it to protect the body from the wind or rain. Several such small buckles were found on the battlefields in Poltava region.

Officers' Belts

The uniform of Swedish officers was regulated, and was essentially the same for all officers, but some items of an officer's equipment, for example, his sword belt was not subject to such regulation. Sword belts could be plain without decorations, made of elk or other leather, or with decoration on them. Officers could have individual buckles and other leatherwear and furniture according to their taste. Judging by portraits and the surviving examples of buckles and harnesses, they could have all kind of decorations. In addition to the most common form of buckle in the form of two joined ovals, there are the some of a similar pattern but with elements of foliate ornamentation, as well as buckles which are oval, rectangular and other forms. The buckle was fastened not as we are accustomed to, on a peg, it was fastened to the belt, but it was fastened on the belt, on the attached and coiled from metal hook, which was inserted into a plate with a hole at the second end of the harness. This was the principle used to fasten all Great Northern War belts and

---

33   A. Homann, 'Kriegerische Symbole barocker Macht am Kragen Mantelschließen der Zeit um 1700 aus Norddeutschland und Südskandinavien', in *Archäologische Nachrichten aus Schleswig-Holstein 2015*, pp.82–87.

OFFICERS' UNIFORM OF THE CAVALRY AND DRAGOONS

harnesses. Sometimes these hook systems were quite complex in shape.

The sword belts used by Swedish officers during the War can be divided into several types:

1. Elk leather belt without any decoration, with a buckle and hook, with a loop on the plate and a pelt-shaped harness, or without it.

2. Elk leather with a buckle, with a loop on the plate and with or without a pelt-shaped harness. The edge of the belt is covered with silver or gold metal thread, galloon lace, or in some cases a metal fringe.

3. The leather embroidered with gold metal thread in floriate motifs, with various shapes of buckle.

4. Sword belt of leather with an archaic method of attaching a pocket in which the sword is inserted, which has a pair of plates with hooks, which are fastened to the belt (see illustration).

5. The belt was made of leather and covered with cloth, with or without galloon lace, but of different variations in construction. It could be an ordinary belt made of a single sheet of leather and covered with cloth, or the variant described above, when a separate sling was suspended from the belt, in which the sword was inserted.

Plain and unadorned shoulder straps are preserved in the collections of both the Stockholm Armémuseum and Livrustkammaren. Galloon lace shoulder straps are recorded in written sources, e.g. for the officers of the Östgöta Kavalleriregemente in 1697,[34] and officers of the Taubes or Schlesiska Dragonregemente in 1704–5.[35] Officers of Stenbocks Dragonregemente in 1705 had their harness edged with silver galloon.[36]

It is possible to see what a shoulder belt with silver stitching along the edge of it looked like from an exhibit in the collection of the Poltava Battle Museum, at Poltava. A shoulder belt from the period of the Great Northern War is inventory no. 48, the belt is made of elk leather with silver stitching. All of metal pieces as well as the buckle are made of brass and gilded. What is interesting is the two-spoke oval buckle. The hook is not simply made of a sheet of metal, but has a complex construction. On the plate in which the hook is inserted there is engraved floreat ornament, it is an interesting detail, because it would not be visible to anyone except to the owner, the plate was covered by the belt.

Facing page:
Top, a cloak from the Armémuseum in Stockholm, inventory no. AM.015490.

Bottom: Cloak of Charles XII, Livrustkammaren.

---

34 Höglund, *The Great Northern War 1700–1721*, p.54.
35 Höglund, *The Great Northern War 1700–1721*, p.97.
36 Höglund, *The Great Northern War 1700–1721*, p.88.

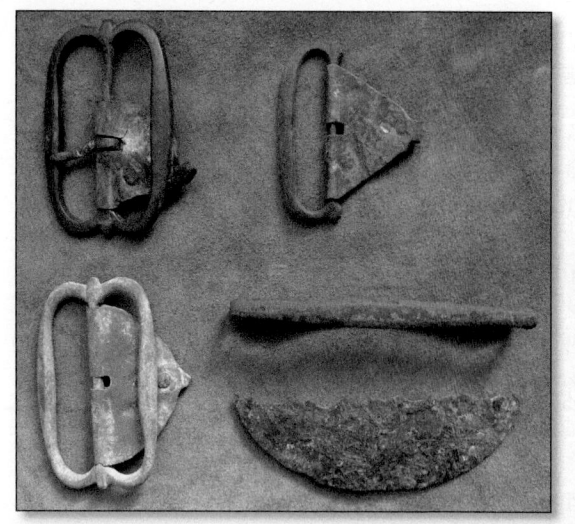

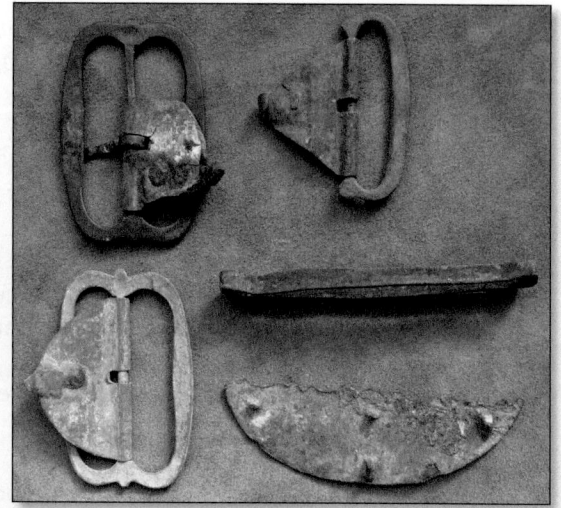

CHARLES XII'S KAROLINERS VOLUME 2

Above: Buckles from archaeological digs. (Author's collection)

Above: A Swedish sword belt in the collection of the Poltava Museum, inventory no. 48.

Right: A sword belt in the collection of the Poltava Museum, inventory no. 47.

OFFICERS' UNIFORM OF THE CAVALRY AND DRAGOONS

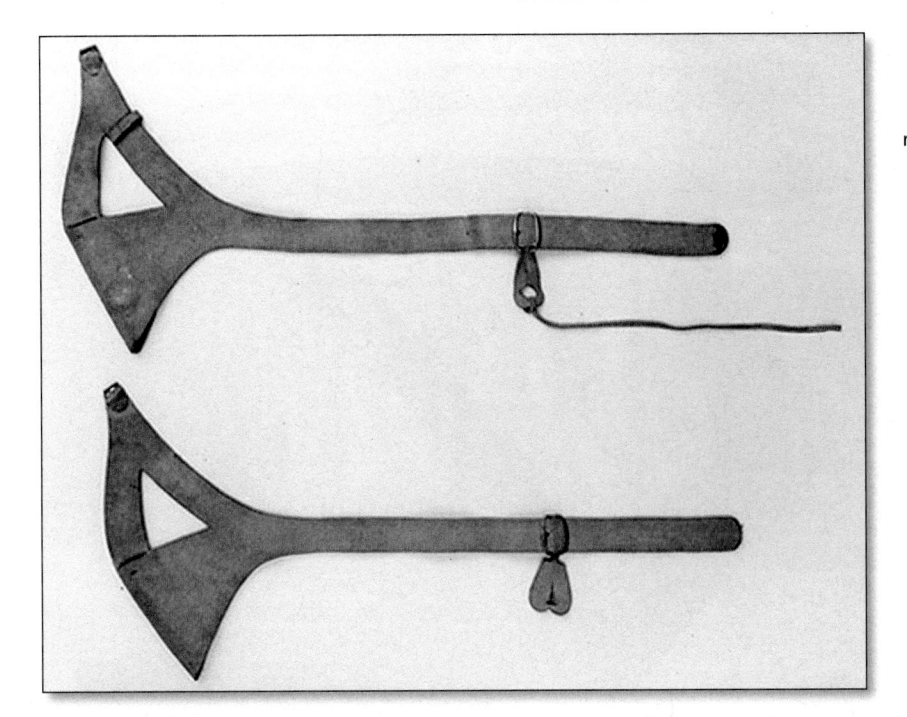

Swedish *livgehäng* sword belt, used by both officers and troopers of cavalry regiments. Livrustkammaren inventory no. 69435.

There are no surviving belts decorated with gold metal and gold thread in the various Swedish museums but they can be seen in portraits of some Swedish officers. Such belts became popular towards the end of the seventeenth century. Also this type of richly embroidered belt is found on portraits of Charles XII,[37] and of some officers. This type of richly decorated in gold sword belt with git buckle is shown on a portrait of 1690s of an unknown, but presumably Swedish officer – it was previously believed, erroneously, to be a portrait of Tsar Peter the Great.[38] Incidentally, several sword belts, decorated with floral motifs from the wardrobe of Peter the Great are preserved in good condition. One of them, unlike the sword belts cut from one thick sheet of leather, is made of several thin sheets of leather glued together and embroidered with gold thread.

A fragment of a sword belts edged with galloon lace and also with fringe (type 4), is preserved in the collection of the Poltava Museum, inventory no. 47. This is the type of sword belt where the hanger attached to the belt with two hooks, in this case two brass hooks shaped in the form of a grenade. An example, listed as a shoulder sword belt in VIMAIV&VS inventory no. 13/1839, is a belt made of elk skin covered with galloon lace, with a fringe on one edge, and a brass clip with rings, is most likely the second part of the same sword belt.[39] A similar system of fastening the sword on hooks, but on a waist strap, is known to us from a Russian sword belt of the

---

37 Pia Ehasalu, *Rootsiaegne maalikunst Tallinas 1561-1710: produktsioon ja retseptsioon*. Dissertation, Estonian Academy of Arts, p.245.
38 Peter the First and his Entourage. Almanac vol. 465, SPb, 2015, p.103.
39 'Perfect Victoria' exhibition catalogue SPb 2009, p.348.

Sword belt in the collection of Muzeum Narodowe w Krakowie (Krakow Museum), inventory no. MNK XIV-4 1-3.

Great Northern War period from the Hermitage Museum.[40] The belt and the hooks are silver-plated, rectangular in shape, with notches on the surface. This is also an example of what looks like a sword belt covered over cloth. An example of this design is described as being in use by the officers of the Kunglig Majestäts Livregemente Dragoner, Livdragonregementet; covered with blue cloth, and panelled with gold galloon lace.[41]

Another interesting belt is kept in the Muzeum Narodowe w Krakowie (Krakow Museum) inventory no. MNK XIV-4 1-3. The museum attribution says that it, together with the sword with it, belonged to Charles XII. The belt is of a design untypical for Swedish sword belts. It is made of red leather, and the carrier for the scabbard is sewn to the waist belt. The buckle, instead of the usual hook with a catch at the other end of the harness, has a shape and construction similar to that described above on the belt from the Poltava Museum.

Gauntlet Gloves

Cavalry and dragoon officers wore leather gauntlet gloves, those of both the former and the latter could be edged with galloon. Gauntlets of senior officers could be additionally edged with a fringe made of metal or metallised thread. Several examples of gauntlets of the period under consideration are preserved in the collection of the Armémuseum in Stockholm. Despite their general similarity, they do differ in the size and shape of the gauntlet cuff.

---

40 'Perfect Victoria' exhibition catalogue SPb 2009, p.302.
41 Höglund, *The Great Northern War 1700–1721*, p.83.

OFFICERS' UNIFORM OF THE CAVALRY AND DRAGOONS

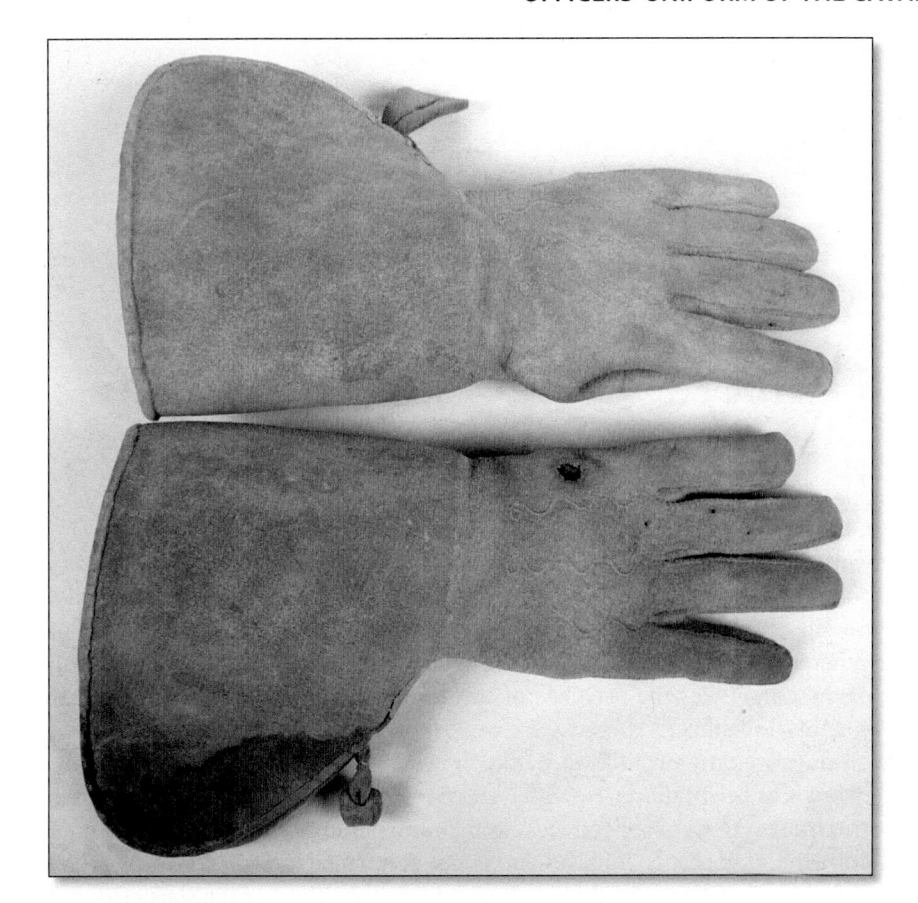

Gauntlets in the collection of the Armémuseum in Stockholm, inventory no. AM.032390.

On some examples these are triangular (inventory no. AM.032362) and on others rounded (inventory no. AM.022998). The gloves could be made either from a single piece of leather, as on the photo, or from a number of pieces. Gauntlets were usually made from yellow-coloured elk skin.

Footwear

Officers of cavalry and dragoons wore boots, which did not differ in any particular way from the above examples of those used by the other ranks. Boots were also present in the wardrobe. The boots were fastened with brass buckles, the soles were attached with wooden pegs. Examples of this type of boots are represented in museum collections, such as in the Armémuseum, Stockholm, inventory no. AM.015472.

7

Officers' Gorgets of Rank

Officers' gorgets (*ringkragar*), decorated according to the officer's rank, were worn by infantry officers, but judging by the number of, for example, trophy gorgets and the number of officers killed or captured in the Battle of Poltava, not all of them wore gorgets.[1] The use of officers' gorgets in the cavalry in general, and in dragoons raises a number of questions. Probably, the wearing of the gorget was the privilege of cavalry colonels. However, it is not clear, whether the officers' gorgets were worn by the latter in mounted units when on duty, or only on foot, in battle, or when simply on duty, or just in on parades or celebrations. However, since many senior officers wore cuirasses, and moreover were obliged to wear them on parades, such a combination of cuirass and gorget is doubtful and is not confirmed anywhere. If the gorget was worn in the mounted units, then it was probably over the waistcoat and under the coat, and not together with the cuirass. A fairly large number of portraits of cavalry officers survive today, but gorgets do not appear on these portraits. Gorgets are shown on two portraits, but for special occasions, and they rather appear as an exception rather than the rule. The portrait in question is the 1704 portrait of Arvid Bernhard Horn af Kanckas, Greve Horn af Ekebyholm, Kapten-Löjtnant vid Kunglig Majestäts Drabanter, Generallöjtnant, in the Armémuseum, Stockholm. The second is a portrait of a Drabant by Peter Ljung, dated to 1704 and already mentioned in the first volume of this study. Ljung is wearing a ceremonial gorget with the Queen Dowager's monogram, and a long buff coat. In the lower corner of the portrait is an officer's gorget, which characteristically is not being worn, but rather serves as a decoration and to emphasise the rank of the officer.

There is one mention in the documentation of officers' gorgets, for the Jämlands Dragonregement in 1708,[2] and one surviving officer's gorget, with a form and decoration common at the end of the seventeenth century – that of the Colonel of the Karelska (Viborgslän) Fördubblingsregemente Till Häst (Karelian Dual Cavalry Regiment), A. G. Muhls. Considering

---

1   S. I. Shamenkov, 'The Uniform of Swedish Officers of the Great Northern War' [Electronic resource], in *History of military affairs: studies and sources*, 2015. Vol. VI. – C. 216.

2   Larsson, *Karolinska Uniformer*, p.26.

OFFICERS' GORGETS OF RANK

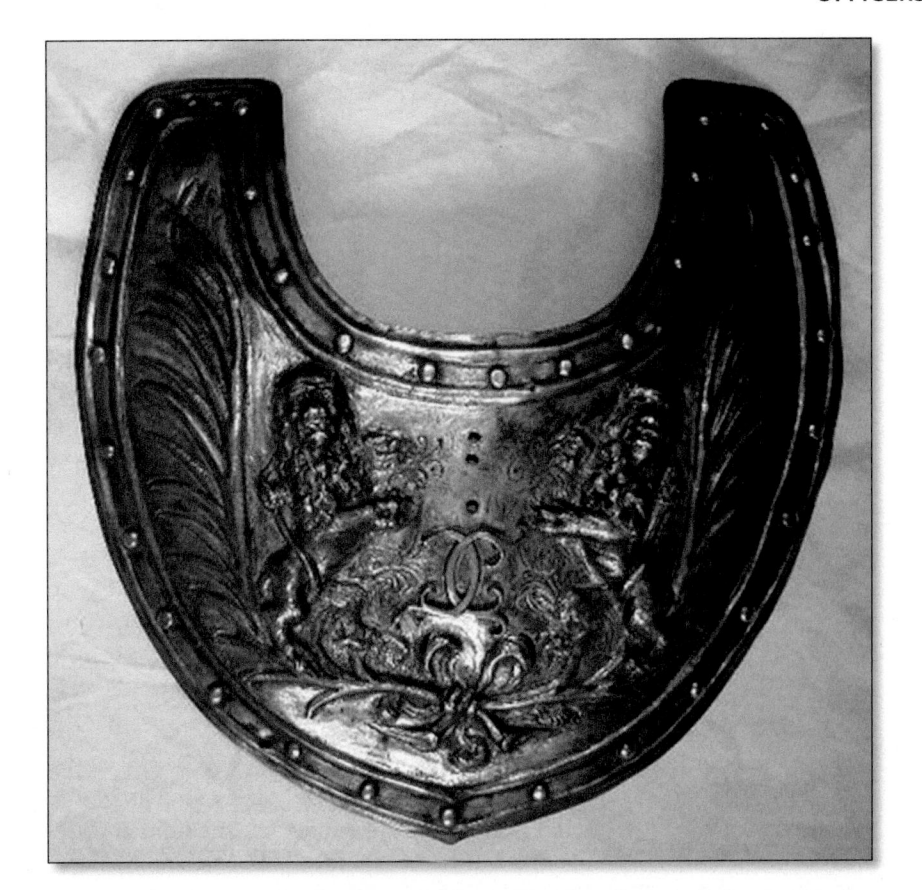

Officer's gorget of Överste A. G. Muls of the Karelska (Viborgslän) Fördubblingsregemente Till Häst. (Photo from the author's collection)

there were such a large number of horse and dragoon regiments, and the numbers of surviving portraits of cavalrymen, the mention of gorgets in only one regiment seems negligible in suggesting a more widespread practice of officers wearing gorgets. Thus, we can only confirm the use of officers' gorgets by some dragoon officers of the Jämlands Dragonregement, and by the Colonel of the Karelska (Viborgslän) Fördubblingsregemente till Häst, and perhaps, from his example, by some cavalry colonels.

8

The Uniform and Equipment of the Drabant Corps (*Drabantkåren*)

Uniform, Equipment, Horse Furniture

The commander (captain) of the Drabant Corps was Charles XII. The Corps (company) of Drabants consisted of five officers and 12 senior ranks, vizt: the Company captain, the captain-lieutenant, the lieutenant, the adjutant, the quartermaster, six corporals and six vice-corporals, plus between 150 and 190 private soldiers. Each Drabant trooper had the army rank of captain. The total number of all ranks varied from 150 to 200 men.

In 1699 the Drabant Corps received new uniforms. This is mentioned in a letter dated 20 April 1699 from Charles XII to the then commander of the Drabants, Överstelöjtnant (Lieutenant Colonel) Carl Nieroth. The new uniforms and equipment of the Drabants cost a considerable sum, about 56,000 silver coins. To put this in context, for this sum, four cavalry regiments of 1,000 men each could be armed with carbines and pistols (a carbine cost seven thalers and a pair of pistols the same amount). The new livery of the four officers cost 3,014 thalers. From the report for 1699 it appears that their annual salary was then 4,752 thalers. If we compare these two sums with each other, we get a pretty good idea of the expense of the new officers' uniforms. Oddly enough, the Crown also paid for new uniforms for senior officers, whose pay supplements were not included.

The new uniform included a camel hair 'carbeck' (*kamelhårs*) hat with a gilt button and gold galloon lace trim. It should also be noted that in images of Drabants, the hats show small bundles of ears of corn inserted behind the brim, a long-standing distinction of Swedish soldiers dating back to the Skanian War. The hat was worn by folding it up on three sides and angling the front corner towards the left eye.[1] The silk cravats were 74 cm long and

---

1 Schreber von Schreeb, *Karolinska Förbundets Årsbok 1936*, p.106.

THE UNIFORM AND EQUIPMENT OF THE DRABANT CORPS (DRABANTKÅREN)

26 cm wide and could be white or black.[2] The officers of the Corps when not mounted could wear an officer's gorget according to their rank. Blue cloth coats and waistcoats with lining of different blue fabrics and embroidered with gold galloon of different widths, were fastened with big and small gilt buttons. Additionally, the officers' waistcoats could be decorated on the front and bottom with gold embroidery in the form of baroque floral ornaments – cf. the portrait of Kaptenlöjtnanten Arvid Horn.

The coat had a falling collar, and the pockets had large pocket flaps, unlike the rectangular three-button pockets of the cavalry. The buttons of the coat and waistcoat were strung on a leather strap inserted into the inside.[3]

The waistcoat of leather or cloth also had pockets and flaps, but these were smaller than on the coat.

The amount and size of the gold galloon lace varied according to the rank of the officer. The breeches were of light yellow leather, with galloon lace for officers, but without for privates. There was one button below the knee. The moose leather sword belt, as well as the bandolier with a metal clip for the carbine, and also the cartridge pouch and belt, were covered with blue cloth and edged with gold galloon. The buckles of the belt was also gold plated. Gloves were also covered with gold galloon.

The cloak was blue, with a braid of gold with a touch of blue silk running down the collar.

The boots of the Drabants were of the same model as those of the rest of the cavalry, with round buckles on the spur leathers, and metal spurs.

Surviving documents detail the materials and quantities used to make the uniforms of the Royal Drabant Corps. The examples below show the variety of fabrics used, perhaps taking into account the personal preferences of some officers.

For the making of the new, lavishly decorated uniform of Öfwerste Lieutenanten Wählborne H:r Carl Nierot in 1699 the following was used: fivecubits of *blått kläde* (blue cloth), 6½ cubits of moire, three cubits of canvas, four lod *blått silcke*, one cubit of *sijdenbast*, one cubit of *dvelck*, 11½ cubits *isabell sammet*, 4 lodh silcke. For wide and narrow gold galloon: *104 lodh breda, 17½ lodh infattning, 121½ lodh gull gallöner*. For the tailoring of

Portrait of Kaptenlöjtnanten Arvid Horn. The waistcoat and decoration described below is accurately shown in this portrait. The coat is shown differently however – without decoration. Armémuseum Stockholm, inventory no. AM.065922.

---

2   Larsson, *Karolinska Uniformer*, p.215.
3   Schreber von Schreeb, *Karolinska Förbundets Årsbok 1936*, p.106.

Details from *The Battle of Düna* by Johan Henrik Schildt, showing senior officers and Drabants in 1701. Armémuseum inventory no. NMA.0025512.

the waistcoat of gold galloon: 27½ *lodh breda*, 4³⁄₁₆ *gull knaphåll*, 48½ *lodh frantzar*. For gold galloon on the breeches: 9⅝ *lodh gull gallöner*.[4]

Various materials were used for panelling of the items of equipment: 47 *lodh frantzar* were used for panelling of the fringed cap, 18½ *lodh frantzar* were used for panelling of the gloves, 43½ *lodh frantzar* were used for panelling of the belt. For the panelling of the hat, the gloves, and the harness, 198⁷⁄₁₆ *lodh gull* galloon was used in all. The waistcoat used 3½ *dusin gull knapphåll* large buttons. Additionally also for the manufacture: buttons 4½ *dusin*, 3 al. *sidenbast*, 5 al. *parckum*, 2 al. *bomersin*, 2 al. *canifas*, 1 al. *franst lärefft*, 4 al. *canifas*.[5] The Öfwerste Lieutenanten's sword is also listed with a *wärje* band, woven from blue and yellow silk thread. In addition, paper for the backing of the galloon was purchased separately.

For making the new uniform and its decoration blue woollen cloth was used for the coat (*blått kläde, canifas, blått parkum*), blue silk velvet (*blått sammet*), blue silk moire (*blått moir*). The whole coat was lavishly decorated

---

4   Schreber von Schreeb, *Karolinska Förbundets Årsbok 1936*, p.135.
5   Schreber von Schreeb, *Karolinska Förbundets Årsbok 1936*, p.136.

THE UNIFORM AND EQUIPMENT OF THE DRABANT CORPS (DRABANTKÅREN)

with various widths of gold galloon lace (*gull gallöner*). This galloon went on the edges of the collar and of the cuffs, and along all the seams and buttonholes. The buttons were gilt. The waistcoat was made of silk velvet, (*isabell sammet*; isabell/isabella is a brownish-yellow colour), with *franzar* (gold fringe), and wide gold galloon lace. A gilded button, probably the one for the hat, and 4½ dozen small gilt buttons, for the waistcoat and breeches, are separately specified in the calculations. The breeches were also decorated with gold galloon, judging by the iconography along the side seam, and possibly in front along the flap.

The two lieutenants were dressed almost identically to the captain-lieutenant. The coat, waistcoat, and breeches were edged with galloon of different widths, measured to weight – *lodh*, and various fabrics were used: *canifas, parckum, bomersin, silcke, schiagg, sidenbast. glantzig dvelck*. For the finishing of the coat, 'the most beautiful silk moires are obtained from the English,' then from French manufactuers semi-silk moire were used.

Since the descriptions mention different types of cloth, it may be useful to explain their texture and what material they were made of. *Kanifas* is a mixed linen, hemp, or cotton cloth. *Parkum* is a cotton cloth of varying thickness. *Bomersin* was made of silk camel hair (i.e. Angora wool) cotton mixed with wool, and wool mixed with silk. *Rusk* is a fine smooth woollen cloth with a

CHARLES XII'S KAROLINERS VOLUME 2

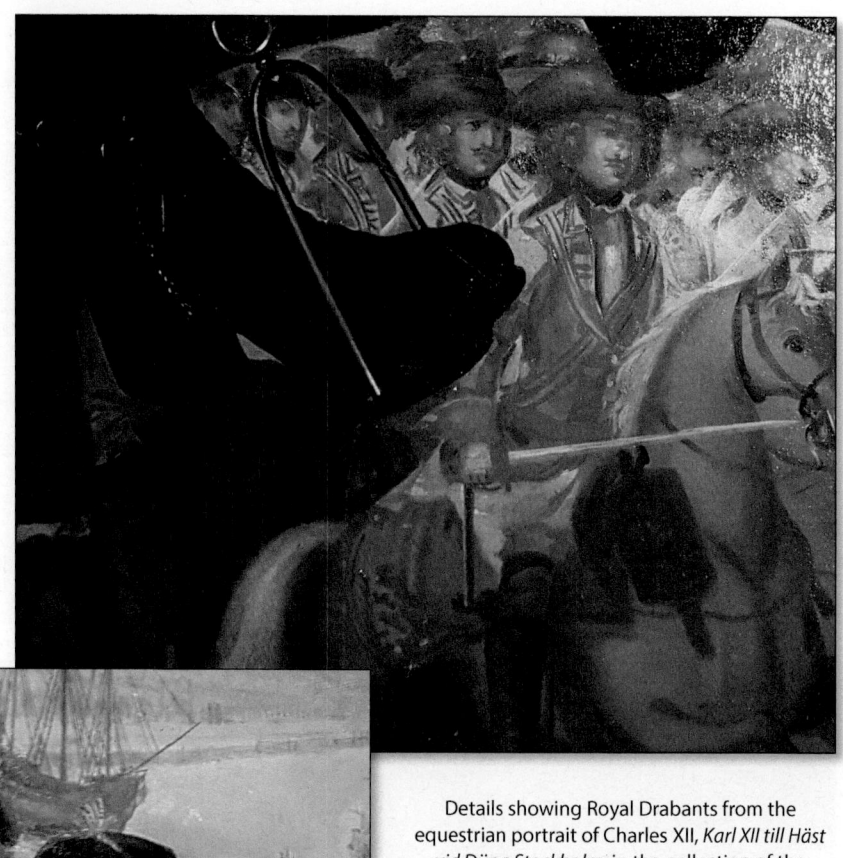

Details showing Royal Drabants from the equestrian portrait of Charles XII, *Karl XII till Häst vid Düna Stockholm*, in the collection of the Armémuseum in Stockholm, AM 065980.

lustre. *Silke* is silk. *Schiagg* is a comparatively thin woollen fabric fashioned with a texture like velvet. An *aln* (elbow) equalled 59.38 cm. *Lod* is a measure of weight of 13.16 g. *Vaxduuk/waxduuk* is waxed cloth.

The new uniform of Kapten Löjtnant Valbome Horn required: for the coat 5½ cubits of blue cloth (*blått kläde*) for its trim and lining: 11¼ cubits of canvas, 2½ cubits of blue parkum (*blått parkum*), 13¾ cubits of blue moir (*blått moir*), 13¾ cubits of blue cloth (*blått sammet*). There were 226¾ cubits of gold galloon of various widths for the edging of the coat and waistcoat, weighing 214 *lodh*. 7½ cubits of gold galloon for the decoration of the sword belt. For the brim of the hat – 3⁵⁄₁₆ measures of *lodh gallöner*. For one pair of gloves; 3⁵⁄₁₆ *lodh gallöner*, 4.56 *lodh gallöner till råcken* (uniform), and 2¼ dozen large gold buttons and five dozen small buttons, seven *lodh* silk.[6]

Löjtnant Wählborne H:r Adolf Johan Kruusbiörn used for his new uniform six cubits of blue cloth (*blått kläde*), 6½ cubits *tafft*, 1½ cubits *canifas*, two cubits *glantzig dvelck*, 4½ cubits skin-coloured cloth (*skinfärga kläde*), three cubits *sijdenbast*, two cubits *canifas*, 2½ cubits *lärft*, 2½ cubits *parckum*, two cubits *bommersin*. A baldric with a gilt buckle, and for decoration, 32 measures of gold fringe (*lodh gull frantzar*), 2½ dozen large gold buttons and four dozen small gold buttons and one button (presumably for the hat).[7]

Löjtnant Högwåhlb. Gref Carl Wrangell chose for his new uniform blue cloth, yellow cloth, lining cloth: six cubits of blått kläde, five cubits of Guult, 12 cubits of lining cloth (*tyg till foder*), five cubits of parkum cloth, three cubits of canvas (*canifas*), nine measures of silk (*lodh silke*). For panelling garments 290⅜ lodh of gold galloon, including a pair of gloves lined with cloth. I. al. blått sammet for panelling a portcullis, and a portcullis gilt buckle.

The lieutenant's hat was also edged with gold galloon, with a gilt button, and is labelled in the document as *Wirgince*. The explanation says that this was the name given to castor hats, which consisted of half beaver's wool and half of hare or camel wool.[8]

Quartermaster's Uniform

The following materials were needed to make the coat of the *Qvarter Mästaren* (Quartermaster): 5¼ cubits of blue cloth (blått kläde), eight cubits of *rask*, 1½ cubits of canvas (*canifas*), 1⅝ cubits of *schiagg*, three skeins of silk (*lodh silke*), ²⁷⁄₁₂ dozen gilded bronze buttons (*stora förgylte mässingz knappar*), ⅚ dozen small buttons of the same kind. Gold galloon (*gull gallöner till råcken*) – 27½ cubits, 54 cubits of narrow, 15 cubits of *infattning*, 17½ cubits for panelling buttonholes (*knapphåhl*).

For the edging of the cartridge pouch and carbine belts (*Patrontaskan och Carbijn Remmen*) 3⅛ cubits of wide galloon lace and 1⅞ of narrow. For the decoration of the sword belt 2⁹⁄₁₆ cubits of gold galloon, 1⅞ cubits for the

---

6   Schreber von Schreeb, *Karolinska Förbundets Årsbok 1936*, pp.137–138.
7   Schreber von Schreeb, *Karolinska Förbundets Årsbok 1936*, pp.138–139.
8   Schreber von Schreeb, *Karolinska Förbundets Årsbok 1936*, p.109.

gloves 2½ cubits for the hat, 2½ cubits for the cap, eight cubits of wide and eight cubits of narrow galloon, as well as eight cubits of gold fringe. Quartermasters' hats, edged with gold galloon, were made of camel hair (*carbeck* [*kamelhårs*] *hatt med gull knap*), for which 2½ cubits of galloon and a gilded button were used. For the decoration of the carbine belt, cartridge pouch and sword belt, 1¾ cubits of blue *schiagg* (*blått schiagg*).[9]

Corporal's Uniform

The uniforms of corporals were the same as those of the quartermaster and adjutant, but the galloon decoration was not as rich, the galloons weighing only 112 *lod*. The whole uniform required 158 *lod* = 2.2 kg.

The following materials were needed to make the corporals' coat: 5¼ cubits of blue cloth (*blått kläde*), eight cubits of *rask*, 1½ cubits of canvas (*canifas*), ⅝ cubits of *schiagg*, three skeins of silk (*lodh silke*), 2⁷⁄₁₂ dozen large bronze gilt buttons (*stora förgylte mässingz knappar*), ⅚ dozen small gilt buttons. Gold galloon for lining the corporal's coat: 27½ cubits of wide and 54 cubits of narrow, and another 21 cubits (*infattning*), as well as 17½ cubits, for edging the buttonholes (*knapphåhl*). There were 3⅛ cubits of wide and 1⅜ cubits of narrow galloon for the lining of a corporal's waistcoat.

For decorating the carbine belt, and for decorating the cartridge pouch, 3⅛ cubits of wide and 1¾ cubits of narrow gold galloon was required. For the decorating of the sword belt 4½ cubits. For the hat 2½ *alns*, and for the gloves 2½ *alns*. For the lining of the carbine belt, cartridge pouch and waist belt 1¾ cubits of blue cloth (*blått schiagg*).

To make the shabraque required 1 cubit of cloth, 1¾ cubits of waxed cloth (*waxduuk*). The decoration of the shabraque required gold galloon – eight cubits of wide and 16 cubits of narrow.

Vice Corporal's Uniform

The uniforms of the Vice-Corporals (*korpralernas*) were improved because 'the King graciously decreed that six of the best corporals should be made corporals.'[10]

To make the coat of the vice-corporals of the Drabants required the following: 5¼ cubits of blue cloth (*blått kläde*), eight cubits of *rask*, 1½ cubits of *canifas*, ⅝ cubit of *schiagg*, three skeins of silk (*lodh silke*), 2⁷⁄₁₂ dozen large bronze gilt buttons (*stora förgylte mässingz knappar*). The edging of the vice corporal's coat required gold galloon of different widths: 8¾, 14¾, and 21 cubits for edging buttonholes. To decorate the waistcoat of a vice corporal, gold galloon of different widths were required: 3⅞ cubits and eight cubits, and for the buttonholes 14 cubits. The edging of the sword belt also required different gold galloon: 2⁷⁄₁₆ cubits and 1⅞ cubits. For the decoration of the carbine belt,

---

9 Schreber von Schreeb, *Karolinska Förbundets Årsbok 1936*, p.141.
10 Schreber von Schreeb, *Karolinska Förbundets Årsbok 1936*, p.110.

THE UNIFORM AND EQUIPMENT OF THE DRABANT CORPS (DRABANTKÅREN)

and of the cartridge pouch it required: 3⅛ cubits and 1⅞ cubits of gold galloon. For the hat, 2½ cubits of gold galloon. For decoration and covering the holsters – 14⅝ *aln.* of gold galloon.[11]

The Uniform of the Drabant Troopers

To make the coat of a trooper of the Drabant Corps, the following materials were needed: five cubits of blue cloth (*blått kläde*), eight cubits of *schiagg* cloth, 6½ cubits of blue *rask* (*blått rask*), and 1½ cubits of white *rask*, 2⁷⁄₁₂ dozen large gilt buttons (*stora förgylte mässingz knappar*), ⅚ dozen small gilt buttons (*små förgylte mässingz knappar*), 2½ skeins of silk (*lodh silke*), 1½ cubits of canvas, 17½ cubits of gold galloon for buttonholes, 11¾ cubits of narrow and 8¾ cubits of wide.

For the brim of the hat, 2½ cubits of gold galloon, and a gilt button.

The following materials were required for the decoration of the waistcoat of the Drabant Corps: 13½ cubits of gold galloon for the edging of the buttonholes (*gull knapphåll*), and eight cubits of narrower gold galloon.[12]

The cravat of the Drabant troopers was of black silk, 74 cm long and 26 cm wide.

For decorating the carbine belt, 5½ cubits of gold galloon were required: 2¾ cubits each of wide, and of narrow. For decorating the cartridge pouch 2¾ cubits of gold galloon. 7¾ cubits of galloon were required for decoration of the belts. For the edging of the belt for the carbine and for the cartridge pouch 1¾ cubits of *schiagg* was required.

The breeches, apparently leather, were the same as those of the officers, but not decorated with galloon lace.

New cloaks are not mentioned for the Drabant Corps, which may indicate that no changes were made to them, and that the blue cloth cloaks acquired in 1695 were in satisfactory condition. These were blue with a lining of yellow wool and with gold galloon on the edge of the collar. The cloak was fastened with gilt buckles, bearing the royal monogram and crown. Also at about the middle of the edge length of the front were small buckles.[13]

The galloon on the uniforms of the Drabants weighed 39 *lod*, and on the whole uniform 74 *lod*, about 1 kg.

On the images of the Drabants during the battles of 1700–1701, attached to the hats can be seen ears of corn. The tradition of inserting ears of corn behind the brim of the hat was known since the Skåne War. The same ears of corn can be seen on the paintings depicting Charles XII in the battles of 1700–1701. For example on the portrait by Anders Johansson von Cöln, *Karl XII till Häst vid slaget vid Düna*, and on the portrait by J. H. Wedekind, showing the same battle near Riga in 1701, the painting also shows the Royal Drabants in detail (the painting is dated 1715).

---

11 Schreber von Schreeb, *Karolinska Förbundets Årsbok 1936*, pp.142–145.
12 Schreber von Schreeb, *Karolinska Förbundets Årsbok 1936*, p.145.
13 Larsson, *Karolinska Uniformer*, p.136.

In 1700 the Drabants received another issue of field uniforms. The black hat, its brim drawn to the crown on three sides, was edged with a broad gold galloon, the length of the galloon was 2½ cubits and it weighed two *lods*. On the left side a gilt button was fastened to a loop. The cravat was of black silk crepe, 74 cm long. The blue single-breasted coat was five cubits if cloth and tapered in at the waist, with a bell-like silhouette at the bottom. The lining of the coat used 6½ cubits of blue *rask*, and 1½ cubits of white undyed *rask*, ⅝ cubit of *shiag*, 1½ cubits of canvas and 2½ cubits of silk. The cuffs used ⅝ cubit of *shiag*. For the decoration of the coat there was 8¾ cubits of wide galloon and 11¾ of narrow, on the lining of the hinges 17½ cubits, the total weight of the galloons was 24 *lod*. Paper was put under the galloon. The coat had 31 large and 10 small gilded buttons. The buttons were strung on a leather strap, which was inserted between the woollen cloth of the coat and its lining fabric.

Taking into account the number of buttons put on the coats of Drabants we can assume that seven buttons were put on the flaps of pockets.

A suede waistcoat of mid-thigh length, with a detachable collar, with eight cubits of galloon, and another 13½ cubits of galloon to cover the seams. The total weight of the galloons was 10¼ *lod*. The waistcoat was fastened with 10 small gilt buttons. It is worthwhile to emphasise the small lapel collar on the waistcoat; such waistcoat collars are shown on some portraits of officers, and also on portraits of Charles XII.

Leather breeches with a small button below the knee. Gloves of elk skin decorated with 2½ cubits of galloon, weighing 2½ *lod*. A belt of moose skin, covered with blue silk velvet with a gilded brass buckle, and with galloon trimming along the edge, using 7¾ cubits of galloon, weighing 8½ *lods*. In 1701 the Drabants received the new model '1701 Drabant sword', with a gilded brass guard, and black scabbard with a gilded throat and chape. The sling for the carbine was of elk skin 10 cm wide, lined with blue *shiagg* cloth, and with the buckles and hook gilded, and edged with 8⅛ *lod* of galloon along the edges. The cartridge box (*ledunka*) was made of leather and the lid was covered with blue cloth and galloon lace.[14]

The Liv Esquadronen in 1717 wore a black hat with gold galloon of a finger's width, with a gilt brass button. Black silk crepe cravat. Blue coat with and English cloth lining with blue collar and cuffs and with gilt brass buttons. A thick leather waistcoat, reaching to the middle of the thigh, with the same buttons as on the coat, but somewhat smaller. Elk skin breeches without a seam between the thighs, narrow at the knee, and with a button to fasten them below the knee, a blue cloak with a blue collar, and a leather-coloured lining of English cloth. Dragoon-style belt with a bayonet compartment and

Cuirasses and boots, above the grave of Drabant Johan Gjertta

---

14 Larsson, *Karolinska Uniformer*, pp.135–139.

THE UNIFORM AND EQUIPMENT OF THE DRABANT CORPS (DRABANTKÅREN)

Image of a cavalryman on the coat of arms of Johan Gjertta.

with a gilt buckle. Carbine belt of ordinary ox skin, but with a gilt buckle. The cover for the cartridge box was made of black leather.[15]

The boots of the Drabants were probably of similar models to those of other cavalry. The preserved boots of Drabant, Baron Johan Gjertta, which are still hanging next to his sword and cuirasses (two of!) with the family coat of arms over his grave in Munsö kyrka.[16]

The Musicians of the Drabants

There was a kettledrummer and trumpeters in the Corps of Drabants, but not much is known about the decoration of the coats of the musicians of the Corps. The uniforms of the Drabant musicians were made of blue cloth, and were decorated with silver galloon. In February 1701, the previous banners to the kettledrums, and the banners and cords and tassels of the trumpets were completely worn out. It is not clear how long they had been in service or when they had been issued – perhaps the banners in question were from the reign of Charles XI. They were of blue silk, with a gold crowned royal monogram framed by palm branches. An idea of the appearance of such

---

15 Larsson, *Karolinska Uniformer*, pp.135–139.
16 <https://kulturbilder.wordpress.com/2017/09/24/begravningsvapen-for-baron-johan-gjertta-f-1666-d-1740>

banners is shown in the drawing of a kettledrum player in the *Karoliner*.[17] Thus, it can be assumed that in 1700 the Drabant kettledrums were adorned with these banners.

The correspondence requested that the banners be replaced and new ones be made. These new banners were to be embroidered in gold with a crown and the royal monogram. As a result, a pair of banners was made of 4½ cubits of white silk damask, five cubits of white silk braid, nine cubits of silk fringe, and 11¾ cubits of gold fringe. The royal monogram below the crown, framed by palm branches, was embroidered in gold onto the white silk. Covers of waxed cloth were also made for the kettledrum and the banners.[18] The horse of the kettledrummer of the Drabants was a grey.

The trumpets of the eight trumpeters in the Drabant Corps were silver-plated, with cords and tassels of mixed gold and silver silk thread, and covers of waxed cloth (*waxduuk*).

Horse Harness

The bridle used by the Drabants was generally indistinguishable from the general army pattern, probably also with plates, possibly with the crowned royal monogram. The saddles of the Drabant Corps were of the German pattern, with shabraques of blue cloth with a double galloon lace on the edge. In 1699, one cubit of blue woollen cloth and one cubit of waxed cloth (*1 Aln. Blått Kläde, 1 Aln. Waxduuk*) were required for the shabraque and for the covering of the holsters. For the decoration of the shabraque and holsters, 7¾ cubits of wide gold galloon were needed, and the same amount of narrow gold galloon.[19]

According to one writer, in 1699 on the rear corners of the shabraques of Drabant troopers were embroidered three small gold crowns below a large gold crown; the officers of the corps had laurel branches on each side of the crowns. Drawings of the Drabant officer's shabraque show a fringe along the edge.[20] On a detail of a painting in the collection of the Armémuseum in Stockholm, *Karl XII till Häst vid Düna* inventory no. AM.065980, images of Drabants, show a shabraque with crowns and laurel branches, judging by the descriptions of the issue of materials, and the absence of fringe on the edge of the shabraque, we can assume that this is the shabraque of a corporal of the Drabant Corps.

From 1696 to 1700 the Drabant's shabraque was of blue woollen cloth with the crowned royal monogram in the rear corner. The shabraque was bordered with yellow cloth and silk cord. The holster had a covering of black leather. In 1700 to the field uniform of ordinary Drabants was introduced a blue cloth shabraque made of one cubit of cloth, in the rear corner was the

---

17 Åberg and Göransson, *Karoliner*, p.39.
18 Schreber von Schreeb, *Karolinska Förbundets Årsbok 1936*, pp.124–126.
19 Schreber von Schreeb, *Karolinska Förbundets Årsbok 1936*, p.146.
20 Åberg and Göransson, *Karoliner*, pp.42–43.

royal monogram below the crown. The edge of the shabraque was covered with a wide and a narrow galloon with a total length of 7¾ cubits and weight of 14¾ aln, one cubit of wire thread was used for making the shabraque. In 1717 a simple leather shabraque and leather holsters were introduced.[21]

The painting *The Battle of Düna 1701* (*Slaget vid Düna*) by Johan Henrik Schildt, Armémuseum inventory no. NMA.0025512, painted a few years after the battle, shows a blue cloth Drabant's holster cap edged with gold galloon. A cloth case decorated with galloon lace was attached to the rear bow of the saddle – this can be seen on the saddle of the Drabants on the same painting depicting the Battle of Düna in 1701.

The Armament of the Drabants

The Drabants had the usual cavalry armour and equipment, but their swords were of a special pattern with a gilded hilt. The Corps had several swords of models 1685, 1695, 1701 and 1707 in use at the same time. The first three batches of swords were made at the Norrköping Armoury. The fourth batch was made in Saxony at the Dresden arms factory on the eve of the Russian campaign. The length of the blade of the Drabant sword was 96.7 cm. The sword was carried in a blackened leather scabbard from a waist belt. In some cases, such weapons were tailored individually according to the height and weight of the owner. The collection of the Kremlin in Moscow contains a sword of a senior officer of the Drabant Corps, inventory no. Or-4044. The heart-shaped cup of the guard is openwork, pierced through with small holes, the upper part of the hilt, the edges of the guard and the tip are decorated with floral ornamentation. This sword corresponds to the 1690 model sword for the senior ranks of Drabant Corps although it was obviously made in the early 1700s.[22]

The swords and sword hilts of the Drabants were often engraved with a crowned royal monogram perhaps framed by laurel branches, and additionally various mottos might be engraved on the blade, for example, *Vivat Carolus, Rex Svegorum*. To the hilt was attached a sword-knot (*templak*) with a tassel (*wärje band*), woven from blue and yellow silk cord. In 1699, such sword-knots were obviously not intended for all Drabants, they are not listed in the calculations of material needed, except for the commander, Öfwerste Lieutenanten Wåhlborne H:r Carl Nierot. There is an example of a Drabant officer's sword in the Livrustkammaren, inventory no. 8 878 (15:150:a) from the period 1700–1709.[23] The sword has a characteristic shape of Walloon type guard, model *Karolinska drabantvärjans fäste*. Length 947 mm, width 40 mm. The blade is straight, sharpened along both, converging, edges. On both sides of the blade are etched decorations consisting of a crowned monogram of Charles XII (double CXII), under which is placed the inscription *SOLI DEO GLORIA* (To God Alone be the Glory).

---

21 Larsson, *Karolinska Uniformer*, p.141.
22 'Perfect Victoria' exhibition catalogue, p.306.
23 <https://samlingar.shm.se/object/ECAF8ED5-DB8C-440A-9C98-729F23C1275B>

Above, and facing page: Trumpeters of the Swedish cavalry on *The Battle of Poltava* by Louis Caravac, 1718.

Carbines and Pistols

Small arms were not highly valued in the Carolinian cavalry, especially in the time of Charles XII. A good proof of this can be found in the provisions of Magnus Stenbock's *Reglemente for den ny Wärfda Svenska Armeen* of 1710, which instructs the cavalryman that he should 'never fire or use his carbine or pistol, except when the enemy is scattered and turns his back, and is driven into swamps and defiles.' During the reign of Charles XI the Drabants were armed with wheelock carbines, and those used at the time of his death were probably made in the 1680s. The calibre was 29 mm, the barrel length was 75.5 cm and overall length of the carbine 223 cm with a weight 3.42 kg.

The Drabants were also armed with a pair of pistols. Until 1700 these were wheelocks, in which case the equipment of the Drabant would have included a spanner for priming the mechanism. This spanner was suspended on a leather loop from the front of the holster belt. From *c.* 1700 each Drabant was armed with two flintlock pistols of 16.03 mm calibre, which were carried in holsters at the saddle bow and protected with leather or cloth covers.

The armament of Drabants included a flintlock rifled carbine of 18.55 mm calibre and weighing 0.5–1 kg. The carbine was carried on a cloth-covered and galloon decorated leather sling with a carbine 'hook' or spring clip (*pantalere*) worn over the left shoulder. In the list of orders of

THE UNIFORM AND EQUIPMENT OF THE DRABANT CORPS (DRABANTKÅREN)

1700 in Stockholm is '212 pcs. Carbines with flintlocks with spring pannier' intended for the Royal Drabants, according to the approved model of 26 April 1699. In the order for carbines intended for the Drabants in 1699, a number were of a smaller calibre, but of better quality. Of these, eight carbines were selected for officers and corporals. As it was impossible to get all the carbines exactly alike, the ones most similar were selected. In 1702 the Drabants recorded rifled flintlock carbines, model 1699.[24] The special *Drabantkarbinen m.1699* carbine, which is preserved in the collection of the Armémuseum in Stockholm (Armémuseum, inventory no. 4094) may be considered the pinnacle of what the weapon technology of that time could achieve. The barrel is smoothbore and 86.5 cm long with a 19 mm calibre. The overall length of the carbine is 220.5 cm, with a weight 3.28 kg. At the end of 1703, the Drabants received the new carbines ordered in 1700, with French flintlocks. These new carbines were sent to Danzig at the same time as the Drabant swords of model m.1701. It is believed that the Drabants carried these throughout the reign of Charles XII. In March 1717 'carbines' were ordered for the Liv Esquadronen, but this weapon, regardless of its name, was a variation of the dragoon musket with bayonet.

---

24 Schreber von Schreeb, *Karolinska Förbundets Årsbok 1936*, pp.78–79.

The carbine was carried from the 'carbine belt' (*pantaler*) over the left shoulder. Carbine belts m/1699 were used by both non-commissioned officers and ordinary Drabants decorated respectively with wide and narrow gold galloon stitched along the edges, on top of a covering of blue *shiag*, the buckles and carabiners were entirely gilded. The carbine belt was made of elk skin and was around 10 cm wide. It had a rectangular iron loop on it and in the centre of the outer long side of this loop was attached a carabiner spring, which hooked into a ring attached to a long metal staple screwed to the inner side of the carbine. When the trooper was mounted, the carbine hung muzzle downward. Musket holster – a case with a strap for attaching the carbine to the saddle into which the butt of the stock was inserted, so that the carbine did not hurt either the rider or the horse, when on the march. There is no convincing information that such a holster was used by the Drabants or in other mounted regiments during the war. All references to such a device in the Swedish cavalry are known only from the second half of the 1710s. Moreover, their absence is clear on the surviving images of the Drabants from the period. They are only referenced on 24 November 1716, when Charles XII in a letter to Öfwerst Löjtnant Lillieström orders him to equip the Livregementet with, among other things, a *karbinskor*.[25]

Ammunition for pistols and carbines was carried in small ammunition boxes (*ladunka*) worn on a belt over the right shoulder. New cartridge boxes were received by the Drabants on 23 July 1703. In 1700, a sheet iron frame was inserted into the middle of the leather box, with space for 11 cartridges and a compartment for an oiler. In 1717 the number of places for cartridges increased by one to bring it up to 12, with a thirteenth compartment for the oiler. The box lid was covered with a wide and narrow galloon on the edges.

The belt for the cartridge box was noticeably narrower than the carbine belt, and could have a gilded buckle, and the end of the belt ended with a pelta shaped plate. In addition to the cartridges in the cartridge box, the pistol holsters had compartments where cartridges could also be kept.

Until 1702, Drabants had armour: breastplates for non-commissioned officers and troopers, and a full back and breast for the officers. The cuirasses of the Drabant troopers and NCOs did not differ from those used by the regiments of horse and they are described in detail in the chapter devoted to the equipment of cavalry regiments. The cuirasses of Drabant officers were decorated in front with chased gilded devices of the royal monogram, lions and palm branches.

During the Polish campaign, Charles XII abolished the cuirass in the Drabant Corps. The King believed that they were ineffective protection against bullets and only fatigued both rider and horse. Officers, however, may have continued to use cuirasses.

---

25 Schreber von Schreeb, *Karolinska Förbundets Årsbok 1936*, p.83.

9

The Uniform of the Musicians of the Cavalry and Dragoons

In cavalry regiments the establishment was supposed to include 8 trumpeters and 1 kettledrummer. Extant information shows that dragoon regiments also had kettledrummers as well as drummers. In addition to these categories of musicians, some regiments at least had oboists, as well as musicians who played the dulcimer and the shalmey (the medieval shawm). Musicians are recorded in the following regiments: in 1700 in the Kunglig Majestäts Livregemente Dragoner; Livdragonregementet, there were five musicians playing the shalmey; in 1705 in Stenbocks Dragonregemente there were four oboists and two musicians playing the dulcimer; in 1700 in Livländskt Dragonregemente there were six musicians playing the shalmey and two the dulcimer; and in 1716 in Skånska Ståndsdragonregemente there were three oboists and one dulcimer player.[1]

According to surviving descriptions, the hats of the musicians in most regiments were edged with silver metallic or silk braid and the inside was lined with black linen.

In general, the coat and livery of musicians was the same cut as that of ordinary cavalry, and repeated the tendencies in the development of single-breasted and double-breasted coats during the war, except for two details. The first distinctive detail of the coat of many musicians was the decoration of the coat with braided cord, braid or galloon in different variants of these materials. Braid, galloon or cord was sewn on the uniform, on the seams, collar, on the edges of pocket flaps, on the front of coats and/or around the buttonholes. The second unique detail is the false sleeves, which were sewn into the seams on the shoulders of the coat. In some cases, the false sleeves may have been decorated at the edges with braid or galloon. It seems that these decorative elements were used for musicians only in the cavalry regiments. Such false sleeves are shown on the coats of kettledrummers and trumpeters of the Royal Drabants, and on two engravings by E. Dahlbergh from the end of the seventeenth century (images of cavalrymen against the

---

1   Larsson, *Karolinska Uniformer*, p.118.

Trumpeters shown on a painting of the Battle of Düna in 1701, by Johan Henrik Schildt. Armémuseum Stockholm, NMA.0025512.

background of Höiientorp, and Wänngarn). On one of the engravings it can be seen that the sleeves have no horizontally arranged galloon, on the second the whole figure is shaded, together with the sleeves. On a painting depicting the Battle of Düna in 1701 by Johan Henrik Schildt, two trumpeters in blue coats are shown in the background, one with a yellow false sleeve with possibly a yellow lining. The coats of neither musician show any decoration with braid or galloon. It is not known if all musicians, even in the cavalry regiments, had false sleeves on their uniforms, and it is likely that dragoon musicians did not have them at all, except perhaps for kettledrummers. The question of horizontal bands of lace or braid along the entire length of the sleeve of cavalry musicians remains controversial; they are not shown on the pictorial sources, and are not in the descriptions of uniforms and materials of the regiments, which are cited below.

The musicians' coats were embroidered with galloon, cord or braid, sometimes with different colours of thread in the braid. According to the descriptions in the documents, there was no universal system of decoration, each regiment having it own individual decoration. That is, in one regiment galloon or braid was sewn on the seams, cuffs, around the pocket flaps, on the collar, on the side, in front and back, and in another, only on the pocket flaps and on the seams. There are difficulties, too, in visualising the appearance of the braid. It is possible to understand what the cord plaited from different

THE UNIFORM OF THE MUSICIANS OF THE CAVALRY AND DRAGOONS

colours of strands may have looked like – it was either a twisted cord or a plaited braid. But what remains a mystery is the pattern of weaving from different coloured strands, and the sequence of the pattern on the braid. All kinds of pattern suggested by reconstructions are entirely possible because the original examples of braids used in the decoration of Swedish musicians' uniforms in 1700–1721, either have not survived or have not, as yet, been found.

According to some accounts, musicians' coats embroidered with galloon or woollen braid were not used in all regiments. For example, the trumpeters of the Smålands Kavalleriregemente in 1710–12 had plain blue uniforms without any decoration. The same was the case in Riksänkedrottningens [Queen Dowager's] Livregemente till Häst, where in 1715 it is recorded that there was no musicians' livery, and the trumpeters wore a plain blue coat.[2] It is possible, of course, that this is a consequence of austerity following the loss of the main army in the 1709 campaign. Additionally, the uniform of the musicians could be in reversed colours, that is, the whole uniform of the musicians of the facing colour of the regiment, for example, yellow. Thus a cavalry trumpeter is shown in this way on the background of the equestrian portrait of Charles XII in the collection of the Statens Historiska Museum, the whole uniform including the false sleeves are shown in yellow, without any edging of braid or galloon,[3] and the timpani player is shown in a similar way on one of the paintings by J. Lembke.

In some cases, the decoration of uniforms in the same regiment could vary from one musician to another. For example, in the Stenbocks Dragonregemente, the drummer had a blue uniform with yellow lining, the seams and edges of the collar cuffs and buttonholes were decorated with blue and yellow braid. While for the other musicians of the regiment, the oboists and the kettledrummer in 1705, the hat was edged with narrow silver galloon and the coat was blue with white lining and blue and white braid on the seams, collar, cuffs and buttonholes. The buttons were silver-plated.

The surviving information on some regiments, provides some understanding of the approximate amount of cloth used for manufacturing uniforms, the number of buttons, the braid or cord to decorate the musicians' coats etc.

Detail of a late seventeenth-century painting by J. Lembke, depicting a kettledrummer in the background. The kettledrummer is shown in a yellow coat with false sleeves, blue cuffs, and the kettledrum banner is also blue.

---

2 Höglund, *The Great Northern War 1700–1721*, p.56.
3 Larsson, *Karolinska Uniformer*, p.85

Above and facing page, two engravings by Erik Dahlbergh from the late seventeenth century, depicting cavalrymen, including kettledrummers and trumpeters, against the background of Höiientorp and Wänngarn.

In the descriptions it is not always possible to understand completely whether the livery is described with false sleeves at the back, or whether it is a simple coat decorated with a braid, except in the few cases when this point is stated in the document.

Adelsfanan i Sverige och Finland. In 1696 they wore a yellow coat edged with blue and gold braid. The braid was sewn on the chest, sleeves and around the coat.

Riksänkedrottningens [Queen Dowager's] Livregemente till Häst. In 1715 trumpeters wore a coat of blue cloth, without any ornamentation.

Kunglig Majestäts Livregemente Dragoner; Livdragonregementet. In 1700 the drummers' hats were edged with white braid. The coat was blue with bronze buttons, and decorated with *camlet* lace. The waistcoat and breeches were of leather.

Skånska 3 Männingsregementet till Häst. In 1700, making a coat required five cubits of blue cloth, eight cubits of blue *rask* and three dozen pewter buttons. For decorating the coat, 64 cubits of wide cord and 16 cubits of narrow cord were required.

Upplands 3 Männingsregementet till Häst. In 1700 making a coat required five cubits of blue cloth, eight cubits of blue *rask*, and three dozen pewter buttons. Decoarting it required 64 cubits of wide cord and 16 cubits of narrow cord.

Karelska Kavalleriregemente. In 1719 the coat used five cubits of cloth and 4¾ cubits of blue lining fabric, and English buttons made of tin.

Smålands Kavalleriregemente. In 1710–12 trumpeters did not have a special musicians' livery, but wore a plain blue coat.

Västgöta 3 Männingsregementet till Häst. In 1701, five cubits of cloth for the coat, eight cubits of blue *rask* for the lining. three dozen buttons, 64 cubits of wide cord and 16 cubits of narrow cord were used for the edging the coat. In 1719 a blue coat with a blue lining and edged with cord. The waistcoat was of elk skin with pewter buttons.

Upplands 3–5 Männingsregementet till Häst. In 1715 the coat had galloon lace. For the eight trumpeters' coats, 200 cubits of cord were used.. The coat had galloon on the collar and the sword belt was edged with galloon.

Pommerska Kavalleriregementet. In 1702, the trumpeters and the kettledrummer of this regiment wore a hat with silver galloon; a light blue uniform with a crimson red lining, cuffs and collar with 2½ dozen silver-covered buttons. The coat was decorated with silver galloon on the seams, collar, pocket flaps, buttonholes, and cuffs, with an epaulette on the right shoulder, or perhaps a small 'wing' in the shape of a crescent moon, also edged with galloon. In addition, the musicians of this regiment are

THE UNIFORM OF THE MUSICIANS OF THE CAVALRY AND DRAGOONS

mentioned as having a blue supravest (or supra vest), with a red lining, with a double row of pewter buttons, the buttonholes and seams of the supravest were edged with white braid. The form of the supravest is not known in detail but we can assume that it would resemble similar items as worn in other European armies. For example, French cavalry musicians in the early eighteenth century wore similar supravests. The musicians of the Pommerska Kavalleriregementet might have had a particularly long example, or it could also be a smaller one, only as long as the waist.

Bremiska Dragonregementet. In 1700 the regiment had oboists on its establishment in addition to drummers. The hats of the oboists were edged with silver braid, the *pajrock* was suede-coloured, with pewter buttons, blue lining and blue cuffs, and covered with blue braid. The coat was blue with suede-coloured lining and cuffs and silver-plated buttons. The coat was decorated with white and silver braid on the collar with pocket flaps, the edges of the cuffs and on the seams. The breeches and waistcoat were leather with silver buttons. The belt was also edged with silver braid. The drummer had a similar appearance, but the coat was edged with silver braid.[4]

Ingermanländska Dragonregementet. In 1708 musicians wore hats with silver braid, blue coats edged with plush braid, and blue breeches.

Verdiska Dragonregemente. The coats of musicians of this regiment stand out from the general range of single-breasted coats of musicians of other regiments. In 1703, the oboist wore a hat with silver decoration. He had a blue, double-breasted coat with blue lining and pewter buttons; the seams of the coat, the buttonholes, and the cuffs were edged with silver braid. The cloak was blue with a blue lining. The kettledrummer wore a similar uniform. The drummer's coat was somewhat simpler decorated but also

---

4   Höglund, *The Great Northern War 1700–1721*, p.84.

double-breasted, with pewter buttons and white silk braid on the seams, the buttonholes were also decorated.[5]

Pommerska Dragonregementet. In 1703–1707, the drummer wore a blue coat with blue lining and cuffs and bronze buttons. The coat was decorated with wide gold and blue thread braid on the buttonholes, seams, collar and pocket flaps. An African musician in the regiment in 1703 wore a red scarf, a blue coat with blue lining and cuffs and with bronze gilded buttons. At the seams and pocket flaps it was edged with gold galloon, he had a leather waistcoat with bronze buttons. The headdress was a red woollen cloth turban, with gold cord along the edge. He wore a woven sash/belt. This exotic outfit was complemented by a sabre, probably of oriental type, a sabre belt, or silk cord belt, was hidden under the sash.

Stenbocks Dragonregemente. In 1705, musicians (oboists, kettledrummer, and dulcimer players) wore hats with silver braid, a red scarf, and blue coats with white wool lining and silver-plated pewter buttons. The collar, cuffs, pocket flaps, buttonholes, and seams of the coat were edged with blue and white braid. The waistcoat and breeches were made of leather. The musicians also wore a blue surcoat (a *pajrock*?) with blue lining and brass buttons, as well as a cloak of blue cloth with yellow lining and brass buckles.[6] The drummer of the same regiment wore the same hat and had a blue coat with pewter buttons. The coat was also decorated on the collar, cuffs, button loops and seams, but in a different colour combination – blue with pale coloured braid.[7] The belts of the musicians and kettledrummer were made of buffalo leather with a silver buckle and a blue and white cord around the edge, while the drummers had the usual belts.

Taubes or **Schlesiska Dragonregementet.** In 1704–1705 the uniforms of oboists and drummers comprised a hat with silver braid, blue cloaks with a yellow lining and bronze clasps. The coat was blue with blue lining and blue cuffs, and bronze buttons; it was edged with braid of alternating blue, white, orange and black piping along the seams and buttonholes. A leather waistcoat with bronze buttons. The buttonholes were panelled in yellow.

Dückers or **Preussiska Dragonregementet.** In 1705, the oboist and drummer wore a hat with a silver band. A blue cloak with a blue lining, the collar was edged with yellow braid. A blue coat with yellow lining, collar and cuffs. Button loops were edged with blue and yellow braid, the buttons were bronze. A waistcoat of light blue colour with bronze buttons, a red lining and edged with yellow braid. Leather breeches.

---

5   Höglund, *The Great Northern War 1700–1721*, p.87.

6   Larsson, *Karolinska Uniformer*, p.117.

7   Höglund, *The Great Northern War 1700–1721*, p.88.

THE UNIFORM OF THE MUSICIANS OF THE CAVALRY AND DRAGOONS

Features and Variations of the Decoration on Musicians' Coats

Lars-Eric Höglund in his book proposed a scheme of arrangement of woollen or woven silk thread braid for the embroidery on cavalry coats and the livery of musicians, which looks to be in the style of the era. A variant of the embroidery of the coats of musicians – the kettledrummer and trumpeter of the Västgöta Kavalleriregemente in the 1700s – is shown in the picture, a reconstruction by E. von Strokirch in 1911. Another plate shows a trumpeter of the same regiment in 1748, in a coat with yellow and blue mixed lace, with yellow and blue segments – rectangles – with bevelled edges. The coat also shows false sleeves decorated on the edge with braid. It is difficult to say today on what evidence the artist based his work on or whether he saw actual lace for Swedish the musicians of cavalry regiments of the first quarter of the eighteenth century. It remains to trust, and hope, that it was painted on the evidence of descriptions or then surviving examples. Few pictorial sources and descriptions have survived to today.

Detail of an engraving from the early 1700s, with kettledrummer and trumpeters, probably showing musicians of the Guard Regiment or Drabants.

CHARLES XII'S KAROLINERS VOLUME 2

THE UNIFORM OF THE MUSICIANS OF THE CAVALRY AND DRAGOONS

Drawing by E. von Strokirch. Västgöta Kavalleriregemente in 1748. The lace is shown with yellow and blue segments in a bevelled edge rectangle. Inventory no.AMA.0006232

Facing page: Drawing by E. von Strokirch of Västgöta Kavalleriregemente in 1700. The lace is shown as being made of multicoloured threads, in a plaited pattern. Inventory no.AMA.0006228

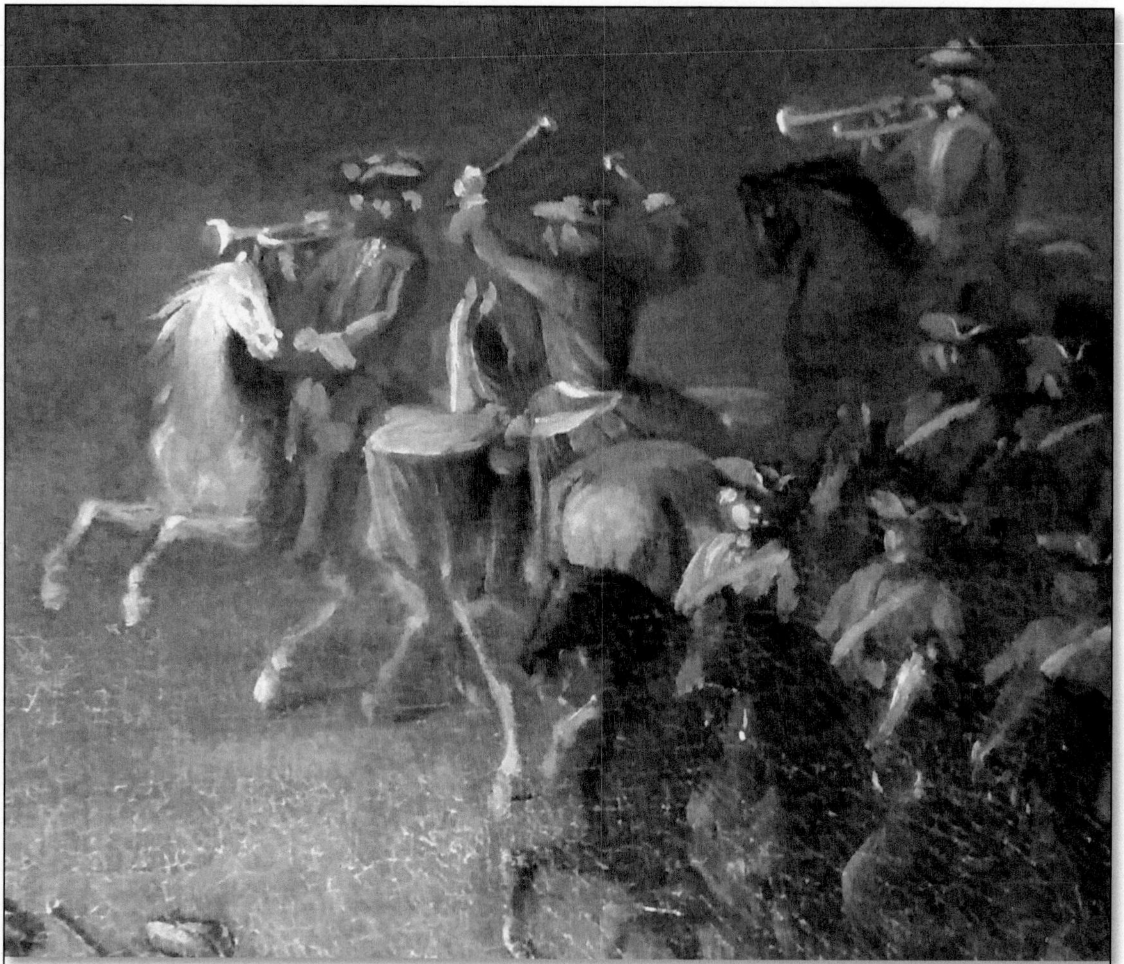

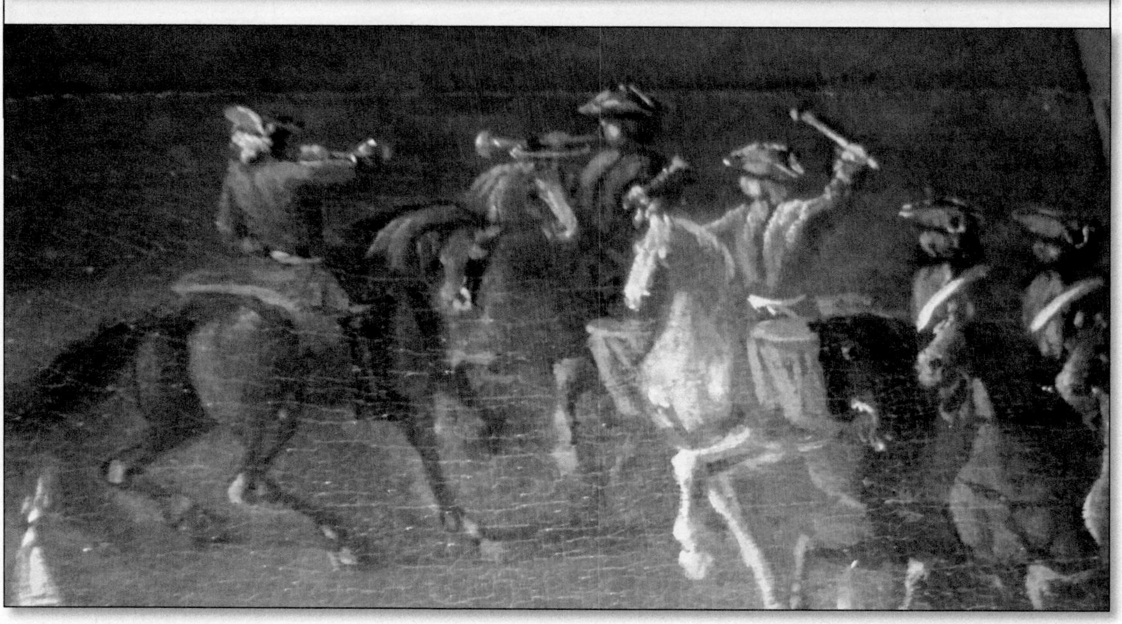

THE UNIFORM OF THE MUSICIANS OF THE CAVALRY AND DRAGOONS

Right: A trumpeter of a cavalry regiment, wearing a livery embroidered with braid or galloon. (Author's illustration)

Facing page: Trumpeters and kettledrummers from *The Battle of Poltava* by Denis Martin.

CHARLES XII'S KAROLINERS VOLUME 2

Kettledrummer of a cavalry regiment. (Author's illustration)

There are some other images from the Great Northern War period which show a slightly different arrangement of the decoration on the coats of cavalry musicians, and which are not presented in Lars-Eric Höglund's book. For example, the engraving detail showing Charles XII mounted is particularly valuable as the engraver paid particular attention to the musicians, especially to the decoration and the arrangement of the trumpeter and kettledrummer lace, this detail from the engraving has already been published several times.[8]

On the livery of the kettledrummer, the galloon or braid is laid out on the chest along the buttonholes, and also symmetrically on the right field of the coat. The galloon or braid goes along the shoulder seam, the armholes of the sleeve, and probably along the edge on the false sleeves at the back. What is especially interesting is that the pattern of laying out the braid or galloon on the pocket flaps can clearly be seen, around, and below the pocket. On the trumpeters standing behind the kettledrummer, the galloon or braid is laid across the coats in a similar manner, although it isn't precisely the same. For example, the braid or galloon below the pocket flap is not laid in a circle like the kettledrummer's, but with a cape. What is interesting is that the seams on the sleeves are not edged with galloon or braid. The sleeves of the livery of the drummer have a similar silhouette to the sleeves of the coat of Charles XII, with the same small cuff, which is not visible because of the gloves. Once again, it is difficult to state unequivocally whether all musicians of the cavalry had such characteristic details of their uniform – details such as the livery of musicians and the false sleeves sewn into the shoulder seams at the back. The schemes of the arrangement of lace and braid on the sleeves are also not clear; it is unclear in what cases musicians' lace would be embroidered horizontally on sleeves, with segments between braids or galloons. The braid or galloon on the uniforms of cavalry musicians was sewn only along the seams, including the back, the middle of the back, the slit, around the edge of the uniform, side slits, collar, pocket flaps, around the pocket flaps, cuffs, in front in two rows along the chest, and on the button loops.

Even more interesting, is the unusual appearance of the musicians – trumpeters and kettledrummers – on the painting of the Battle of Poltava by Louis Caravac from 1718. The Swedish kettledrummer is shown in a blue uniform with a yellow collar and seven buttons up to the level of the breastplate. The coat is not embroidered with galloon or braid, but instead has a yellow cord lanyard attached to its right shoulder. The hat is edged with yellow galloon lace, somewhat wider than that of the troopers next to him. It is difficult to say what regiment is represented on the canvas. With regards to the lanyard on the right shoulder, there are four similar coats, *justokors*, known from late seventeenth century, in the collection of the Armémuseum in Stockholm inventory no. AM 17539.[9] Maybe this decoration of the uniforms of musicians could be from

---

8   Pavel Konovaltjuk, *Einar Lyth Vägen till Poltava : slaget vid Lesnaja 1708* (Stockholm: Svenskt Militärhistorisk biblioteks förlag 2009), p 49; O. Sokirko, *The Ukrainian Rubicon. The Battle of Poltava, 1709*. Ch. III (Kiev: 2009), p.59.

9   Klas Kronberg and Tomas Roth, *The French Uniforms Mystery* (Stockholm: Armémuseum, 2010), p.32.

Oboist and drummer of the Drashun Regiment. (Author's illustration)

THE UNIFORM OF THE MUSICIANS OF THE CAVALRY AND DRAGOONS

some recruited regiments, perhaps from the Germany. For example, on the images of the Reiter Kurbrandenburgisches Garde du Corps (Brandenburg Guard Cavalry) in 1698 there are images of lanyards. The kettledrums on the painting are shown with red banners embroidered in yellow or gold. Trumpeters next to each other, probably of the same regiment, are shown in the same uniforms with yellow cuffs and half coat lapels, these are also without any embroidery, braid or cord on the uniform. Lanyards are shown in the same way. The banners on the pipes are red with yellow or gold silk fringe. The red covers of the pistol holsters should also be noted. The painting by Louis Caravacca is full of a lot of authentic details, in addition to his client – Tsar Peter the Great – gave descriptions. Thus this solution to the decoration of the uniform looks quite probable. In the Swedish Army, several cavalry regiments had red holster covers; Östgöta Kavalleriregemente, Nylands och Tavastahus Läns Kavalleriregemente, Pommerska Regementet. The artist may have depicted musicians from one of these regiments. It is also possible that the Swedish uniforms depicted on the painting may not be from the time of the Battle of Poltava, but later, perhaps from the 1710s.

Denis Martin's painting *The Battle of Poltava* in the collection of the Museum of the Battle of Poltava shows Swedish squadrons in the background, behind the Swedish infantry in battle order. On the right flank, two of them, the trumpeters and kettledrummers are clearly visible, they are depicted in ochre-coloured uniforms, the banners on the kettledrums are red. It is difficult to judge to what extent the colour scheme actually reflects reality, as the cavalry of the squadrons are also depicted in dirty ochre uniforms. This combination of colours for the musicians is known, but it is impossible to say which regiment is represented. Also the musicians are shown without any embroidery on the uniforms or any galloon or braid. Nonetheless it is a rare example of the depiction of Swedish musicians, and in particular Swedish kettledrummers in battle.

10

Musical Instruments, their Decoration and Banners

Cavalry trumpets could be without additional decoration or could be decorated with a silk cord with tassels, in some cases this could be a mixture of coloured silks, and/or metal silver or gold threads. The trumpets could also be decorated with fringed banners of silk or other cloth of the regimental colour. There is evidence of banners decorated with the royal monogram. Kettledrum banners could also be decorated with the royal monogram or a crowned monogram, in some cases flanked by palm branches. The ways of decorating the trumpet banners varied, it could be by appliqué or embroidery, or by painting the decoration onto the silk. Not all banners necessarily had a royal monogram and palm branches. Trumpet banners could also have tassels attached to them, probably at the bottom corners. The monograms and palm branches were not of a uniform design, and in every example known to us there are variations in the actual form of the design.

The Swedish cavalry also used kettledrums originating both from Sweden proper and also captured trophy drums. One example of this latter practice are the Saxon kettledrums captured at the Battle of Klishov on 2 July 1702 and later given to the Swedish Guards cavalry by Charles XII as a reward. After the Battle of Poltava they were, in turn, given as a trophy to the life-squadron of Prince A. Menshikov. In the Armoury Chamber is kept a set Swedish kettledrums, MMK inventory no. Or-4688, which survived by almost a miracle. They are of 52.5 cm diameter and 32 cm deep. These are one of eight pairs of kettledrums taken in the Battle of Poltava from the Swedish regiments of cavalry. All of these kettledrums were kept in the Armoury Chamber, but in 1737 were badly damaged by the fire of that year and lost all their banners.

Above are described illustrations of cavalry trumpets with red trumpet banners and red kettledrum banners. A painting of 1862, *Victory at Poltava* by Alexander Kotzebu, shows Swedish kettledrums in the foreground among the trophies, with yellow banners with silver embroidery in the form of a crowned royal monogram, framed by silver palm branches and embroidery. The artist is known to have used objects from the trophy collection as models for the painting. It is reasonable to assume therefore that the kettledrums depicted are not the artist's fantasy, but depictions of a real artefact, which in

MUSICAL INSTRUMENTS, THEIR DECORATION AND BANNERS

Details of a cartouche of Nylands och Tavastahus Läns Kavalleriregemente, showing the kettledrums and trumpets. The blue banners with gold royal monogram are clearly visible.

the middle of the nineteenth century was still kept in the trophy collection. The kettledrums depicted on the canvas do actually confirm our knowledge of the colour and decoration of the Swedish cavalry's kettledrum banners.

An important and rare image for understanding the appearance of kettledrums and the kettledrum banner decoration is in T. Jacobsson's book.[1] It shows the kettledrums of the Swedish artillery in 1716 on their kettledrum. The decoration in the form of the crowned royal monogram framed by palm branches, is still present, and the proportions and length of the banners are clearly visible.

Surviving banners in the Livrustkammaren Museum, inventory no. 17253 (889), give us a idea of the size and materials of kettledrum banners. They are made of white silk damask, and the overall dimensions are 800 mm wide and 500 mm top to bottom. The size of the decoration is 660×250mm. The banners are decorated in the centre with the painted monogram of Charles XII – a double letter 'C' surrounding the figure 'XII', all surmounted by a Royal Crown, and surrounded by two palm branches. The edges are bordered with a stylised floral design. In the corners, above the monogram, which frames the edge of the banners, are small wreaths. All decoration is painted in gold with brown highlighting, the crowns are shown with a red lining.[2] Judging from the colour and decoration, it is likely that this banner belonged to Livregementet till Häst.

---

1 Jakobsson, *Artilleriet under Karl XII:s-tiden*, p.408.
2 <https://samlingar.shm.se/object/AAEAF89F-B742-4EE6-B234-C485DD3A5307>

CHARLES XII'S KAROLINERS VOLUME 2

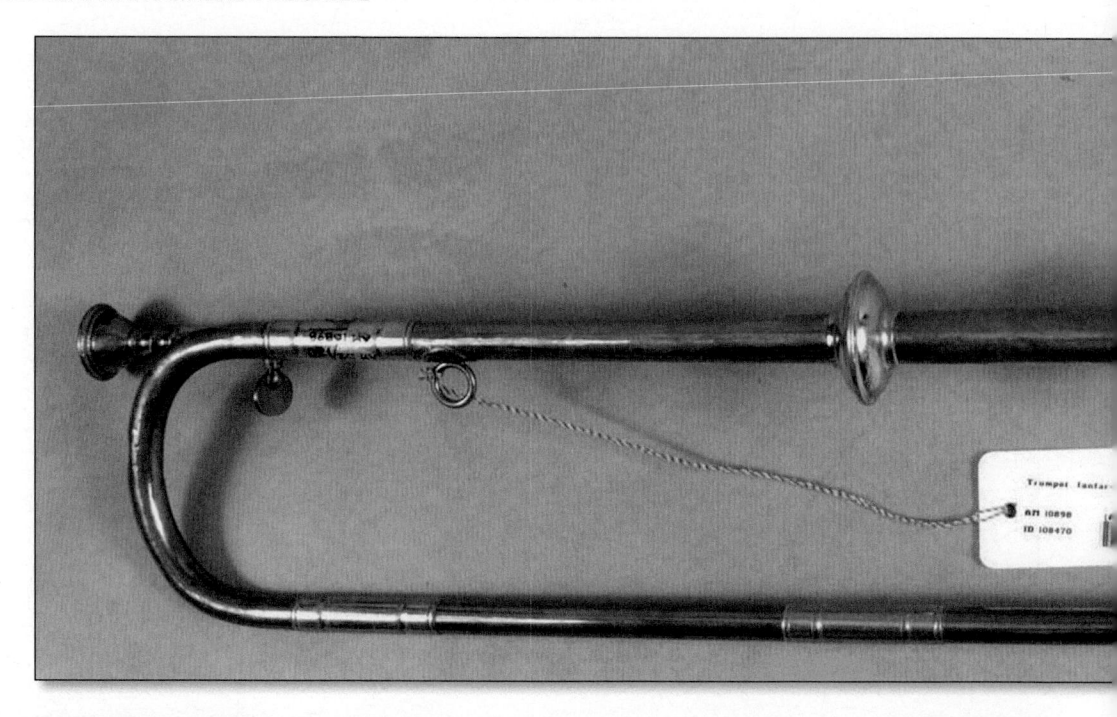

Top: Trumpet from the collection of the Armémuseum, Stockholm, inventory no. AM.010898.
Above: trumpet with decorative tassels, drawing by J. Ph. Lemke, Nationalmuseum, Stockholm. Inventory no. AM.010898.
Facing page: Trumpet tassels. Collection of the Armémuseum, Stockholm, inventory no. AM.010908.

MUSICAL INSTRUMENTS, THEIR DECORATION AND BANNERS

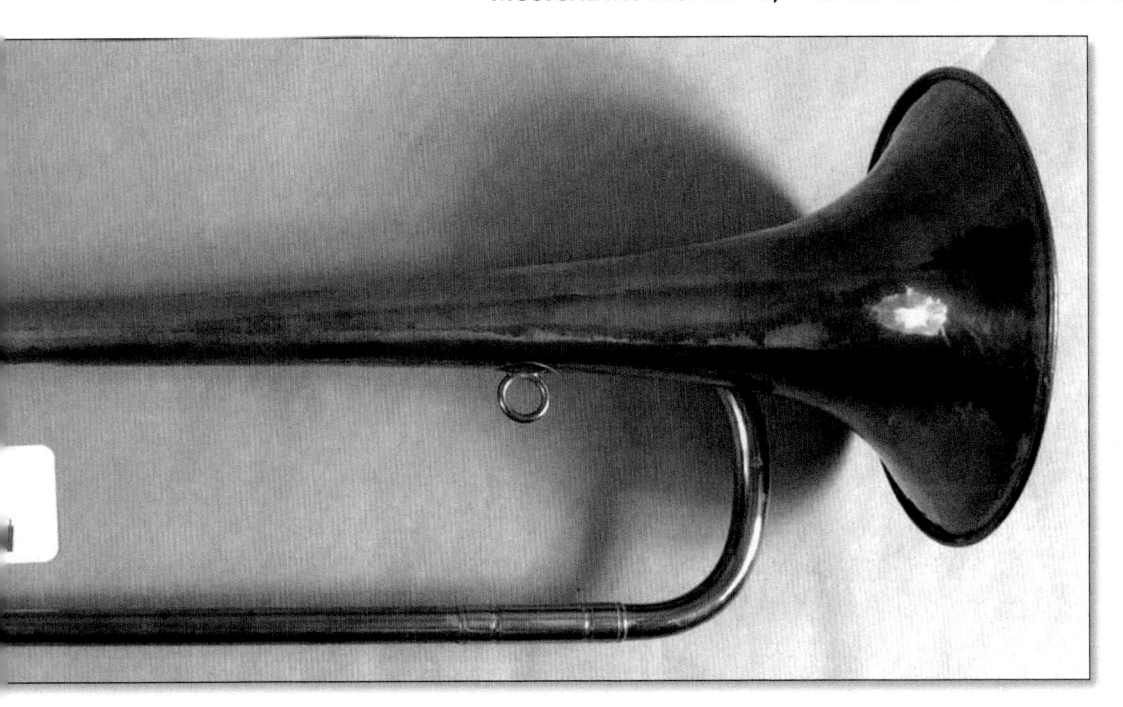

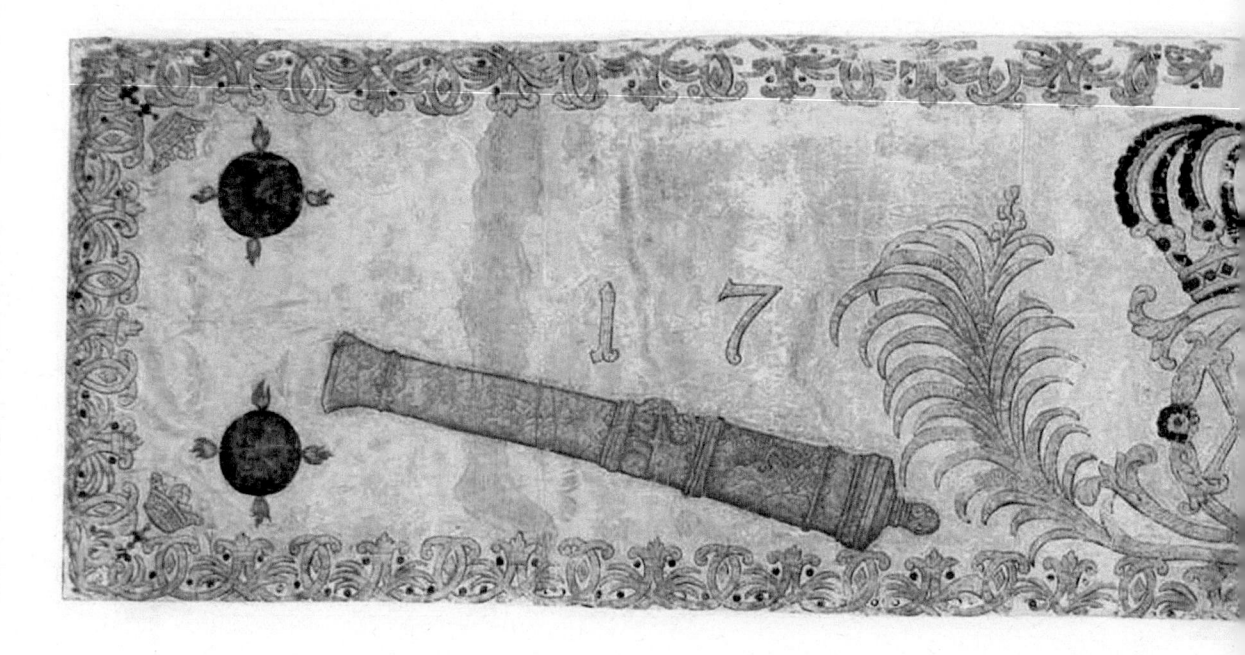

Kettledrum Banner from the collection of the Armémuseum, Stockholm, inventory no. AM.089915.

Another banner that has survived (see overleaf) belonged to the kettledrums of the Artillery.³ This banner is dated to 1716 and is also made of silk damask with a woollen lining. Brown, red, blue, and gold paints have been used in the decoration. The decoration is similar to that of the Livregementet till Häst, showing the monogram of Charles XII, the double C, surmounted by a crown and flanked by two palm branches. The sides carry the date 1716, plus a gun, and two flaming grenades in the corners of each side. The cloth is bordered by stylised floral ornamentation.

A little-known description of trophies from the collection in Russian museums may show the materials and decoration of the banners from a different perspective. After the battles of Lesnaya and Poltava in 1709, by a decree of Peter the Great a record was made of the reception into the Armoury Chamber of the captured banners, weapons, officers' gorgets, etc., including kettledrums and curtains. The following are among these trophies:

> A pair of azure coloured banners, different coats of arms sewn in gold and silver, gold and silver fringe and tassels. A pair of yellow banners, emblems sewn with gold and silver, fringe and silk tassels with gold. A pair of crimson banners without coats of arms, they have two tassels of silk with silver, fringe of silk with silver. A pair of banners, herbs written in gold and silver, silk fringe. Six pairs of banners in all. Eight covers of soft leather.⁴

---

3   <https://digitaltmuseum.se/011024453860/pukfana>

4   Y. N. Bolotina and V. R. Novoselov, 'Captured in the battle Swedish guns, and banners, and kettledrums, and other all kinds of military supplies to taken to the Armoury Chamber.' Documents of the Russian State Archive of Documents on the trophies taken from the Swedes after the Poltava Victory on 27 June 1709, in *Historical Archive*, 2009, No. 3. C. 25.

MUSICAL INSTRUMENTS, THEIR DECORATION AND BANNERS

In addition to the inventory of banners, covers for the kettledrums made of leather are also mentioned, though they were in a dilapidated state.

In the inventory of memorable and non-memorable items kept in the hall, among the trophies of the Great Northern War, item no. 1283 is 'two yellow silk kettledrum banners, in the middle is sewn in gold a double C monogram with a crown above it. 1682.'[5] It is quite possible that these are the banners which were used as the model by Alexander Kotzebu, and had miraculously survived the fire of 1737.

From surviving documents, for some regiments, we have the following descriptions of the details of the decoration of musical instruments:

Norra Skånska kavalleriregementet. Blue–yellow cords with two tassels.

Adelsfanan. Trumpet cord made of silver coloured silk

Smålands Kavalleriregemente A cord to a cavalry pipe made of blue and yellow silk with silver thread mixed through.

Nylands och Tavastahus Läns Kavalleriregemente. On a map of 1696, which shows details of the equipment and armament of this regiment, the trumpets have blue banners fringed yellow and displaying the royal monogram. The kettledrums are decorated with similar banners.

Pommerska Kavalleriregementet. In 1702 the banners were crimson red, covered with white and silver thread.

---

5   Talyzin, *Description of the Artillery Hall of Memorable and Unmemorable Objects 1862*, p.71.

CHARLES XII'S KAROLINERS VOLUME 2

Right: Detail of kettledrums from *Victory at Poltava* by Alexander Kotzebu.

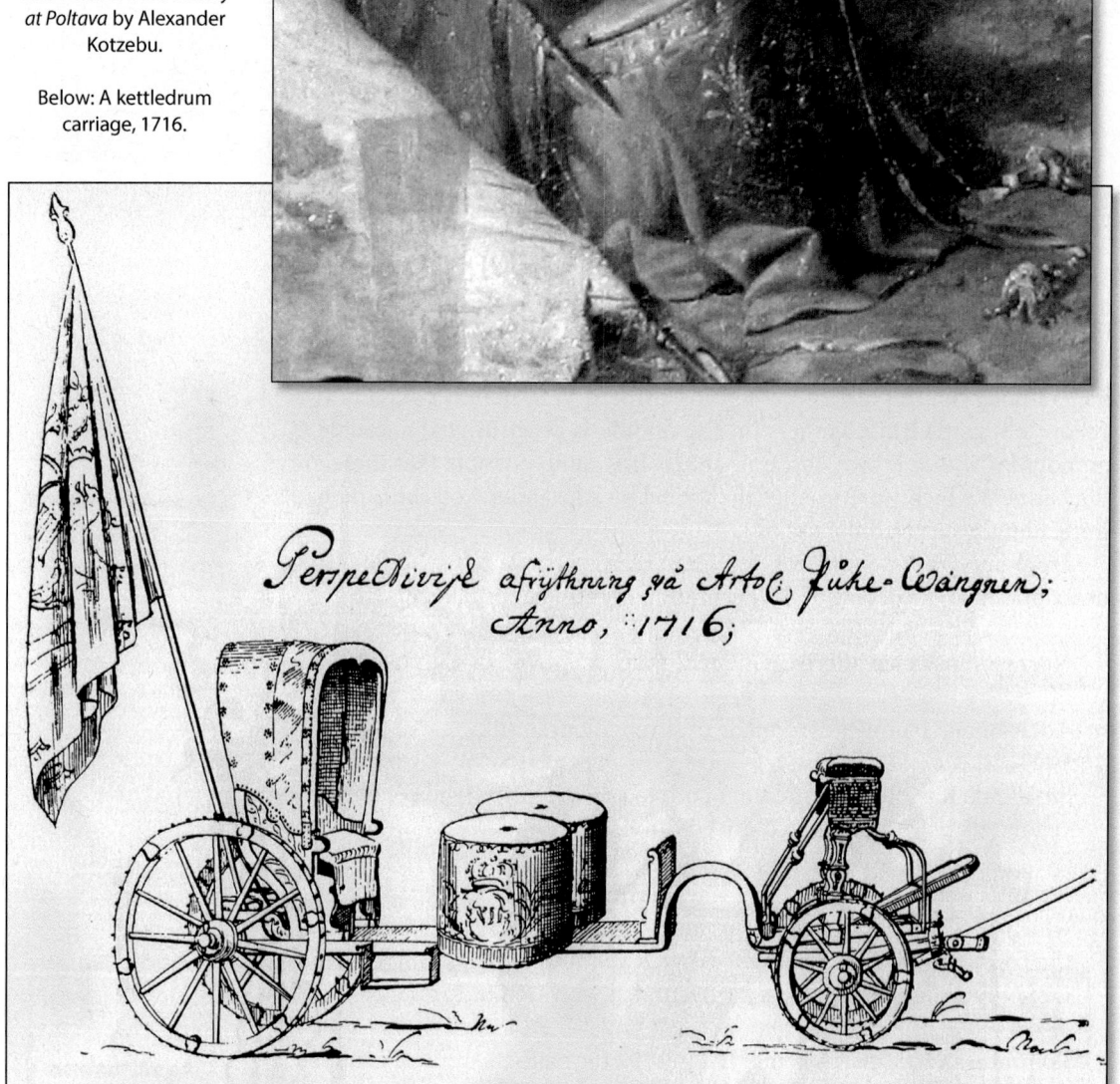

Below: A kettledrum carriage, 1716.

MUSICAL INSTRUMENTS, THEIR DECORATION AND BANNERS

Verdiska Dragonregemente. Kettledrum banners of blue panelled in silver. The drums were coloured light yellow. The drum strap is made of yellow buff leather.

Pommerska Dragonregementet. In 1703–1707, kettledrums with blue-coloured charges with a golden Royal Monogram and Crown.

Stenbocks Dragonregemente. In 1705, the drum is painted in blue and yellow flames, with the Stenbock coat of arms. The banding of the drum is panelled in blue with pale camel hair binding. The laths are yellow, sewn with gold and silver.

Taubes or **Schlesiska Dragonregementet** – the drum is painted blue with the Taube coat of arms. The kettledrums are also blue with the Taube coat of arms, panelled in yellow and gold.

Dückers Dragonregemente. In 1705 drum straps had blue and yellow braid.

Schwerins Dragonregemente. In 1711 the drum straps were buff leather, panelled with a braid of red and white camel hair.[6]

A kettledrum banner of the Livregement from 1716. It is the only one from the Guards cavalry that has survived from the time of Charles XII. Livrustkammaren inventory no. 17253 (889).

---

6   Information on the colour of the shabraques is taken from Larsson, *Karolinska Uniformer*, and Höglund, *The Great Northern War 1700–1721*.

11

Horse Furniture For Troopers and Distinctions for Officers

Cavalry Troopers' Horse Furniture

The Swedish Army used saddles of the German cavalry type, with iron stirrups. In the Armémuseum in Stockholm is a saddle of this German type, probably belonging to the Adelsfan Regiment, inventory no. AM015468. Another saddle is in the collection of the Skolkoster Museum, inventory no. 12646SKO. The saddle is well preserved and it is a good example of the saddles that were used in the Swedish cavalry. The saddles are covered with black leather, to the front bow of the saddle in the Skolkoster collection are attached, on brackets, straps for the pistol holsters and to the back straps for saddlebags. On the troopers of the Nylands och Tavastahus Läns Kavalleriregemente depicted on the map cartouche the saddle, holsters and straps are particularly well shown.

To briefly describe the peculiarities of the German saddle design. The basis of the saddle was a wooden tree glued with veins and leather, with front and back bows, and wings stuffed with horsehair. Under the saddle was a blanket made of felt, with canvas or cloth lining, and between the saddle and the rider was a cover made of leather. The saddle was kept on the horse by means of various straps. A wide strap, the girth, ran under the belly of the horse, and a pastern with a tailspin. Iron stirrups were attached to the stirrup leathers which in turn were attached to the saddle. In some cases, the Swedish Army used special holsters – a bucket suspended on the right side of the saddle in which the barrel or the butt of a musket were inserted. Under the saddle was placed a leather or cloth, coloured according to regimental colours. To the front bow of the saddle were attached straps for fastening pistol holsters to it, which in their turn could have black rectangular leather overlays, as well as cloth covers. Holsters were made of wood and glued with black leather. The headband was also of the German type, *mundstunchnoe*, of black leather with metal buckles. In some cases in the Swedish Army at the side of the bridle, at both sides, was attached a bronze oval shoe – the so-called *puckla*. The *puckla* could have decorations in the form of notches or baroque style ornaments. An interesting variations are *puckla* with engraved

HORSE FURNITURE FOR TROOPERS AND DISTINCTIONS FOR OFFICERS

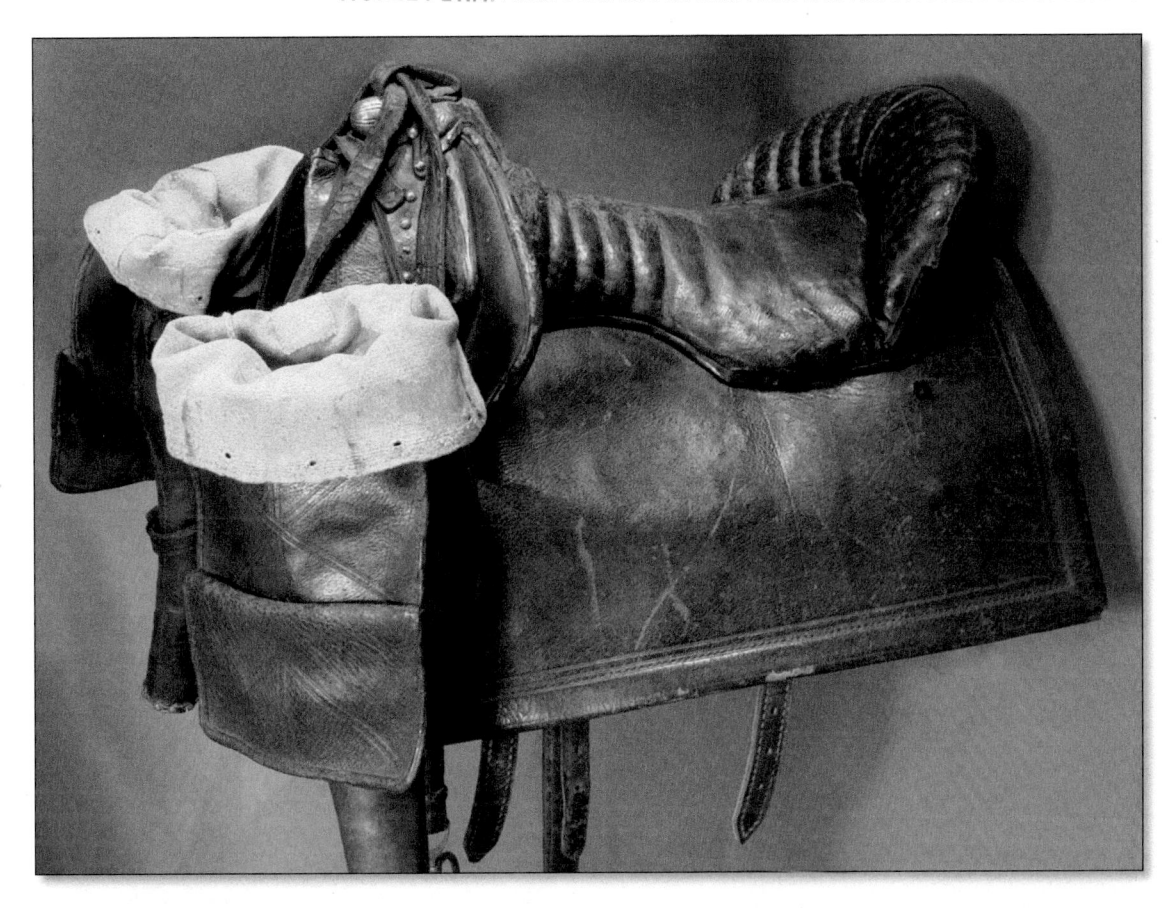

Saddle. Collection of the Armémuseum, Stockholm, inventory no AM.015468.

royal monograms, there are less than a dozen such *pukla* with a monogram known to exist today, one of which is in the collection of the Armémuseum, Stockholm, inventory no. 096137, a second in the collection of the author – found during agricultural work in the Poltava region, this *pukla* is five centimetres long and four wide.

The Volosh Regiment used saddlery and horse furniture of an Eastern European pattern.

An example of a Swedish cavalry cap from the Great Northern War can be found in the collection of the Armémuseum in Stockholm, inv. no. AM.067149. It is probable that this and another one, AM.115615, are slightly later than the period, but they have preserved the main features and the style of decoration. The shabraque is made of blue cloth, lined with canvas, and edged with braid 4.2 cm or 2.2 cm wide, with crowns embroidered at the corners. The width is 110.5 cm and the height 52.5 cm.

For Östgöta Kavalleriregemente in 1717, one cubit of red cloth, 2½ cubits of felt, ¼ cubit of yellow caraze, ½ cubit of yellow cloth and three cubits of cord were used.

The saddle, headband and shabraque of officers could have non-regulation decorations and ornaments. As a rule officers had several horses at their disposal at any one time and it is unlikely that all of them had identical sets of horse furniture with decorated lace and embroidered holster caps.

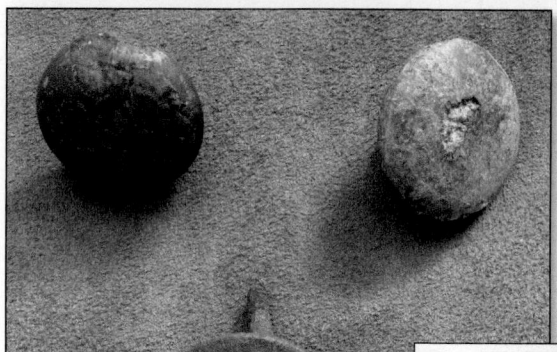

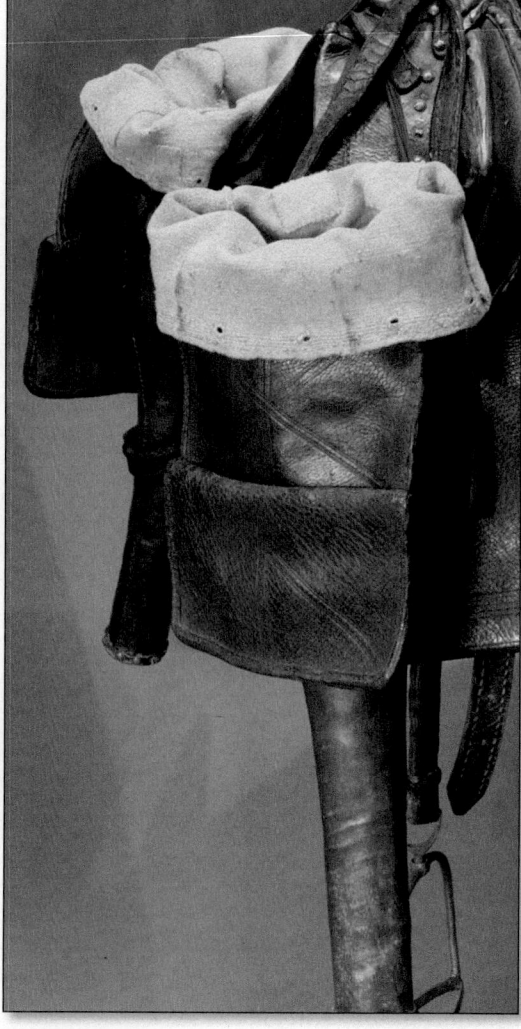

CHARLES XII'S KAROLINERS VOLUME 2

Above: holsters. Collection of Armémuseum, Stockholm, inventory no. AM.067152.

Above: front and back of a bridle *puckla* and two buttons. (Author's collection)

Right: A *puckla* in the collection of the Armémuseum, Stockholm, inventory no AM.096137.

152

HORSE FURNITURE FOR TROOPERS AND DISTINCTIONS FOR OFFICERS

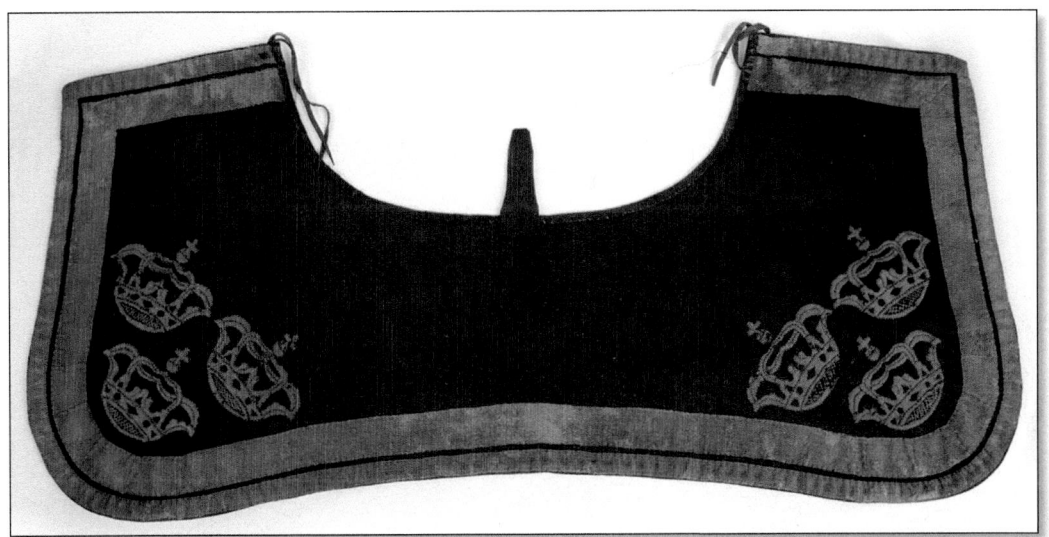

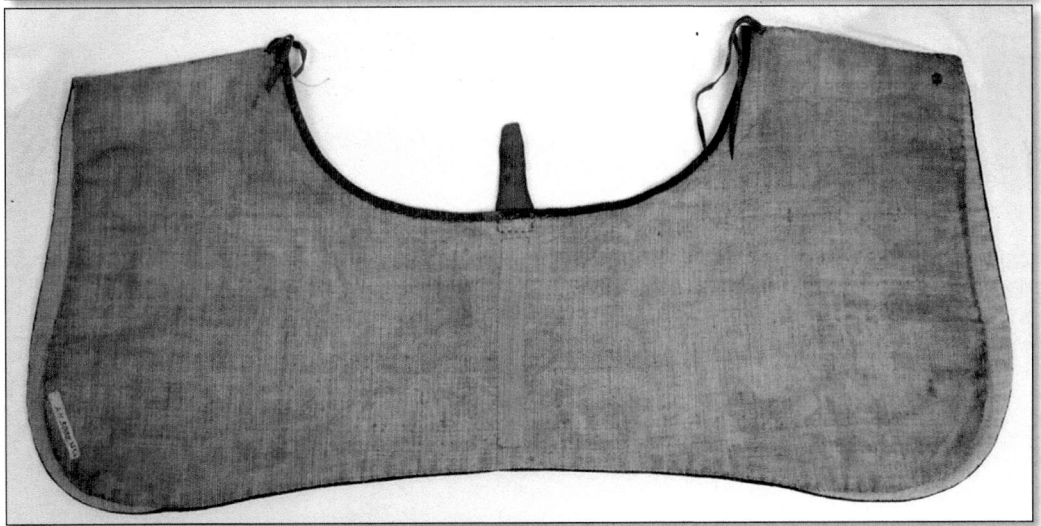

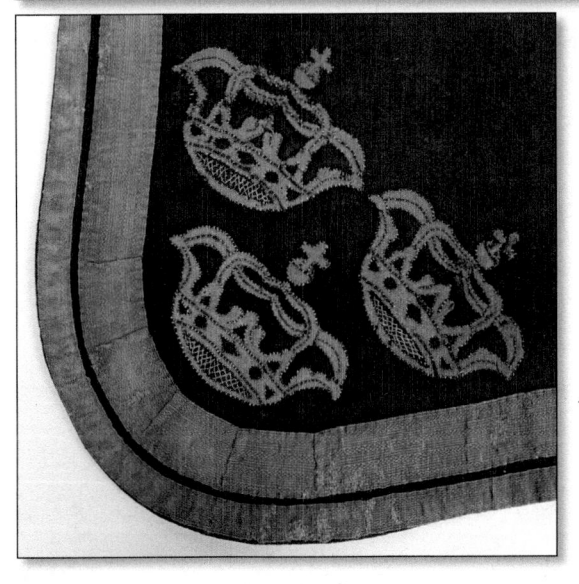

Shabraque from the collection of the Armémuseum, Stockholm, inventory no. AM.067149.

153

CHARLES XII'S KAROLINERS VOLUME 2

Shabraque and holster caps (covers). Västmanlands Läns Museum, and AM.115615 in the collection of the Armémuseum, Stockholm.

It is also questionable how widespread the practice of showing the royal monogram and monograms on the holster caps was. On the map with a cartouche showing the cavalrymen Nylands och Tavastahus Läns Kavalleriregemente (see above), the royal monogram is clearly visible, in yellow or gold on the black leather covering of the holsters. From this image it is difficult to understand whether such decoration belonged only to the officers of cavalry, or whether it applied to all members of the regiment. The available images of cavalrymen on other pictorial sources of the Great Northern War period do not show such monograms on the covers of pistol holsters.

Unfortunately, there is no complete data for the whole period of the war with details by regiment. Below is a list of the surviving information which helps to give an idea of the changes in the decoration of the shabraques, and this may give an idea of shabraques for the regiments where information has not survived.

Shabraques of Officers of the Cavalry and Dragoon Regiments

Livregementet till Häst. A blue shabraque with gold galloon lace and gold crowns in the corner of the shabraque.

Adelsfanan i Sverige och Finland. In 1697, a blue velvet shabraque with gold galloon lace and cord on the edge, in the corners an embroidered crowned royal monogram.

Bremiska Dragonregementet. In 1700 a blue shabraque with suede-coloured edging and silver galloon lace, the crown and monogram of the King in silver embroidered in the corners. The pistol holster covers are blue with silver panelling.

Pommerska Dragonregementet. In 1703 shabraque and holster caps were blue with gold galloon, between them a narrow wavy galloon, and gold fringe three fingers wide on the edge. For captains and lieutenants the same but without the fringe, and for lieutenants and cornets, narrow galloon.

Verdiska Dragonregemente: In 1703 a blue cloth shabraque with silver galloon lace and fringe, between the galloon lace striped, a narrow silver piping.

Stenbocks Dragonregemente. In 1705, a shabraque of yellow cloth with silver galloon lace and narrow silver galloon lace around the edge.

Taubes or **Schlesiska Dragonregementet.** In 1704 a blue cloth shabraque and holster cover with gold galloon lace 'three fingers wide', gold crowned royal monogram in the corner, with narrow galloon on the edge.

Shabraque and Holster Covers (Caps) of Non-Commissioned Officers, Musicians, and Troopers of the Cavalry and Dragoon Regiments (shabraque colour information from Larsson, *Karolinska Uniformer,* and Höglund, *The Great Northern War 1700–1721*)

Livregementet till Häst. In 1700 non-commissioned officers had a blue cloth cap with yellow piping and a silver cord around the edge, while other ranks had a blue cap with yellow piping and three yellow crowns in the corners. In the autumn of 1709, when describing the new uniforms and equipment, the trooper's shabraque was mentioned as being blue with black leather edging. In 1720 they had blue shabraques with two borders, one wide and the other narrow.

Adelsfanan i Sverige och Finland. In 1696, the non-commissioned officers' caps were blue with silver and gold edging, the corporal's cap was blue with gold lace. The troopers' shabraques and covering of pistol holsters were yellow, with blue braid and a blue crown. In 1712 the trooper's shabraque was of yellow cloth, covered with leather.

Västgöta Kavalleriregemente. In 1700 the troopers had a yellow shabraque and holster caps. In 1715 it was a yellow shabraque with leather edging.

Smålands Kavalleriregemente. In 1714, non-commissioned officers had a black leather shabraque with a gold monogram and crown in the corners. Troopers in 1700 had a yellow shabraque.

Smålands Kavalleriregemente. Black shabraque with gold Royal monogram and crown.

Nylands och Tavastahus Läns Kavalleriregemente. A red shabraque with yellow edging.

Östgöta Cavalleriregemente. In 1700 a red shabraque with yellow edging. Later, the regiment's coat of arms of a griffin was embroidered in the corner of the shabraque.

Karelska (Viborgs och Nyslotts län) Kavalleriregementet. A blue shabraque.

Norra Skånska [North Scania] Kavalleriregementet. In 1702 the regiment had yellow shabraques with blue-yellow edging, with the royal crown and monogram in the corners.

Södra Skånska [South Scania] Kavalleriregementet. In 1701 a blue shabraque with yellow edging.

Riksänkedrottningens [Queen Dowager's] Livregemente till Häst. In 1715, a blue shabraque with leather edging.

Bohus Dragonskvadron. In 1702 green shabraque with a yellow edge. 1712 a shabraque of yellow cloth.

Jämtlands Kavallerikompani. In 1695, a blue shabraque.

Adelsfanan i Estland och Ingermanland. A yellow shabraque and holster caps.

Adelsfanan i Livland och pä Ösel. A yellow shabraque and holster covers.

Upplands 3-Männingsregementet till Häst. In 1721 a blue cloth shabraque with yellow cord.

Västgöta 3-Männingsregementet till Häst. In 1719, non-commissioned officers had a black leather shabraque.

Bremiska Kavalleriregementet. In 1696 the shabraque and holster caps were blue with white braid and the royal monogram in white. In 1701 non-commissioned officers had a blue shabraque, with gold lace and monogram. The privates had a blue cap with a yellow and blue edging, and a yellow royal monogram and crown.

Kunglig Majestäts Livregemente Dragoner; Livdragonregementet. In 1700 non-commissioned officers had a blue cloth shabraque with a yellow edge and a silver cord on the edge.

Drottningens [The Queen's] Livregemente till Häst or **Estniska Kavalleriregementet.** A white shabraque.

HORSE FURNITURE FOR TROOPERS AND DISTINCTIONS FOR OFFICERS

Pommerska Kavalleriregementet. In 1702 the kettledrummer's cap was of blue cloth with a white-yellow-red braid edging and a white monogram and crown in the corner. In 1702 the trooper's shabraque was of blue cloth with red-yellow-white edging and the coat of arms of Count Mellin in the corner of the shabraque.

Bremiska Dragonregementet. In 1700 the non-commissioned officers had a blue English cloth shabraque with a suede-coloured edge, palm-wide, with a blue-yellow-silver cord around the edges. The corporals had a blue-blue-silver cord. Private soldiers had a blue cloth shabraque with silver-blue-yellow cord on the edge.

Livländskt Dragonregemente. In 1703–07 a blue shabraque with yellow holster covers.

Pommerska Dragonregementet. Non-commissioned officers in 1703 had a blue shabraque with two yellow laces on the edge, one wide and the second narrow.

Verdiska Dragonregemente. Non-commissioned officers in 1703 had a blue shabraque with a double silver lace on the edge and a narrow lace in between.

Meierfelts Dragonregemente. A blue shabraque with yellow edging.

Stenbocks Dragonregemente. In 1704, the troopers had blue shabraques with yellow and black woollen galoon with a yellow royal monogram, and yellow and black cord on the edge. In 1705 the non-commissioned officers had blue shabraques with yellow wool and with silver braid, with yellow braid on the edge. Musicians (timpanist, oboists) had a blue shabraque with white-blue silk cord on the edge. The troopers had a yellow cap with a blue cloth edging.

Taubes or **Schlesiska Dragonregementet.** In 1704, non-commissioned officers had a blue shabraque with yellow braid and blue/yellow cord around the edge, yellow crown and King's monogram in the corners. The privates had a blue shabraque with blue-yellow woollen edging and a yellow monogram with a crown on the edge of a blue-yellow cord. Yellow holster covers with blue edging.

Dückers or **Preussiska Dragonregementet.** For non-commissioned officers in 1705, a blue shabraque with black lining with wide and narrow yellow braid, with blue-yellow cord. The troopers had blue shabraques with yellow woollen edging and blue-yellow cord on the edge.

Bassewitz Dragonregemente or **Dragonregemente i Wismar.** A blue shabraque with blue and white edging.

Schwerins Dragonregemente. Non-commissioned officers in 1711 had a blue shabraque with white woollen cord on the edge. In 1711 the troopers had a blue shabraque with a white camel's wool cord, of a finger's width, and a second white-red cord on the edge. For musicians, the shabraque was edged with the same cord as the uniform: red and white camel hair.

Vietinghoff's or **Barthska Dragonregementet.** A a blue shabraque with white edging.

Upplands Ståndsdragonregemente. In 1716 the troopers had a blue shabraque with suede-coloured edging.

Bohus Dragonskvadron. In 1694, green shabraques.

Colour Plate Commentaries

Plate 1. A trooper from the reign of Charles XI. Ears of corn are inserted behind the hat brim – a kind of cockade, the tradition of using these ears of corn continued under Charles XII. The trooper is dressed in a buff coat under a cuirass. Despite the archaic character of the buff coat (*colette*) during the Great Northern War, it was used partially or even fully in several regiments: Riksänkedrottningens [Queen Dowager's] Livregemente till Häst, in Adelsfanan i Estland och Ingermanland, Drottningens [The Queen's] Livregemente till Häst; in Estniska Kavalleriregementet, Karelska (Viborgs och Nyslotts Län) Kavalleriregementet, Norra Skånska (North Scanian) Kavalleriregementet. The horse furniture did not change much, and in some cases the same suites of equipment remained in use for many years. In many regiments, especially in the early years of the war, wheelock carbines and older models of pistols continued in use.

Plate 2. Trooper, Riksänkedrottningens Livregemente till Häst (Hedvig Eleonora) [Queen Dowager's Regiment], and Estniska Kavalleriregemente. The two looked similar. In buff coat and cuirass and armed with a sword and a wheelock carbine, with a spanner for spanning the lock attached to the belt on the right-hand side. Ammunition is carried in a cartridge box on the belt over the right shoulder.

Plate 3. Trooper of the Västgöta Kavalleriregemente *c*.1700. The hat is trimmed with silver galloon, the coat is without a collar and lined in yellow.

Plate 4. Trooper of the Östgöta Kavalleriregemente *c*.1700. The hat is edged with silver galloon; the coat is collarless and lined yellow. In this case a slightly different type of coat is shown, with buttons on the side only down to the level of the pockets.

Plate 5. Trooper of the Smålands Kavalleriregegemente 1700–1704. Hat with gold galloon, blue coat with lined yellow with yellow metal buttons, leather waistcoat and breeches. On top of the coat he wears a cloak of grey cloth lined in yellow at the front, on the side, the collar and the back at the cut. At the throat the cloak is fastened by two buckles of yellow metal. In the front, two similar but smaller buckles are attached in the middle on the front edges.

COLOUR PLATE COMMENTARIES

Plate 6. Trooper of the Adelsfanan of Estonia, Ingria, Livonia and Ösel (Saaremaa). Troopers of these regiments wore similar uniforms – grey hats with white and blue trim, grey coats with yellow lining. Both regiments also continued to wear buff coats.

Plate 7. Trooper of Livregementet till Häst, 1706–1709. Hat with gold galloon lace, light blue coat, with the same lined in light blue, yellow metal buttons (from Wolke's *The Swedish Army of the Great Northern War, 1700–1721*).

Plate 8. Trooper of Nylands Kavalleriregemente, 1696–1701. The regiment wore hats and grey carpus, grey coats with red lining and with pewter buttons. The regiment wore cuirasses (from Wolke's *The Swedish Army of the Great Northern War, 1700–1721*). A similar uniform, grey coats but with grey lining instead of red was used from 1701 until 1708 by Åbo och Björneborgs Läns Kavalleriregemente.

Plate 9. Dragoon trooper, Livonian Dragonregemente W. Shlippenbach 1702–1703. He is dressed in a captured Saxon coat, in this case a coat of the Saxon Foot Guards (Polish). A powder horn is suspended from the belt.

Plate 10. Dragoon of the Livonian Dragonregemente W. Shlippenbach, 1703–1707. The dragoon is wearing a hat with yellow braid, a blue coat with yellow metal buttons, a blue waistcoat and leather breeches. He is armed with a hand mortar for throwing grenades, which are carried in a grenadier bag over his left shoulder.

Plate 11. Corporal of the Verdiska Dragonregementet, 1703. The corporal's hat is edged with silver braid, and coat of blue cloth with blue lining is of the double-breasted pattern with buttons covered with blue cloth. The collar and pocket flaps are edged with silver braid. He is depicted during training at the moment of preparing to throw a grenade. A grenadier's bag is worn over the left shoulder, to the strap of which a bronze pipe enclosing a burning match is attached.

Plate 12. Trooper of Dückers or Preussiska Dragonregementet, 1705. Privates wore hats or blue karpus with yellow braid. Coats were blue with yellow lining. He is armed with a dragoon musket, sword, and bayonet for the musket.

Plate 13. Colonel (Överste) A. G. Muhl Karelska (Viborgs Län) Double Regiment of Horse, 1703. The colonel is shown in a ceremonial uniform, heavily embroidered with gold galloon according to his rank. Under the collar of the uniform he is wearing a lavishly decorated gorget (*ringgraph*) of a pattern that was used in the time of Charles XI, again it is decorated according to his rank with a crown above the King's monogram supported by a pair of lions, flanked by palm branches. The engraving is reproduced from a surviving gorget (see main text).

Plate 14. Staff officer, Adelsfanan of Estonia and Ingermanland (Swedish Ingria), 1700. The portrait of the colonel of the Regiment F. Wachtmeister forms the basis for this reconstruction. The hat is edged with gold cord or perhaps narrow gold galloon. As in the portrait, this officer is wearing a double-breasted 'everyday' uniform over a cuirass.

Plate 15. Second Cornet, Adelsfanan of Sweden and Finland, 1700. The Sekundkornetten is dressed in an everyday coat, as would probably be worn on campaign. The leather cornet belt is decorated with cloth and galloon.

Plate 16. Staff officer of a cavalry regiment in a ceremonial coat worn over a double-sided ceremonial cuirass, with decoration.

Plate 17. Officer, Adelsfanan of Sweden and Finland, 1700, in a ceremonial coat in mounted order.

Plate 18. Cavalry officer in an unadorned service coat and wearing a leather waistcoat and breeches.

Plate 19. Officer of Livregementet till Häst in a non-regulation service coat with additional decoration. On the horse's bridle are attached *puckla* displaying the Royal monogram.

Plate 20. A cavalry officer in a service coat with buttonholes edged in gold galloon lace over a breastplate.

Plate 21. Officer, Kunglig Majestäts Livregemente Dragoner; Livdragonregementet, 1700, in a ceremonial uniform and wearing a plain cuirass. Note the decorated belts covered in cloth.

Plate 22. Officer, Verdiska Dragonregementet, 1703. He is wearing a service uniform according to the Royal Decree. The coat has buttons covered with blue cloth, and the hat, collar and cuffs are edged with silver galloon. The cloth covered belt for the musket is also edged with silver galloon. The sword is worn from a waist belt.

Plate 23. Non-commissioned officer, Bremiska Kavalleriregementet, 1701. The non-commissioned officer's hat is covered with a wide gold galloon, as are the cuffs, the buttonholes and the pocket. The coat is blue with a blue lining, and a full back and breast is worn over the coat. Note the pouch/bag for the queue.

Plate 24. Non-commissioned officer, Bremiska Dragonregementet 1700. His hat edged with silver galloon. The blue coat has the lining, collar and cuffs of a 'suede' colour. The collar, cuffs and pocket flaps are all edged with silver galloon. The strap for the dragoon musket and the sword belt are also edged with galloon.

Plate 25. Drabant, 1701 (from Wolke's *The Swedish Army of the Great Northern War, 1700–1721*).

COLOUR PLATE COMMENTARIES

Plate 26. Trumpeter, Adelsfanan of Sweden and Finland 1700. Hat with gold galloon lace, coat heavily decorated with braid.

Plate 27. Drummer, Stenbocks Dragonregemente 1705. The hat is trimmed with silver galloon, the coat has pewter buttons, and the seams, collar, cuffs, and buttonholes are edged in blue and pale yellow braid. The drum strap is edged with the same braid, the drum is painted with yellow and blue flames and with the coat of Arms of Stenbock.

Plate 28. Pommerska Dragonregementet kettledrummer, 1703–07. The kettledrummer wears a red turban covered with gold cord. The coat is of blue cloth with gold galloon lace on the seams and on the pocket flaps. It is belted with an orange silk scarf, under which is a belt supporting a sabre. In the background is a regimental kettledrum.

Plate 29. Musician of the Stenbocks Dragonregemente playing the hautbois, 1705. The hat is edged with silver galloon lace, the coat is blue with white collar and cuffs. The buttons are pewter and silver plated. Unlike the drummer's uniform, the coat is edged with blue and white braid on the seams, collar, cuffs, buttonholes as is the belt.

Plate 30. Cavalry staff officer in double-breasted service coat (from Wolke's *The Swedish Army of the Great Northern War, 1700–1721*).

Plate 31. Kettledrummer of the Drabant Corps, 1700. The kettledrummer's blue uniform is decorated with silver galloon in a ladder design on the front, and galloon on the seams, collar, cuffs, around the bottom edge and on the false sleeves on the back.

Plate 32. Breeches from the Hermitage, St Petersburg, G. E. inventory no. ERT-8458 (author's illustration).

Plate 33. A buff coat from the Hermitage, St Petersburg, G. E. inventory no. ERT-8521 (author's illustration).

Plate 34. Details of sword belts of the Great North War period, showing variations of decoration and cut.
　1. Sword belt from the Artillery Museum in St Petersburg. Elk skin with silver thread with a red linen lining, brass buckle and hook to attach to the belt, possibly both originally gilt.
　2. An elk skin belt made of several layers of fine elk leather with a gold-embroidered floral decoration along the edge.
　3. Part of a sword belt from the collection of the Battle of Poltava Museum at Poltava. Elk skin with galloon and fringe trim, gilt brass hooks for fastening to the belt.
　4. Sword belt from the collection of the Battle of Poltava Museum at Poltava. Moose leather with silver thread stitching along the edge and with brass buckles.

Bibliography

Åberg, A., and G. Göransson, *Karoliner* (printed in Yugoslavia, 1989)

Alf Åberg, Alf, *Fångars Elände: Karolinerna i Ryssland 1700–1723* (Stockholm: Natur och Kultur, 1991)

Arteus, G., Krigsteori och historisk forklaring II. 'Karolinsk och europeisk. stridstaktik 1700–1712', *MHI*, 5. 1972

Bellander, E., *Dräkt Och Uniform* (Stockholm, Norstedt, 1973)

Danchenko, V., *Swedish Banners and Flags*, exhibition catalogue (St Petersburg: State Hermitage Museum 2021)

Höglund, Lars-Eric, *The Great Northern War 1700-1721. Colours and Uniforms* (Karlstad: Acedia Press, 2000)

Homann, A. 'Kriegerische Symbole Barocker Macht am Kragen Mantelschließen der Zeit um 1700 aus Norddeutschland und Südskandinavien,' in *Archäologische Nachrichten aus Schleswig-Holstein 2015*

Jakobsson, T., *Artilleriet under Karl XII:s-tiden*, Armemusei Skrifter I (Stockholm: 1943)

Konovaltjuk, Pavel, *Einar Lythvägen till Poltava : Slaget Vid Lesnaja 1708* (Stockholm: Svenskt Militärhistorisk Biblioteks Förlag, 2009)

Kronberg, Klas, and Tomas Roth, *The French Uniforms Mystery* (Stockholm: Armémuseum, 2010)

Kroon, K., *Kolme Lovi ja Greifiall Pohjasojas* (Tallin: Argo 2007)

Krotov, P. A., *Battle of Poltava* (for the 300th anniversary of the Battle of Poltava)

Kungl. Lifregementets Till Häst Historia: Utarbetad Efter Samlingar Generalmajoren M. M. O. Bjornstjerna, M. F., Och Rlksheraldikern M. M. C. A. Klingspor. Uppsala & Stockholm Lifregementet Till Häst Aren 1667–1723

Larsson, Anders, *Karolinska Uniformer och Munderingar åren 1700 till 1721* (Tallinn: Jengel Förlag, 2022)

Letin, C. and O. Leonov, *Russian Military Costume From Peter I to Peter III* (Moscow: 2008)

Lundblad, Knut, *Geschichte Karl des Zwölften Königs von Schweden*, Band 1 (Hamburg: Friedrich Derthes 1835)

Olin M., *Det Karolinska Porträttet Ideologi, Ikonografi, Identitet* (Stockholm: Raster 2000)

Palli, H., *Between the Two Battles for Narva. Estonia in the First Years of the Great Northern War 1701–1704* (Tallinn: 1966)

Pia Ehasalu, *Rootsiaegne maalikunst Tallinas (1561–1710): produktsioon ja retseptsioon*. Dissertation, Estonian Academy of Arts.

Rangstöm, L. (ed.), *Modelejon Manligt Mode 1600 -tal 1700-tal 1500-tal* (Stockholm: Livrustkammaren, 2002)

Schreber von Schreeb, Tor, Karolinska Förbundets Årsbok 1936: Kongl. Maij:tz Drabanter, 1695–1718: deras organisation, beväpning och mundering

'Perfect Victoria' exhibition catalogue (St Petersburg, 2009)

Shamenkov, Sergey, *Charles XII's Karoliners, Volume 1: The Swedish Infantry & Artillery of the Great Northern War 1700–1721* (Warwick: Helion & Company, 2022)

Slisarenko, O. Voloski, 'Polks of The Armies of Karl XII and Peter I In The Campaigns 1708–1709', in *Ukrainian Historical Journal*, 2017, No.1

Talyzin, I. D., *Description of the Artillery Hall of Memorable and Unmemorable Objects 1862* (St Petersburg: 2006)

Tatarnikov, K. *Building Statutes and Instructions of the Russian Army of the XVIII Century*. Collection of materials, vol. I (Moscow: 2010)

Tatarnikov, K. *Stroevye ustavs instructions and instructions of the Russian Army of the XVIII century*. Collection of materials, vol. I (Moscow: 2010)

Tatarnikov K., Officers' Tales of the First Quarter of the Eighteenth Century, *Otstavnye Chiny I Zapoloshnye Chiny*, vol. 2 (Moscow: 2017)

Velikanov V., 'Swedish Cavalry 1700–1709' in *Voin Magazine*, no. 6

Wolke, Lars Ericson, *The Swedish Army of the Great Northern War, 1700–1721* (Warwick: Helion & Company 2018)

Peter the First and his Entourage . Almanac vol. 465, (St Petersburg, 2015)

Letters and Papers of Peter the Great. – T.VII. – Vyp.2 Vyp.2 (Moscow: Leningrad, 1946)

Sokirko O., Ukrainian Rubicon Poltava battle 27 Chervnya 1709 r. Ch.II (Kiev 2009)

The Royal Facade. Karl XII in the Armoury (Stockholm, 1998)

Electronic Resources

Lewenhaupt, Adam: Karl XII.s officerare. Biografiska anteckningar. 1920.
<http://runeberg.org/karlxiioff/0145.html>
<https://kulturbilder.wordpress.com/2017/09/24/begravningsvapen-for-baron-johan-gjertta-f-1666-d-1740/>
<http://emuseumplus.lsh.se/eMuseumPlus?service=ExternalInterface&module=collection&objectId=55942&viewType=detailView>

Other titles in the Century of the Soldier series

No 1 *'Famous by my Sword'*: The Army of Montrose and the Military Revolution
No 2 *Marlborough's Other Army*: The British Army and the Campaigns of the First Peninsular War, 1702–1712
No 3 *Cavalier Capital*: Oxford in the English Civil War 1642–1646
No 4 *Reconstructing the New Model Army*: Vol 1: Regimental Lists April 1645 to May 1649
No 5 *To Settle the Crown*: Waging Civil War in Shropshire, 1642–1648
No 6 *The First British Army, 1624–1628*: The Army of the Duke of Buckingham
No 7 *Better Begging Than Fighting*: The Royalist Army in Exile in the War against Cromwell 1656–1660
No 8 *Reconstructing the New Model Army*: Vol 2: Regimental Lists April 1649 to May 1663
No 9 *The Battle of Montgomery 1644*: The English Civil War in the Welsh Borderlands
No 10 *The Arte Militaire*: The Application of 17th Century Military Manuals to Conflict Archaeology
No 11 *No Armour But Courage*: Colonel Sir George Lisle, 1615–1648
No 12 *Cromwell's Buffoon*: The Life and Career of the Regicide, Thomas Pride
No 14 *Hey for Old Robin!* The Campaigns and Armies of the Earl of Essex During the First Civil War, 1642–44
No 15 *The Bavarian Army during the Thirty Years War*
No 16 *The Army of James II, 1685-1688*: The Birth of the British Army
No 17 *Civil War London*: A Military History of London under Charles I and Oliver Cromwell
No 18 *The Other Norfolk Admirals*: Myngs, Narbrough and Shovell
No 19 *A New Way of Fighting*: Professionalism in the English Civil War
No 20 *Crucible of the Jacobite '15*: The Battle of Sheriffmuir 1715
No 21 *'A Rabble of Gentility'*: The Royalist Northern Horse, 1644–45
No 22 *Peter the Great Humbled*: The Russo-Ottoman War of 1711
No 23 *The Russian Army In The Great Northern War 1700-21*: Organisation, Matériel, Training, Combat Experience and Uniforms
No 24 *The Last Army*: The Battle of Stow-on-the-Wold and the End of the Civil War in the Welsh Marches, 1646
No 25 *The Battle of the White Mountain 1620 and the Bohemian Revolt, 1618–22*
No 26 *The Swedish Army in the Great Northern War 1700-21*: Organisation, Equipment, Campaigns and Uniforms
No 27 *St. Ruth's Fatal Gamble*: The Battle of Aughrim 1691 and the Fall Of Jacobite Ireland
No 28 *Muscovy's Soldiers*: The Emergence of the Russian Army 1462–1689
No 29 *Home and Away*: The British Experience of War 1618–1721
No 30 *From Solebay to the Texel*: The Third Anglo-Dutch War, 1672–1674
No 31 *The Battle of Killiecrankie*: The First Jacobite Campaign, 1689–1691
No 32 *The Most Heavy Stroke*: The Battle of Roundway Down 1643
No 33 *The Cretan War (1645–1671)*: The Venetian-Ottoman Struggle in the Mediterranean
No 34 *Peter the Great's Revenge*: The Russian Siege of Narva in 1704
No 35 *The Battle Of Glenshiel*: The Jacobite Rising in 1719
No 36 *Armies And Enemies Of Louis XIV*: Volume 1 - Western Europe 1688–1714: France, Britain, Holland
No 37 *William III's Italian Ally*: Piedmont and the War of the League of Augsburg 1683–1697
No 38 *Wars and Soldiers in the Early Reign of Louis XIV*: Volume 1 - The Army of the United Provinces of the Netherlands, 1660–1687
No 39 *In The Emperor's Service*: Wallenstein's Army, 1625–1634
No 40 *Charles XI's War*: The Scanian War Between Sweden and Denmark, 1675–1679
No 41 *The Armies and Wars of The Sun King 1643–1715*: Volume 1: The Guard of Louis XIV
No 42 *The Armies Of Philip IV Of Spain 1621–1665*: The Fight For European Supremacy
No 43 *Marlborough's Other Army*: The British Army and the Campaigns of the First Peninsular War, 1702–1712
No 44 *The Last Spanish Armada*: Britain And The War Of The Quadruple Alliance, 1718–1720
No 45 *Essential Agony*: The Battle of Dunbar 1650
No 46 *The Campaigns of Sir William Waller*
No 47 *Wars and Soldiers in the Early Reign of Louis XIV*: Volume 2 - The Imperial Army, 1660–1689
No 48 *The Saxon Mars and His Force*: The Saxon Army During The Reign Of John George III 1680–1691
No 49 *The King's Irish*: The Royalist Anglo-Irish Foot of the English Civil War
No 50 *The Armies and Wars of the Sun King 1643–1715*: Volume 2: The Infantry of Louis XIV
No 51 *More Like Lions Than Men*: Sir William Brereton and the Cheshire Army of Parliament, 1642–46
No 52 *I Am Minded to Rise*: The Clothing, Weapons and Accoutrements of the Jacobites from 1689 to 1719
No 53 *The Perfection of Military Discipline*: The Plug Bayonet and the English Army 1660–1705
No 54 *The Lion From the North*: The Swedish Army During the Thirty Years War: Volume 1, 1618–1632
No 55 *Wars and Soldiers in the Early Reign of Louis XIV*: Volume 3 - The Armies of the Ottoman Empire 1645–1718
No 56 *St. Ruth's Fatal Gamble*: The Battle of Aughrim 1691 and the Fall Of Jacobite Ireland
No 57 *Fighting for Liberty*: Argyll & Monmouth's Military Campaigns against the Government of King James, 1685
No 58 *The Armies and Wars of the Sun King 1643-1715*: Volume 3: The Cavalry of Louis XIV
No 59 *The Lion From the North*: The Swedish Army During the Thirty Years War: Volume 2, 1632–1648
No 60 *By Defeating My Enemies*: Charles XII of Sweden and the Great Northern War 1682–1721
No 61 *Despite Destruction, Misery and Privations..*: The Polish Army in Prussia during the war against Sweden 1626–1629
No 62 *The Armies of Sir Ralph Hopton*: The Royalist Armies of the West 1642–46
No 63 *Italy, Piedmont, and the War of the Spanish Succession 1701–1712*
No 64 *'Cannon played from the great fort'*: Sieges in the Severn Valley during the English Civil War 1642–1646
No 65 *Carl Gustav Armfelt* and the Struggle for Finland During the Great Northern War
No 66 *In the Midst of the Kingdom*: The Royalist War Effort in the North Midlands 1642–1646
No 67 *The Anglo-Spanish War 1655–1660*: Volume 1: The War in the West Indies
No 68 *For a Parliament Freely Chosen*: The Rebellion of Sir George Booth, 1659
No 69 *The Bavarian Army During the Thirty Years War 1618-1648*: The Backbone of the Catholic League (revised second edition)
No 70 *The Armies and Wars of the Sun King 1643–1715*: Volume 4: The War of the Spanish Succession, Artillery, Engineers and Militias
No 71 *No Armour But Courage*: Colonel Sir George Lisle, 1615–1648 (Paperback reprint)
No 72 *The New Knights*: The Development of Cavalry in Western Europe, 1562–1700
No 73 *Cavalier Capital*: Oxford in the English Civil War 1642–1646 (Paperback reprint)
No 74 *The Anglo-Spanish War 1655–1660*: Volume 2: War in Jamaica
No 75 *The Perfect Militia*: The Stuart Trained Bands of England and Wales 1603–1642
No 76 *Wars and Soldiers in the Early Reign of Louis XIV*: Volume 4 - The Armies of Spain 1659–1688
No 77 *The Battle of Nördlingen 1634*: The Bloody Fight Between Tercios and Brigades
No 78 *Wars and Soldiers in the Early Reign of Louis XIV*: Volume 5 - The Portuguese Army 1659–1690
No 79 *We Came, We Saw, God Conquered*: The Polish-Lithuanian Commonwealth's military effort in the relief of Vienna, 1683
No 80 *Charles X's Wars*: Volume 1 - Armies of the Swedish Deluge, 1655–1660
No 81 *Cromwell's Buffoon*: The Life and Career of the Regicide, Thomas Pride (Paperback reprint)
No 82 *The Colonial Ironsides*: English Expeditions under the Commonwealth and Protectorate, 1650–1660
No 83 *The English Garrison of Tangier*: Charles II's Colonial Venture in the Mediterranean, 1661–1684
No 84 *The Second Battle of Preston, 1715*: The Last Battle on English Soil
No 85 *To Settle the Crown*: Waging Civil War in Shropshire, 1642–1648 (Paperback reprint)
No 86 *A Very Gallant Gentleman*: Colonel Francis Thornhagh (1617–1648) and the Nottinghamshire Horse
No 87 *Charles X's Wars*: Volume 2 - The Wars in the East, 1655–1657
No 88 *The Shōgun's Soldiers*: The Daily Life of Samurai and Soldiers in Edo Period Japan, 1603–1721 Volume 1
No 89 *Campaigns of the Eastern Association*: The Rise of Oliver Cromwell, 1642–1645
No 90 *The Army of Occupation in Ireland 1603–42*: Defending the Protestant Hegemony
No 91 *The Armies and Wars of the Sun King 1643–1715*: Volume 5: Buccaneers and Soldiers in the Americas
No 92 *New Worlds, Old Wars*: The Anglo-American Indian Wars 1607–1678
No 93 *Against the Deluge*: Polish and Lithuanian Armies During the War Against Sweden 1655–1660
No 94 *The Battle of Rocroi*: The Battle, the Myth and the Success of Propaganda
No 95 *The Shōgun's Soldiers*: The Daily Life of Samurai and Soldiers in Edo Period Japan, 1603–1721 Volume 2
No 96 *Science of Arms: the Art of War in the Century of the Soldier 1672–1699*: Volume 1: Preparation for War and the Infantry
No 97 *Charles X's Wars*: Volume 3 - The Danish Wars 1657–1660

BIBLIOGRAPHY

No 98 *Wars and Soldiers in the Early Reign of Louis XIV:* Volume 6 - Armies of the Italian States 1660–1690 Part 1

No 99 *Dragoons and Dragoon Operations in the British Civil Wars, 1638–1653*

No 100 *Wars and Soldiers in the Early Reign of Louis XIV:* Volume 6 - Armies of the Italian States 1660–1690 Part 2

No 101 *1648 and All That:* The Scottish Invasions of England, 1648 and 1651: Proceedings of the 2022 Helion and Company 'Century of the Soldier' Conference

No 102 *John Hampden and the Battle of Chalgrove:* The Political and Military Life of Hampden and his Legacy

No 103 *The City Horse:* London's militia cavalry during the English Civil War, 1642–1660

No 104 *The Battle of Lützen 1632:* A Reassessment

No 105 *Monmouth's First Rebellion:* The Later Covenanter Risings, 1660–1685

No 106 *Raw Generals and Green Soldiers:* Catholic Armies in Ireland 1641–1643

No 107 *The Khotyn Campaign:* Polish, Lithuanian and Cossack armies versus the might of the Ottoman Empire

No 108 *Soldiers and Civilians, Transport and Provisions:* Early modern military logistics and supply systems during the British Civil Wars, 1638–1653

No 109 *Batter their Walls, Gates and Forts:* The Proceedings of the 2022 English Civil War Fortress Symposium

No 110 *The Town Well Fortified:* The Fortresses of the Civil Wars in Britain, 1639–1660

No 111 *Crucible of the Jacobite '15:* The Battle of Sheriffmuir 1715 (Paperback reprint)

No 112 *Charles XII's Karoliners:* Volume 2: The Swedish Cavalry of the Great Northern War 1700–1721

SERIES SPECIALS:

No 1 *Charles XII's Karoliners:* Volume 1: The Swedish Infantry & Artillery of the Great Northern War 1700–1721

About the Author

Sergey Shamenkov graduated from the Academy of Arts in Lviv. He lives and works in Odesa, Ukraine. He is the author of articles, books and scientific graphic reconstructions on the subject of clothing, materiel and military culture of the Ukrainian Cossacks and in the Swedish and Polish-Lithuanian Commonwealth armies. His artwork can be found in many books published by Helion & Company.